EXAMINATION COPY

Scholarly Resources is pleased to send you this book ~~for~~
your examination. When you have reached ~~a decision we~~
request that you complete this brief form ~~and return it to the~~
address given below.

Book Title: _____

Name: _____

Institution: _____

Department: _____

I am adopting this book for use in:

Course title: _____

Term:_____   Enrollment: _____

_____As a Primary Text   _____As a Supplementary Text

_____As Recommended Reading

_____I am not adopting this book for the following reason(s):

Scholarly Resources Inc.
104 Greenhill Avenue • Wilmington, DE 19805-1897
800-772-8937 • 302-654-7713
E-mail: market@scholarly.com • www.scholarly.com
Contact: Toni Moyer, Marketing Manager

Entangled in Terror

Entangled in Terror

The Azef Affair
and
the Russian Revolution

Anna Geifman

A Scholarly Resources Inc. Imprint
Wilmington, Delaware

© 2000 by Scholarly Resources Inc.
All rights reserved
First published 2000
Printed and bound in the United States of America

Scholarly Resources Inc.
104 Greenhill Avenue
Wilmington, DE 19805-1897
www.scholarly.com

Library of Congress Cataloging-in-Publication Data

Geifman, Anna, 1962–
    Entangled in terror : the Azef affair and the Russian Revolution/
Anna Geifman.
        p.   cm.
    Includes bibliographical references and index.
    ISBN 0-8420-2650-9 (cloth : alk. paper). — ISBN 0-8420-2651-7
(pbk. : alk. paper)
        1. Azef, Evno Fishelevich, 1869–1918.   2. Revolutionaries—Russia
Biography.   3. Terrorists—Russia Biography.   4. Informers—Russia
Biography.   5. Partiia sotsialistov–revoliutsionerov Biography.
6. Russia—History—Nicholas II, 1894–1917.   I. Title.
DK254.A8G45   2000
947.08′092—dc21
    [B]   99–38693

Photos courtesy of Gosudarstvennyi Arkhiv Russiiskoi Federatsii, Moscow,
Russia and Hoover Institution Archives, Stanford University, Stanford,
California.

⊗ The paper used in this publication meets the minimum requirements of the
    American National Standard for permanence of paper for printed library
    materials, Z39.48, 1984.

To Abe and Rita Geifman

About the Author

A nna Geifman was born in 1962 in Leningrad. In 1976 she and her family emigrated to the United States. She received her B.A. and M.A. from Boston University and her Ph.D., from Harvard. She is currently Associate Professor of History at Boston University. Dr. Geifman is the recipient of numerous awards and grants, including the John M. Olin Faculty Fellowship and the IREX Faculty Research Grant. She is the author of *Thou Shalt Kill: Revolutionary Terrorism in Russia, 1894–1917* (Princeton University Press, 1993) and the editor of *Russia Under the Last Tsar: Opposition and Subversion, 1894–1917* (Blackwell, 1999).

Contents

Note on Names and Dates

This book follows the Library of Congress style in transliterating Russian words, such as names of people and geographical locations. In reference to events taking place within the Russian Empire, all dates appear in Old Style, in accordance with the Julian calendar, in use in Russia until February 1917. The Julian calendar was twelve days behind the Gregorian calendar in the nineteenth century and thirteen days in the twentieth century. Unless indicated otherwise, the Gregorian calendar is used in reference to events beyond the borders of the Russian Empire.

Acknowledgments

It is a great pleasure for me to convey my gratitude to the many institutions, granting agencies, colleagues, and friends whose help and encouragement were essential for the completion of this book.

I began preliminary research at the International Institute of Social History in Amsterdam and the Hoover Institution of War, Revolution, and Peace in Stanford, California, and am always thankful for all support and assistance from their archival and library staffs. Also at the initial stage of research, I received a Seed Grant from the Boston University Graduate School, which allowed me to travel to Russia to begin archival investigation in Moscow and St. Petersburg.

Most of the research for the book was conducted in Moscow archives and libraries in 1996–97, in part supported by several short- and long-term grants from the International Research and Exchanges Board (IREX), with funds provided by the Andrew W. Mellon Foundation, the National Endowment for the Humanities, and the U.S. Department of State. I am greatly indebted to the staff of the State Archives of the Russian Federation (GARF) and am particularly grateful for the invaluable assistance offered by L. I. Petrusheva and especially Z. I. Peregudova, who was invariably supportive and willing to share her extensive knowledge of sources.

I would further like to extend my sincere appreciation to Victor V. Leonidov, the curator of the archival library of the Russian Cultural Fund (Arkhiv-Biblioteka Rossiiskogo Fonda Kul'tury), for guiding me to important new materials. I am equally thankful to Feliks Lur'e for his help in locating many essential documents from the Russian State Historical Archive (RGIA) in St. Petersburg. Dr. Lur'e was also my opponent in a passionate television debate in St. Petersburg in 1996, demonstrating once again that the controversy over Evno Azef's role and personality is still meaningful and pertinent. Dr. Oleg V. Budnitsky, my distinguished colleague from Rostov-on-the Don, helped me a great deal by providing key information about Azef's youth, as well as by offering perceptive observations relevant to other periods of his life. My thanks are also due to another colleague, Leonid Praisman from

Jerusalem, who was very generous with essential archival references and interesting comments about Azef's Jewish identity.

The Humanities Foundation at Boston University, chaired by Katherine T. O'Connor, supported me with a grant that allowed for a semester free of teaching so that I could start writing this biography. Of equal value were several travel grants offered by Boston University's History Department, enabling me to participate in professional conferences and present my current work to interested scholars.

I owe a great debt to Norman Naimark, Richard Pipes, Philip Pomper, and especially Jonathan Daly and Michael Melancon, all of whom read either the entire manuscript or significant parts of the text and showed remarkable generosity with their time, constructive advice, and kind encouragement. None of these people or organizations are of course responsible for any error of judgment, fact, or scholarship.

I must express deep appreciation to Linda Montgomery and Leslie McGann for their friendship and helpful editorial assistance. I am also thankful to Ella Pechnikova, Anya Sosinskaia, and Dr. Victor V. Lebedinskii, who shared their expertise in discussions of personality types and the applicability of psychology to historical writing. Serezha Sossinsky-Semikhat and Dr. A. Lexis provided firsthand family memories of the revolutionary events in Russia—something which in more ways than one proved so pertinent for writing this book. Nor should I forget Galya Dobrushina, who was always willing to share her perceptive analysis of intricate problems in human relationships, confirming this book's assumption about the possibility of seeing personalities from "yet another angle." I must also mention my Russian friends and colleagues T. Filipova, D. Oleinikov, L. Gatagova, A. Bakhanov, S. Antonenko, and A. Levandovskii, all of whom contributed so much to the many memorable and professionally, as well as emotionally, stimulating evenings during my stays in Moscow. Finally, among those who stoically endured my preoccupation with the darker sides of human personality and activity, I owe the world to the one who always seeks life beyond its formalities, to N. and A. Arko, and to K. Otovsky—for their love.

Introduction

Nothing is so much to be feared as Fear.
—Henry David Thoreau, *Journal*[1]

With the 1905–1907 countrywide revolt at an end, Christmas of 1908 did not promise much international publicity for Russia, Tsar Nicholas II, or the daredevils who had sought to overthrow him by violent action. The 1905 revolution had already wound down. Launched largely as a constitutional movement of the educated elites, it quickly degenerated into a bacchanalia of brutality that took the form of mass peasant uprisings and workers' strikes, military and naval mutinies, pogroms, armed demonstrations, student protests, and—the most extreme and sanguinary manifestation of Russian radicalism—a myriad of terrorist acts. Yet, having caused enormous physical, moral, and spiritual devastation, the insurrection eventually succumbed to the proportionately ferocious repressions of the imperial government. The acute crisis, an ominous symptom of both the unhealthy state of Russia's internal life and the deep sociocultural trauma of its Silver Age, was now in the domain of history, having bled the country and leaving it with little sense of political destiny. Disappointment and the rejection of radical ideals and practices now seemed to dominate Russia's stagnant recuperation from the revolutionary turmoil, and the West could hardly have expected a new outburst of political passion in this disillusioned country. Then, in the winter of 1908–09, a bombshell exploded, but this time not in the form of social upheaval. The new assault on Russian public life resounded as a great political scandal associated with the secret life of a single man.

Newspaper headlines introduced Evno Filipovich Azef to the world as a "twentieth-century Judas," and, since this initiation to the most notorious villains' club, for the entire century his name has remained in the Russian tradition as a common noun and a synonym for shameless duplicity, unscrupulous perfidy, and criminal provocation. It entered the lexicon of every educated Russian as a symbol for falseness, corruption, and readiness to betray friends and enemies alike for personal

1

profit. Novelists, playwrights, and poets used Azef's name (and a derogatory neologism derived from it—Azefshchina) to condemn the baseness of human nature.[2] His life became a parable, and his image was employed to depict such wonders of nature as "the night, tenebrous like Azef."[3] In Germany in 1935 an adulated movie star of the Third Reich, Olga Chekhov (Tschechowa)—niece of Russia's most celebrated playwright—played a part in the movie called *Provocateur Azef*. The main character appeared as an ideal candidate to resurrect the notion of a classic "vile character" of the Shakespearean theater: "Azef is a sophisticated villain.... In contrast to him, Iago is a baby."[4] Contemporaries noted in surprise that in certain people the Azef affair even elicited a perverse feeling of national pride. Many Russian nationals in Europe appeared quite pleased with all of the publicity and fanfare that the scandal begot, and their elated faces in Parisian cafes seemed to be saying "We, Russians, showed those Europeans, didn't we?"[5] For decades, Azef's reputation was such that, in comparison, even "Judas was a child and a puppy,"[6] and in many eyes he was indeed none other than a "demon" or the "devil incarnate."[7]

Remarkable as it was, Azef's enduring reputation has always been of a scandalous nature. No other controversy surrounding a single person associated with the radicals' struggle against the government of the last Russian tsar elicited such heated debate and incandescence of passion in the years prior to the collapse of the imperial regime in 1917. Still surrounded by mystery, Azef remains one of the most obscure figures in Russia's political history and is certainly the most enigmatic personality in the country's revolutionary movement.

The story of Evno Azef, who also called himself Azev, Ivan Nikolaevich, Valentin Kuz'mich, Vinogradov, Raskin, Tolstyi (the Fat One), and used a score of other aliases, is inseparable from the history of the Socialist Revolutionary Party, or PSR, the largest subversive militant formation in prerevolutionary Russia. Although the PSR was not unique in proclaiming political assassination a mandatory tool of insurrection, its successes in the combat arena earned it the rank of the "most important terrorist organization known to history"[8] at the time, and justified its reputation as the party of terror. As far as the authorities were concerned, it was the most formidable political foe of the tsarist regime. No other revolutionary organization could claim responsibility for so many sensational shootings and dynamite explosions aimed primarily at high-posted members of the central government in the two Russian capitals, St. Petersburg and Moscow. And of all the prominent party activists, no one was more familiar with these daring terrorist exploits than Evno Azef.

A full-fledged member of the PSR Central Committee, Azef was a principal link between this brain center of the Socialist Revolutionary movement and the main conspiratorial terrorist unit within the party structure, which operated under the title of Combat Organization *(Boevaia organizatsiia)*. This small contingent of professional terrorists came into existence in late 1901 with one specific purpose: to stage, in compliance with direct orders from the party's headquarters abroad, a series of centralized political assassinations targeting the highest-ranking state leaders and officials in St. Petersburg, Moscow, and the larger provincial cities.

From the outset, the party leaders and combatants *(boeviki)* firmly believed that the key to the terrorists' success was the strictest secrecy, achievable only by ensuring the maximum separation of terrorist operations from all other party activities. As a result, members of the Combat Organization isolated themselves from the rest of the PSR cadres and led the life of a tiny militant sect, a quasi-religious cult, in which the revered deity was sacred terror itself. For their part, the Central Committee and other prominent SR leaders rarely interfered in the internal affairs of the terrorist detachment. This was not solely because most of them had no personal inclination toward violence and evidently preferred to preserve their peace of mind by limiting their involvement with combat work to the theoretical justification of violent tactics without exposing themselves to the gruesome details of terrorist operations. The few who did consider it expedient to exercise a certain amount of control over combat affairs encountered staunch defiance on the part of the *boeviki*, who tenaciously resisted any intrusion from the civilians with a typically sectarian distrust of the outside world.[9]

Members of the SR Central Committee therefore had little choice but to rely on the belief that its interests in terrorist ventures were well represented by Azef, the PSR's most respected and trusted veteran. After several sensational political assassinations in 1904–05, he was at the zenith of his popularity: the esteem comrades had for him was unquestionable, deference to his authority was universal, he was idolized by the combatants, and regarded as a hero by the party civilians. Any revolutionary would have dismissed as sheer madness the slightest suspicion that one of the founding fathers of the party, a man of the highest stature and credentials in the radical world, was a secret agent on the payroll of the Russian secret political police, the Okhrana.

Yet this was indeed the case. Nearly a decade prior to the formation of the PSR, Azef had offered his services to the Imperial Police Department and received a warm welcome as a very junior informer with the modest salary of fifty rubles a month.[10] Initially, his contribution as a spy was as limited as his experience in antigovernment circles, but as he broadened his contacts in the radical milieu, built a solid revolutionary reputation, and rapidly advanced in the SR hierarchy toward the pinnacle of his party career as the terrorists' chief, his reports became progressively more vital to his police superiors. As he rose through the SR ranks his secret income from police funds increased accordingly.

By the end of 1904 he had already entered the SR Committee Abroad (*Zagranichnyi komitet*), and in 1906 he became a fully empowered member of the party's Central Committee. Simultaneously, until his formal retirement from police service in the spring of 1908, Azef maintained contact with several high-level Okhrana officers, providing them with firsthand information on various activities of the Central Committee and other leading organs of the PSR, as well as on the plans and operations of the Combat Organization. Due to his efforts the authorities were able to disrupt a large number of terrorist plots, some of which—particularly those aimed at Prime Minister Petr Stolypin and the tsar himself—may have drastically altered the course of Russian history.

There were several occasions when Azef's ties with the Okhrana weakened, and during one period, from the end of 1905 to mid-April of 1906, they were severed altogether as a result of personnel shifts in the police high command.[11] Nevertheless, considering that a two- or three-year term was usually the maximum length of service for an informer,[12] Azef's fifteen-year tenure as a police agent at the heart of a major antigovernment organization was unprecedented in duration and significance. That the authorities were as appreciative of his role in the party as were his credulous comrades in the PSR was reflected in his remarkably large pay, which was close to the salary of a minister: at the end of Azef's police service, he was receiving as much as a thousand rubles a month, not counting bonuses.[13]

The fact that Azef played his dangerous game so well does not explain what his personal stakes in it were, and to this day his motives and behavior remain a "psychological riddle."[14] Was he stimulated by money, or did he seek adventure and the thrill of a double life? Was he a devoted servant of the tsarist regime, ready to betray its enemies who trusted him unconditionally and were prepared to die if their respected leader so ordered them? Perhaps he was a sociopath, seizing an opportunity to assert himself at the expense of both the police and the revolutionaries and enjoying his position of power between them. Azef was undoubtedly under the influence of deep psychological and pragmatic motives in pursuing his long career as a spy, which involved facing the daily risk of exposure followed by immediate and merciless revolutionary vengeance. If we are to understand Azef's actions, it is essential to examine his motives for choosing and following this dangerous path. To undertake such an examination is a primary concern of this study.

Here lies the central paradox of Azef's personality: a sequence of indeterminate, or free-floating, fears rooted in his early years seems to have been the catalyst that drove him toward his initial perilous involvement with the revolutionaries and the police. The inner mechanism is activated by a familiar impetus—motiveless panic, which "comes from within, from deep within, and it bears no relation to the existence of any *exterior* threat."[15] This unconditional fear, a cardinal psychological stimulus that may realize itself in a variety of anomalous responses, appears to be the relentless force that served as inducement and kept Azef entangled in the life-threatening business of political treachery. Indeed, it would be appropriate to speculate whether this life of permanent danger was not persistently, albeit subconsciously, concocted by Azef himself as a means of rationalizing his intrinsic predicament. It has long been noted that something objectively frightening may be extremely attractive to a person who is running away from a vague, yet powerful inner dread. "Fascination with fear is an indication that we are ignoring whatever frightens us enough to warrant this attention."[16]

Initially, Azef could perhaps have avoided this pattern by recognizing his fear as a thing in itself, not necessarily rooted in external causes, rather than rationalizing and fixating on economic, occupational, interpersonal, and other factors as sources of his chronic anxiety. With time, however, his initial psychological condition was thoroughly concealed by the practical aspects of his dangerous existence. There is a sad irony in the fact that in his desperate determination to rid himself of what he perceived, rationally or not, to be the causes of this all-pervasive fear and the associated anxiety, he invariably immersed himself more deeply in the quagmire of risk and physical threat nearly until the end of his life. Azef's behavior thus provides an illustration of a description of fear made decades later: "Under its influence, and trying to escape its influence, we seem fated to give it a yet stronger hold upon us."[17] Various forms of anxiety, including phobias, perpetual agitation, and insecurity in social situations, "move us to actions that are the opposite of those that might redeem us from fear. Trying to protect ourselves, we injure ourselves."[18]

Considering that "of all the emotional forces that pattern our individual and interpersonal behaviors, fear has the most insidious power to make us do what we ought not to do and leave undone what we ought to do,"[19] it is truly surprising that historians and other students of human affairs, particularly those working in the biographical genre, have taken fear for granted and overwhelmingly failed to recognize it for what it is: one of the most influential drives in man's behavior and thus in the entire historical process. Perhaps the most plausible explanation of this unfortunate conceptual flaw in our attempts to understand past human motives and actions is that "no other emotion wears so many disguises—convincing disguises that make us, time and again, treat it as something other than itself." Failing to penetrate the inherent symptoms that fear conceals under its various masks, historians habitually treat it as other sentiments, modes of behavior, or problems.[20] This book is written in the hope of avoiding this pitfall and is, to this end, based on the assumption that any biography requires an interdisciplinary approach, incorporating contemporary findings in human psychology and behavior patterns.

As part of its general aim to shed light on Azef's fascinating story, this study demonstrates the crucial impact that fear had on his personality—perhaps at the risk of offending scholars who reject any transgression of the rigid dividing lines between disciplines as frivolously eclectic. In fact, it is not sufficient to argue that fear had a primary impact on Azef's decision making in his professional life, since it also affected his relations with others, his tastes, and probably even his physical appearance. In short, it ran like a red thread through his entire existence, and one of this book's ambitions therefore is to present Azef's life as a historical case study in fear.

Equally challenging is the strictly historical task of resolving the major controversy that broke out immediately following the scandalous exposure of Azef's true role in the party and the government. In addition to an infinite number of newspaper and magazine articles replete with "fantastic inventions, criminal ornamentations, absurd psychological constructions," and all sorts of imaginative stories about this "infernal Dostoevskian type,"[21] the primary sources of information about Azef's exploits are the statements selectively issued by his former comrades in the PSR. Given their stake in the matter, however, the SRs could hardly be expected to remain impartial and objective observers of what became known as the Azef affair.[22]

The official SR interpretation on numerous occasions reiterated by the party leaders underscored the argument that if the purity of sacred terror had been stained by the dirty hands of a police spy, the reputation of the tsarist regime was also hopelessly soiled, for, according to the radicals, the government had been implicated in the crime of provocation as part of its efforts to combat the revolution. The authorities not only knowingly had employed and paid a man who selectively initiated and executed terrorist acts, and had relied upon him for information while tolerating his criminal activities, but through their secret agent in the PSR, they had also instigated political assassinations.

According to the SRs, Azef's paymasters, driven by personal ambition and internal rivalries, sanctioned political assassinations for two fundamental reasons: first, to demonstrate to the government and the public that there was a major terrorist menace that justified political repression and extensive police involvement in state policy—efforts for which all major participants received promotions, honors, and material rewards; and, second, to eliminate political or personal enemies in their own ranks. Although supposedly a pawn in their hands, Azef, the SRs contended, also must have had his own stakes in this bloody game. Motivated by insatiable greed, he was said to have assumed the role of paid agent provocateur, receiving generous remuneration for helping his high-ranking police employers make use of revolutionaries to stage terrorist acts against their rival colleagues in the government. The SRs further claimed that this was only one aspect of his activity. To secure his position in the PSR—which was essential not only to ensure his physical safety but also to bring him significant financial profits at the revolutionaries' expense—Azef, as a leader of the Combat Organization, had to prove his loyalty to the radical cause by arranging the assassinations of a number of prominent personalities in the tsarist administration. He was alleged to have played a leading role in staging many other terrorist undertakings that he deliberately neglected to report to his police superiors, thus qualifying the agent provocateur also as a double agent.[23]

If the SR public statements were accepted as the truth, as indeed it is in revolutionary lore and in today's scholarship, the Russian police authorities must be pronounced guilty of malfeasance and veritably criminal practices, as must their agent, the "provocateur-virtuoso,"[24] who betrayed both his comrades and his paymasters and was, according to the revolutionaries' verdict, nothing but a "common criminal, always led only by his own goals."[25] This book thus has a dual goal: while seeking insight into Azef's personality, it will also attempt to determine whether the historical evidence supports what is by now the traditional, yet genuinely questionable, assumption that this master spy was also an agent provocateur and a treacherous double agent.[26]

There remains one last mystifying question concerning the Azef affair: How, after so many years of successfully leading a double life, did he come to be exposed as a police informer among the SRs? Did this shrewd, calculating, and experienced man compromise his impeccable revolutionary reputation by one careless faux pas? Did he lose his nerve when the radicals took decisive steps to discover and punish an unknown spy in their midst? Or was it the police who failed to take proper precautions to protect their agent? Like nearly all aspects of Azef's life, his unmasking is obscured by a potpourri of facts, speculation, myths, and fables.

The person most closely associated with Azef's exposure was Vladimir L'vovich Burtsev, a forty-six-year-old independent revolutionary and editor of the historical journal, *The Past (Byloe)*. In May 1908 he informed the PSR Central Committee that he had reason to believe Azef to be a police spy. Initially, few of the SRs were prepared to listen to Burtsev's arguments or to accept his claims as anything other than a malicious insult to the party's most distinguished member. Facing a hostile revolutionary court of honor, convened by the incredulous and angry revolutionaries for the sole purpose of convicting the foolhardy accuser of libel, Burtsev displayed his trump card—definitive compromising evidence against Azef—the oral testimony of a former director of the Police Department, Acting State Councilor Aleksei Aleksandrovich Lopukhin (1864–1928), who from May 1902 until his retirement in March 1905 had been responsible for Azef's activities as a secret agent.[27] Allegedly, as a result of a chance encounter and the ensuing conversation, Lopukhin had disclosed to Burtsev the identity of the spy within the PSR Central Committee. Presented with such an incontrovertible indication of Azef's guilt, the dumbfounded and nonplussed SRs had no choice but to initiate the formal investigation that led to public acknowledgment of Azef's police connections.

The announcement produced a sensation, with Burtsev lauded as the "Sherlock Holmes of the Russian revolution."[28] For a number of subsequent years he edited two newspapers, *The Common Cause (Obshchee delo)* and *The Future-L'Avenir (Budushchee-L'Avenir)*, whose primary purpose was to persuade their readers of Azef's alleged double treachery and involvement in state-sponsored provocation. In issue after issue, Burtsev contended that Azef, acting on the orders of Prime Minister Stolypin and the director of the St. Petersburg Okhrana, General Aleksandr Gerasimov (whom Burtsev labeled a "common criminal" and a "genuine provocateur"), was responsible for a score of terrorist acts in the first decade of the twentieth century.[29] Simultaneously, Burtsev sought to enhance his own reputation as a spy hunter, expounding enthusiastically on the more than questionable story of how he had procured information compromising not only Azef but also the entire tsarist regime from one of its luminaries. The gullibility of Azef's contemporaries—and all subsequent commentators—in accepting Burtsev's version of the events is truly astounding, for great naïveté would have been required of anyone who accepted without question the ease with which Lopukhin is said to have accommodated the revolutionaries' need to identify the spy in their midst. The final objective of this book is therefore to demystify the circumstances behind Azef's exposure, after which he "immediately became one of the most famous people in the world."[30]

His fame notwithstanding, the first and only original attempt to write a complete life story of the "greatest provocateur of modern times,"[31] and "a *classical* example of provocation,"[32] is Boris Nicolaevsky's narrative study, *Istoriia odnogo predatelia* (The story of a traitor), translated into English under the title *Aseff the Spy*. A Russian Social Democrat who was personally acquainted with many participants in the revolutionary events and whose lifelong interest lay in the history of the antigovernment movement, the author was also a well-known archivist and collector of Russian historical records, accounts, and stories. As a result of Nicolaevsky's scrutiny of the predominantly left-wing sources available prior to the completion of his book in 1931, supplemented by somewhat sporadic police materials, his saga largely reproduces the traditional portrait of Azef as it was sketched by Burtsev and the SRs.[33]

Although *Aseff the Spy* contains many valuable insights, Nicolaevsky's inquiry (punctuated by jots of fiction) is deficient in two critical respects, the first being that the official SR documents throw little light on Azef's police connections, dealing primarily with the situation within the PSR that had allowed a government agent to penetrate its central organization.[34] Perhaps even more significant is the other problem characteristic of Nicolaevsky's sources, namely, the ideological tendentiousness that is particularly evident in the personal reminiscences of various revolutionaries. These memoirs are full of assumptions typical of the radicals who were only too willing to accept any information compromising the imperial government, for each stain on the tsarist regime served as an indirect justification of their own involvement in the revolution. To make matters worse, Nicolaevsky was apparently unaware of the extent to which these personal accounts solely present the official version of SR history. Suffice it to say that a published volume of recollections by Boris Savinkov, Azef's closest colleague in the Combat Organization, written in 1908–09 was amended twelve or thirteen times as the result of ultimatums handed down to the author by members of the party's Central Committee: Savinkov would either revise his memoirs or be expelled from the PSR.[35] This repeated revision was certainly not an isolated instance of the party editing personal testimony in accordance with its own vision of the truth,[36] and Nicolaevsky's analysis inevitably reflects the biases of his sources.

His own biases exacerbate this shortcoming. By the 1930s, Nicolaevsky was not entirely free of the political passions of his revolutionary youth and exhibited a somewhat categorical, if not downright opinionated, outlook strongly colored by an underlying conviction that the tsarist authorities were unscrupulous and shamelessly engaged in shadowy enterprises bordering on criminality. This assumption, characteristic of Nicolaevsky the Menshevik, largely disappeared in his later years. But, in his study of Azef, Nicolaevsky the historian still considered government sources to be a priori less credible than those depicting Azef as a criminal and heartless monster, and he retained a romanticized view of the revolution as a panacea for all evil in Russia, with the terrorist struggle a thing of great "purity and beauty."[37]

To Nicolaevsky's credit as a scholar, in the latter part of his life he recognized the serious shortcomings of his earlier work; his death in 1966 prevented him from completing the task of revising it significantly on the basis of newly available evidence.[38] Nevertheless, all subsequent students of the Russian revolutionary movement, most of whom barely touched upon the Azef affair, invariably adopted Nicolaevsky's viewpoint as a common denominator for their own interpretations, accepting the insights of his dated book almost verbatim and never seriously challenging any aspect of his analysis.[39]

Azef left no memoirs, and what biographer would not lament this lacuna in the information about the character under investigation, and the lack of the potential key to his self-perception?[40] On the bright side, the accretion of previously inaccessible sources—historical, psychological, and literary—by itself warrants a fresh look at the extraordinary life of Russia's master spy. We may never be entirely sure about certain details relevant to Azef's formative years, and, admittedly, parts of this book—particularly those that seek to scrutinize the development of his personality—are speculative. In these sections, far from professing an axiom or making a definitive statement, the author aspires to introduce an original and illuminating hypothesis about Azef's psychological profile.

This biography's primary objectives are thus to delineate the spy's discernible image and to reconstruct his extraordinary life of deceit, cruelty, and fear. As if to compensate for some speculative interpretations, as well as for the decreased heat and urgency in today's writing about Russian revolutionaries, the secret police, and terror, the greater temporal distance liberates the historian from many obsolete passions and prejudices. It calls for recompense for the flaws in the tale of the Azef affair, which has never been fully unraveled, leaving ample opportunity for rumor, legend, and historical distortion.

1

A Frightened Child

Terror! What can terror not accomplish? What can reason or religion do to stay the Monster's icy embrace?
—Friedrich Schiller, *The Robbers*, Act 2, Scene 1

In our post-Freudian world there is little need to be reminded of the importance of childhood in the maturation process. At the risk of repeating a truism, the earliest experiences and impressions, external and internal, physical and emotional, intellectual and spiritual, work in their multiplicity to construct a framework for the individual's conceptions of his environment and of himself.[1] Giving tribute to these assumptions, our story begins in the tiny rural town of Lyskovo,[2] in the Grodno province of the Russian Empire, where on 11 July 1869 Evno Azef was born to a very poor Jewish family.

As was true for most Jews in Russia at the time, Azef's life was restricted from the moment of his birth, for he was born in one of the regions of the so-called Pale, peripheral areas specifically designated by the government for Jewish settlements. Of the seven million Jewish inhabitants of the Russian Empire, only an insignificant number succeeded in breaking out of the Pale; the overwhelming majority were permanently confined within it. These Jews lived the life of the semifictional characters portrayed in Shalom Aleichem's stories: with no legal rights to the ownership of farmland, most of them found themselves residing in the semiurban communities known in Yiddish as *shtetls* and in Russian as *mestechki* (literally, "small places"), varying in size from large villages to small towns. In these peripheral settlements everything spoke of habitual poverty:

> the teeming market place, the unpaved streets, the shabby wooden buildings. In summer the dust piles up in thick layers which the rain changes to mud so deep that wagon wheels stick fast and must be pried loose by the sweating driver, with the assistance of helpful

bystanders.... When the mud gets too bad, boards are put down over the black slush so that people can cross the street.

The thirsty dust is further moistened by the dishwater and other liquid refuse of the *shtetl* which is emptied out in the streets. "By the smell of the street water," it is said, "you can tell what day of the week it is."

The main street of a large *shtetl* may be paved with jagged stones, set in as they are found, with no attempt to shape or smooth them.... A few buildings may have two stories, the others will be shabby, unadorned, one-story structures, some with a yard and perhaps a small vegetable garden surrounded by a fence, often broken down.

There is no "Jewish" architecture. The characteristic features of the buildings are their age and their shabbiness....

The general appearance of neglect declares in addition the fact that the house is viewed as a temporary shell ... inhabited for a brief moment of history. Doctrine teaches that only the mind and the spirit endure—"life is a hallway to heaven"—and even the least soulful Jews of the *shtetl,* through force of circumstance if not of conviction, treat their physical dwelling places in accordance with this teaching.

A long history of exile and eviction strengthens the tendency.... True, it is not ... uncommon for a *shtetl* family to inhabit the same house for a hundred years. Yet at any moment the fatal decree may strike, and they may be tossed from the homestead into the deep dust of the road.[3]

Most men in a *mestechko* tried to make a living as petty artisans and craftsmen, salesmen, retail merchants, or small-scale businessmen, and with rare exceptions, the Jews of the Pale barely made ends meet, as the whole contents of many of their so-called "stores" could be bought for "a bit of cash." Their typically large families thus dwelled in overcrowded quarters filled with crying, sickly babies, noisy and messy children of various ages, rushing women dressed in similar "drab mended dresses, a shawl over the shoulders," and grumbling grandparent patriarchs—all living side by side with "the chickens, geese, perhaps a goat or even a cow ... who share[d] the streets, the yards, and on occasion the houses."[4]

Their life was that of the traditional Jewish community, resting on thousands of years of religious orthodoxy. Russian Jewry had a unique diaspora culture with distinctive legends and songs, respect for seniority, and inherited family values, as well as devotion to learning and bookish wisdom. The Jews lived as double outcasts—from both their historical homeland in Palestine and from the mainstream of Christian society in Russia, their geographical homeland. But for all their hardships and the humiliating knowledge of their oppressed status as pariahs in this prejudiced stepmother-country, the gray of their daily life was brightened by splashes of colorful and joyous moments: merry, yet meaningful, holiday celebrations, the happiness of weddings and childbirth, and the quiet exaltation of prayer and traditional storytelling.

Still, their life also included a strong element of fear springing from the eternal threat that their perpetual privation and dearth could all too easily evolve into total impoverishment. Azef's family, of which Evno was the second child, was certainly not exempt from this downtrodden people's dread. His parents, the very poor tailor Fishel' Azef and his wife Sara, had three sons and four daughters, and "for every bite of food there were many hungry mouths."[5] The adults were absorbed in their routine of hard work. His father, equipped with needles and scissors, was always bending over a pile of fabrics, and his mother, weary from childbirth and incessant nursing, yet determined to maintain the household, constantly cooked, washed, cleaned, scolded, and spanked. While still too young to take part in the daily chores, the children were "left to their own devices" (to avoid the more contemporary term "neglected"), free to play among themselves with their few simple toys, to fight for sweets and the other occasional gifts that life brought them, to grow, and, God willing, become a relief and comfort to their aging parents, as was expected of every decent member of the Jewish community. The life of this small and stable community was open to their observation, and very early the children knew its rules and expectations. Since it did not occur to anyone to shelter them from the perpetual trepidations of poverty, that inherent attribute of their milieu, their childhoods were inevitably marked by an awareness of this adult anxiety. For any child, "thrust by birth into an environment he can neither interpret nor control is ... fated to experience as security or insecurity ... both the passing moods and prevailing attitudes of the adults who shape the home."[6]

Nothing distinguished the Azef family from their neighbors in the little town in the Pale until in 1874, when Evno was five years of age and his father decided to risk seeking a better fortune in a place far away. Along with thousands of other indigent migrants from all over provincial Russia, he chose Rostov-on-Don as their new home.[7] Rostov was at the time a rapidly developing industrial and commercial center in southeast Russia, a "merchant city," or the "Russian Chicago," as it was nicknamed for its unexpected economic boom in the third quarter of the nineteenth century. With its ample opportunities Rostov held a magnetic attraction for enterprising upstarts[8]—particularly among the Jews. The Jewish community of Rostov was one of the largest outside the Pale, and although Jews comprised less than 7 percent of the city's population, their economic and cultural influence was impressive and disproportionate to their number. The Jews headed various commercial and financial institutions in Rostov; they ran a number of industrial enterprises; and many lawyers, doctors, and journalists in the city were Jewish.[9] Among Rostov's poor folk rumors and success stories spread about local business magnates ("cavaliers with golden bracelets") who had begun their illustrious careers as vendors and retail salesmen and by the end of their lives had accumulated enormous fortunes in family enterprises. Such tales stimulated the imaginations and acquisitive instincts of many people.

So it was that Fishel' Azef also decided to pursue a career in commerce after his resettlement. Not daring enough to venture into an unfamiliar trade, he opened a modest drapery shop. Still, except for the fact that the family now had to become accustomed to the busy life of a larger town, which was "growing like a mushroom in rainy weather," the Azefs' lifestyle improved little, if at all. The family business failed to make a fortune.[10]

Unable to afford high-priced "civilized" living quarters in the Old Town, with its paved, clean, and brightly illuminated streets, its bustling industrial and commercial life, and its abundance of expensive—and gaudy—shops and European-style restaurants, the Azef family remained outside the nouveau riche Rostov. Separated by poverty from the middle-class glamor of the city's center, they lived in a neighborhood that was a model of slovenly indigence. "If I were a hard-core criminal and had to choose one of two punishments: Siberian exile or a journey . . . along the streets of Rostov, I would have preferred the former,"[11] a contemporary summed up his springtime travel experience, for during every rain whole sections of the city turned into impassable swamps. In the fall, the mire and manure reached above people's knees, and occasionally a family would not dare to leave the house for several days, lest they be immersed in a mud bath. The unpaved streets resembled poorly maintained dirt roads, and were so scantily lit by kerosene lanterns that a local joke declared these drab neighborhoods to be "illuminated exclusively by the moon."[12] Shabby little houses surrounded by filthy yards intensified the sense of destitution, as did the sight of the habitual beggar with a languid hand stretched out for alms, or a drunk, with his sluggish jabber and coarse songs.

Geographical relocation thus did not reverse the wheel of fortune for the Azefs, and it did not alleviate Evno's earliest experiences of impediments and deprivation. In fact, the child probably felt his inferiority even more keenly, for while most inhabitants in Lyskovo, segregated as they were from the Russian Orthodox population, shared the egalitarian life of the dispossessed, in Rostov-on-Don the Azefs were exposed for the first time to much greater ethnic, religious, and social stratification, as well as to the wonderful new temptations that money could buy.

Poor as they were, the Azefs were not homeless or starving; in other words, they were not in the very last stage of deprivation, when a person is totally crushed by the constant struggle to survive physically and no longer considers his condition in relationship to that of the others. Evno was certainly pressed by his family's unfortunate circumstances, yet, as he grew, he still had the drive to assess his predicament. As he came into contact with and involuntarily compared himself to others his age whose households did not bear the devastating stigma of poverty, Azef must have begun to develop a love for money and jealousy of those who had it.[13]

The move could have hardly eliminated an equally strong age-old anxiety that, overt or concealed, had left a permanent psychological imprint on every Jew residing in the Russian Empire—the ever-present threat that the Russian Orthodox majority's conventional antipathy and bigotry toward the Jewish inhabitants of a particular locality would rupture into something worse. Such anti-Semitic outbursts frequently assumed the most barbarous forms of popular hatred and mass violence, culminating in haphazardly organized pogroms that terrorized the Jewish population in the Pale and beyond. The very word "pogrom" elicited panic, and legends of past brutalities kept painful memories and fears alive for generations. Like other children, Evno absorbed these fears as part of his typical Jewish upbringing.[14] For even though the Azefs no longer lived within the Pale, where episodes of anti-Jewish brutality occurred periodically, the prior agonizing experience of the oppressed minority prescribed perpetual alarm. Those who were born in that traumatized environment commonly took for granted a time-proven conjecture that one evening, stunningly quiet and filled with dark foreboding, their timid hopes of avoiding catastrophe could be shattered by the sound of a broken window and by coarse voices from an angry crowd of drunken savages at their doorstep, yelling insults and curses, breaking in, smashing plates and furniture, beating, raping, and looting.

Family ambience and spirit "constitute the most important single factor in the child's climate of emotional growth,"[15] and insecurity and threat were forever present in Evno's household. Hence, in psychiatric terminology, from his earliest years Azef was at great risk of "translat[ing] his experiences into . . . self-doubting" and mistrust. Moreover, in the initial stages of the strenuous and agitated process of building a self-image, a process at work from the moment of birth, the only status a child assigns to himself is that granted him by others, and therefore the only way a small child "can estimate his worth is by the treatment meted out to him" by caretaking adults.[16] The apprehensive, inhibited, and fearful Fishel' and Sara Azef, perceiving themselves as ill-omened and hapless survivors, could not but project this self-image onto their young son, who in their eyes must have been as pitiful as his unfortunate parents.[17]

Whereas mutual kindness and warm caring among family members might have alleviated the crude effects of poverty, Azef's household was well short of being an idyll of love: "There were always quarrels and fights.... A real drama in their family."[18] At least once Azef's mother ran away from home—and in the days when wife battering was almost routine, it took exceptional abuse to drive a subdued woman, unprotected by an independent income, out of the house. No wonder that in the midst of a never-ending family conflict "the children were going crazy" and the relations among the siblings seemed to follow the rueful patterns set by their parents.[19] And—at least so it appeared to the neighbors—of all the Azef children Evno elicited particular antipathy for being "rude and callous."[20]

Evno's father, however, in at least one respect attempted to overcome their accursed fate—by sending his sons to school, despite the tremendous strain on the family's already meager resources. Even away from the Pale, Fishel' Azef retained one of the fundamental beliefs of *shtetl* culture—that education was the key to success and a source of pride:

> A boy who'll study the Gemara
> The father will listen with happiness and joy[21]

In Rostov, however, Azef's father disregarded the traditional wisdom of Jewish orthodoxy that dictated that all learning was to center around the study of the Torah and the Talmud, and he sent his son to the all-male Petrovskii Technical High School. The choice was quite natural for anyone of Fishel' Azef's background. Hoping that strictly utilitarian training would enable a Jewish boy to help his family, and regarding secular education as a major financial investment, fathers were typically inclined to enroll their sons in occupational schools, which had the additional appeal of being less expensive than a gymnasium with a classical curriculum.[22]

Evno Azef thus became the happy beneficiary of a secondary education, a rare luxury for Jewish boys of his background. Yet his scholastic experience seems to have fallen short of redressing either his lack of confidence or his inclination for self-pity—a penchant that he would retain throughout his life and verbalize frequently and explicitly in his adulthood.[23] His school years were also the time when he seemed to have developed a strong tendency to cut corners and seek easy and immediate gains, probably justified in his eyes by the fact that life (especially his life) was tough and it would be foolish not to grab whatever it had to offer.[24] Thus, the unresolved tensions that dominated Azef's early childhood likely reinforced the emerging young opportunist's gradual estrangement from a milieu in which he felt unsafe, turning him into the personality we encounter in his adult years—a wary loner. The same tensions also seem to have contributed to the development of a most agreeable climate for converting many new external circumstances and stimuli into perceived threats.[25]

One of the circumstances was the humiliating awareness of his own poverty, which followed Azef like a shadow into his new social settings. It haunted him more persistently than ever when he began to study side by side with the sons of more prosperous families. Not that his economic disadvantage was merely an exaggerated product of the young man's insecurity—it did present him with very real difficulties. The one most degrading for his ego was that due to his father's inability to meet the costs of his education, Evno apparently had to extend his studies over a period longer than the typical eight-year course. This explains why Azef graduated from his technical school in 1890, when he was already twenty-one; that is, three or four years older than most of his peers.[26] Still, of the many young men who experienced similarly unfortunate circumstances, surely not all suffered from the same devastating insecurity. What appears to have been Azef's troubled emotional reaction to his poverty most likely did not result from a realistic assessment of a complicated social situation; rather, one is led to conjecture that it might have been largely based on psychologically preconditioned and uniquely personal "hangover responses from past ego-defeats."[27]

Nor did Azef seem to possess enough self-confidence to overcome his innate sense of inferiority or to assert his Jewish identity in the atmosphere of official Russian Orthodoxy that at the time was obligatory in his school, as it was in most secondary institutions.[28] To be sure, the task was not an easy one, especially for someone from a family with earlier experiences in the Pale, where the very lifestyle of the *shtetl* community implied distrust of its Gentile or "goy" neighbors.[29] Nothing but harm could be expected from their Christian Orthodox neighbors—such was the traditional assumption of the Russian Jews, many of whom feared and simultaneously despised the Gentiles nearly to the point of considering them crude and aggressive barbarians, prone to unmitigated lawlessness and violence. Fated to live in their midst, the Jewish minority instinctively sought to protect itself by attaching the utmost value to its own community, which isolated itself from most outside influences as its only chance to survive. This prevailing collective attitude—legitimate to a large degree and based on the centuries-long diaspora experience— required constant affirmation by individual members. Accordingly, it is perhaps not very surprising that the Azefs' habitual circumspect withdrawal from the Russian world did not end after their relocation to the more cosmopolitan Rostov. And the young Evno, still very much part of his community and his family, probably continued to perceive his environment as hostile and threatening to people of his kind.

Many Jewish students had to cope with occasional humiliating instances of discrimination on the part of the school administration and teachers. These acts were aggravated by the fact that a majority of the pupils were Christian. But Azef never seemed to have acquired the assertiveness, or what might be called Jewish pride, essential for a sense of inner invulnerability.[30] Evno was thus hardly in a position to make realistic judgments about the attitudes of his Russian Orthodox peers toward his Jewish background and identity, and consequently he retreated into self-imposed alienation from those who might have been his friends. Evidently, he preferred to maintain rather distant, lukewarm, and strictly intellectual relations with his fellow students without becoming emotionally involved[31]—perhaps a result of being incapable of intimacy, which presupposes both courage and trust.

To use a contemporary term, Azef was never "popular" among his schoolmates and, according to some accounts, his relations with his peers were "most odious." At this point in his life, he was not yet fully proficient in concealing his attitudes and emotions, and so other pupils probably could not help developing a certain intuitive awareness of his troubled self-image and repressed fears. He always seemed to be hiding his real thoughts and did not inspire confidence as a faithful friend.[32] What was worse, his fellow students considered him guilty of the most despised of all possible schoolyard crimes: complaining to school authorities and "squealing."[33] Like most insecure individuals, he sought to assert himself at someone else's expense, was rude, and "liked to jeer at other people's failings"; his acquaintances considered him a selfish person who "never forgot an injury and was revengeful."[34]

The other students could hardly be blamed for dealing with him on his own terms. They were not guilty of snobbery, contempt, or prejudice when they reacted to him with the same halfhearted, detached, and somewhat phlegmatic way of communicating and socializing, as well as occasional outbursts of undisguised hostility. In addition, Azef seemed immune to one genuine obsession enthralling numerous teenagers at the time: "the problem of ethics—a virtuous private and public life."[35] Conversely, the fact that Azef "was never noted for his scrupulousness regarding other people's money, a trait that had already shown itself in small ways" while he was still at school, when "many considered him capable of anything that might bring him a profit,"[36] caused even the most congenial of his peers to look askance at him. Finally, there was another and equally crucial factor that alienated and repelled the people around Azef, one which completed the transformation of this already apprehensive and uncertain youth into a lonely, surreptitiously bitter, and intensely frightened adult: Evno Azef had an extremely unattractive physical appearance.

Indeed, by all conventional standards Azef was hopelessly ugly, a circumstance never taken lightly by a young person. "Unprepossessing and heavily built, with a puffy yellow face, large stuck-out ears, a low forehead narrowing towards the top, thick lips, and a flattened nose," Azef resembled a ridiculous caricature. His looks were rendered even more grotesque by his "squeaky high voice that seemed bizarre and ludicrous," and somehow incongruent with the gross and troll-like body resting on thin legs.[37] His grumbling manner of speech seemed particularly disagreeable. He did not look at his interlocutor and instead directed his voice "somewhere down under the table, under his feet."[38] Azef was of above-average height, reduced somewhat because of his slouched posture; he had a short rotund neck; and his hands and feet were small and disproportionate to his bulky figure.[39] Some ill-wishers among his schoolmates called him "a fat pig"[40] and the nickname stuck, for he repulsed people physically at first contact and, since he was inauspiciously slow and cautious in establishing closer relations, he only rarely gave them a chance to reevaluate their first unfavorable impression.

Azef also lacked any of the advantages supplied by stylish clothes, habitual ease at witty conversation, or self-assurance in small talk, all of which were highly valued by teenagers then as they are now. He could not have failed to realize that his unfavorable appearance created an additional obstacle in his deficient relations with others. He was undoubtedly embarrassed by his unrefined manners, the uneasiness and discomfort that betrayed his plebeian upbringing and caused him to be even more clumsy and restrained in the company of those he considered better bred. Not knowing how to correct this image, he sought on occasion to conceal his awkward inferiority behind exaggerated displays of tactlessness bordering on coarseness, when he deliberately offended others with his brazenness and arrogance. This self-defeating game, however, could not alleviate his social complexes, and proved of no avail in winning him success in the student milieu, especially among those of the opposite sex. As he also failed to impress his acquaintances by any gift for warm sensitivity, affection, or empathy, Azef was virtually forced to compensate for his lack of physical charm and social finesse by what would seem to have been his last resort: superior mental and rational faculties.

It is not atypical for an emotionally and psychologically deficient personality in immediate need of recognition to begin to rely almost exclusively on intelligence as a means of self-assertion. And so Azef showed perseverance in developing his intellect, a process that had begun early in his childhood, stimulated and intensified by the supreme "veneration for the power of the mind" in the Jewish community.[41]

While no culture considers stupidity and ignorance virtues, or holds them in esteem, few other groups have as much scorn for them as the Jewish people. Russians, for example, are easily able to tolerate folly and even idiocy; in their tradition, the "Fool in Christ" (*iurodivyi*), a half-crazy beggar clowning barefoot in the churchyard snow and mumbling prayers to God and curses to sinners, is invariably respected as a holy man and a popular prophet. But all spirituality aside, the Russians treat a simpleton, someone akin to "Ivan the Fool," the famous hero of Russian folklore, with good-natured humor and even sympathy if his intellectual flaws are compensated for by naive affability and unassuming kindness. The Jews, on the other hand, are most reluctant to allow for such excuses, especially when an individual fails to make a genuine effort at book learning.[42] "Not every Jew . . . is a scholar or even a learned man, but intellectual achievement is the universally accepted goal," and diligent study is the expectation.[43] To a great extent the traditional intellectual inclination stems from the essence of the Jewish religion, which "imposes a law on its believers." This law "wants to be accessible to reason (the Talmud is nothing but the perpetual rational analysis of God's commandments). . . . The criterion of good and evil is objective: it is a matter of understanding the written law and obeying it."[44] "In the Talmud . . . man's highest distinction is considered in terms of the intellectual and ethical perfection epitomized in devotion to the legacy and in the study of the law, the Torah." And "the holiness and greatness of the Torah are passed onto those who study and develop it. The great sages, who have penetrated the Torah deeply, were equal to angels, became immortal, and acquired powers to create and destroy the universe, raise the dead, etc."[45]

Considering such potential advantages, it is no wonder that from infancy a Jewish boy is guided and prodded toward endeavors of the mind, even through the lullabies his mother sings him while he is still in the cradle:

My Yankeleh shall study the Law
The Law shall baby learn
Great books shall my Yankeleh write
Much money shall he earn.[46]

As a young man Azef found only the last line of this simple yet revealing song truly meaningful. As part of the process of transforming his childhood and adolescent experiences and their psychological repercussions into well-developed penchants, preferences, interests, and general attitudes toward life around him, he gradually reduced his intellectual orientation to sheer practical judgment and shrewdness. Naturally bright, Azef possessed a strong analytical mind and evident abilities for learning, reinforced by a good memory. At the same time, he never developed a liking for theory and was not known for a propensity to contemplate abstract philosophical matters. He did not turn into an erudite, fond of knowledge for its own sake. Nor did he even become a lover of prolonged study who would spend an exciting night over a bulky tome. He lacked inquisitiveness, as well as wit and creativity, and simply was not sufficiently fascinated with any particular area of the humanities or science to be a scholar or thinker. It is perhaps even more interesting that he gravitated toward a purely technical knowledge of practical and rigidly functional disciplines at a time when many of his peers were absorbed by belles lettres and the arts.[47] Azef may have been less interested in literature than in hard sciences because the latter entailed operating with well-defined, concrete, and objective phenomena that demanded strictly intellectual approaches and rational analysis, while the former presupposed, and indeed required—at least in the minds of his contemporaries—greater spiritual and emotional involvement.

Isolated from most of his young peer-intellectuals by his all-encompassing and overpowering rationality, Azef was quite conscious of his intellectual superiority, even if he was unaware of the fact that his mental facilities could hardly compensate for his inmost emotional deficiencies. He refused to associate with students regarded by the school elite as mediocrities, buffoons, and dimwits without any cultural interests, and he did not fit well into any of the school circles. He thus remained a loner until his final years of study in Rostov, when he made the acquaintance of a group of radical-minded youths who were

thinking up revolutionary schemes in their spare time between geom-
etry and chemistry lessons.

This bunch of nonconformists included a few young idealists and
dreamers who were appalled by the stagnant provincialism of bourgeois life in Rostov and had become captivated by the romanticized
image of the heroic freedom fighters glorified in revolutionary publications. All of them were amateurs at politics, having only recently
begun to flirt with radicalism by reading forbidden literature and discussing the views of famous proponents of antigovernment activity,
from the fathers of populism to the Social Democrats and Marx himself, who was already very much in vogue in Russia in the late 1880s
and early 1890s. Perhaps even more noteworthy is the fact that at the
time they were all going through the common hazards of adolescent
rebellion, subjecting to doubt every belief and value expressed by their
families and mentors, and trying to assert themselves as individuals
with unique identities, a developed set of values, and well-formulat-
ed world outlooks. In the process of filling in the gap left by their rejection of traditional values, these youngsters had little choice but to
internalize other people's concepts, validating them as their own.

The emerging passion for revolution in Russian society as a whole
was extremely advantageous to the young, for in addition to providing
them with an elevated outlook and a program for action that offered
ample opportunity for them to prove themselves as heroes, it justified
the spontaneous and often irresponsible decision-making inherent in
their rather prosaic private struggles against the authority of the elders.
These students thus "sought, on the one hand, to liberate themselves
personally from the control of authoritarian parents and teachers, and,
on the other, to legitimize this natural desire for independence by adopting an intellectually or morally justifiable public cause for rebellion"
that would provide them "a seemingly lofty outlet" for their typically mundane drives.[48]

For some of these restless teenagers, their families' economic hardship was an additional, strictly practical incentive for becoming involved
in the revolution. Frustrated by their inability to escape poverty and by
the lack of opportunities for social advancement within the traditional establishment, these dispossessed youths with bleak prospects of success in life enlisted in the struggle against the socioeconomic conditions
endorsed by the tsarist regime. Naive, self-assured, and reckless, they
failed to appreciate the grave consequences of their eagerness to participate in the revolution, seeing it as their only chance for a better future.

Similar motives turned out to be even stronger influences on a
number of Jewish students, whose fiery enthusiasm for radicalism was

reinforced by still vivid memories of the wave of anti-Semitic violence that swept through Russia and Ukraine in the early 1880s. The humiliation of the Pale, state-imposed restrictions on higher education, and multiple obstacles to careers that could have provided many assimilated Jews new long-term interests and objectives, strongly predisposed them to embrace the revolution, in which they then invested all their hopes.

Regardless of the objective circumstances, some youngsters espoused radical activity as part of a general personal proclivity toward felonious behavior and a criminal lifestyle. Among these shady characters, one of Azef's close acquaintances deserves special mention for his notoriety. Young Solomon Ryss began his illustrious career as a revolutionary by forging gymnasium diplomas and claiming that he used the profits from their sale for the purpose of inciting an insurrection in Rostov. Wanted by the city police, he soon fled to Germany, where he eventually joined the Maximalists and assumed the alias Mortimer.

Distinguished for his blatant frivolousness with ethics, Ryss, always more than negligent as far as scrupulousness of methods was concerned, culminated his stay in Europe by stealing and selling rare library books to finance his return trip to Russia. There, in June 1906, he was arrested during an attempted robbery targeting a workers' association (an artel) in Kiev. At that point, Ryss offered his services to the police, and for several months supplied the authorities with a concoction of facts and fibs regarding the affairs of the Maximalists. At the same time, he assured the revolutionaries that he was feeding the Okhrana false information, and even managed to convince some of his radical comrades that his activities were of great revolutionary value. The game did not last long, however, and police suspicions forced Ryss to flee once more. He was arrested again in April 1907, and after the police officers summarily rejected his brazen offer of a fifty-thousand-ruble bribe in exchange for his release, Ryss was sentenced to death and ended his life on the gallows in February 1908. Back in Rostov, Azef, of course, could not have foreseen that the biography of this pretentious, excitable, harlequin-like, waggish young man would develop into an instructive parable of a fraudulent life. The weight of the coincidence is not diminished, however: Solomon Ryss was the only person that sources show Azef to have been on especially good terms with during his early youth.[49]

Azef's background hardly predisposed him to be a champion of the Russian autocracy, but in his case, another far more potent psychological drive stimulated his initial association with its adversaries. His exasperated egocentrism clearly interfered with his ability to immerse himself in an idealistic crusade, yet by joining radical student circles, this self-absorbed, disheartened, and leery young man found an opportunity to make at least a superficial escape from his perpetual isolation for the first time in his life. He was able at last to unite himself with others his age in support of a common cause. Azef's initiation into the revolutionary camp does not seem to have stemmed from a philosophical position; first and foremost it was a result of the need to be a member of a group—something which was also true for countless other adolescents craving a sense of identity and security.

Joining a collective is frequently tantamount to taking a developmental shortcut, and for Azef it was manifestly so, as it promised him painless, if perfunctory, relief from many tormenting anxieties.[50] No longer was he under pressure to synthesize and shape his singularity and to struggle for its recognition, since the radical circle now provided him with a group identity. From the moment of his enrollment in the subversive student cell, Azef could simply identify himself as a revolutionary, a term that encompassed an assortment of assumptions and characteristics common to every member of the secret group. These characteristics included preformulated intellectual postulates and tenets, as well as preestablished ethical principles—the adamant values of the clandestine collective that Azef claimed to have adopted in order to avoid the difficulties inherent in developing values of his own.

For members of this group (as for all like-minded rebels in Russia) the evil nature of the autocracy was an axiom requiring no further consideration. Incompetent, corrupt, and responsible for all the misfortunes that had ever befallen the country, the government of Alexander III was destined to be overthrown by the forces of enlightenment and progress, whose ultimate goal was the complete destruction of the decaying socio-economic, political, and cultural establishment for the sake of a just, humane, and efficient future order to be founded on benevolence, rationality, and law. By the close of the nineteenth century, an increasing majority of opponents of the tsarist regime envisaged this free and egalitarian society as socialist. Even the skeptics who insisted that class analysis was too schematic to be accurate and doubted the expediency of building a new society in accordance with socialist principles considered participation in the revolutionary process an ethical obligation. Not logic alone, but morality itself required them to assume the role of defenders of the oppressed and exploited masses, to liberate them from the tyranny of the all-powerful and unscrupulous autocratic colossus. For generations this was the leitmotif of the intelligentsia's revolutionary credo.

To suppose that Azef was intellectually or morally inclined to become a servant and guardian of the Russian people would be incongruous with our knowledge of his personality. Nevertheless, he readily endorsed all aspects of the creed professed by his radical acquaintances, and they welcomed him as their new comrade. This acceptance gave him at least the illusion of fraternity and rapport with others, which, along with a set of surface values, and supposedly a distinct area of competence, provided a core for his identity, and constituted some of the significant gains resulting from his affiliation with the radical brotherhood. A long craved sense of self-worth was his other important psychological acquisition.

Azef's association with school rebels hardly counteracted altogether the detrimental impact of his earlier experiences: it did not provide him with sufficient self-assertiveness and emotional maturity to deal effectively with the reality of every new situation, nor did it free him from grappling compulsively with unsolved issues from the past.[51] Still, the group's clandestine and illegal nature, which presupposed its seclusion from the outer environment, coupled with the circle's cohesion, magnified as it was by external dangers that tended to unite its members against a world of strangers and enemies, allowed Azef to supplant his old exclusion complex with the previously unknown satisfaction of belonging to a restricted guild closed to the outsiders—to an elite of sorts. This new status in turn augmented his sense of self-importance. However undeservedly, his self-pride could feed off yet another feature of "the group mind"[52]—an implicit belief in the radicals' moral superiority as the only honest and virtuous altruists, as selfless heroes among a multitude of cowards, philistines, and rapacious careerists with no consciences.

Azef and his comrades quickly developed revolutionary connections in the adult world beyond the school walls, an accomplishment that brought them additional confidence and a new boost for their self-esteem. The experienced radicals acknowledged the activities of the youngsters and enthusiastically encouraged their yearning to become full-fledged freedom fighters. Lacking the dexterity and probably the desire for self-awareness (which cannot be attained except through the painfully onerous process of casting aside self-protective reasoning), Azef was obviously not inclined to consider how shaky his revolutionary convictions really were, and, always hungry for approval from his peers and elders, he did not falter in accepting what was not really his. At this point, he may already be regarded as an unconscious imposter guilty of falsely accepting facile praise, but by the same token it is also possible to pity this vulnerable youth for becoming even more dependent on his revolutionary colleagues for self-respect.

Azef's new acquaintances appreciated his intelligence, shrewdness, and especially his matter-of-fact way of handling practical difficulties. Yet, his repellently morose, reserved, and dispassionate demeanor, as well as his pragmatic, business-like approach to revolutionary affairs, perplexed other members of his radical circle, in which, as in most similar groups, fiery slogans, inflated, pompous rhetoric, and ostentatious political demagoguery were almost obligatory and apparently inseparable from genuine conviction. Conversely, Azef demonstrated a positive aversion to high-flown speeches and, indeed, to speeches in general: while taking part in late-night student meetings devoted largely to discussions of underground literature and to tackling the complexities of revolutionary dogma, "he only rarely and even then reluctantly and cursorily inserted a word; to all questions he answered with an abrupt 'yes' or 'no', as if he resented breaking the concentrated silence into which he hastened to submerge himself again."[53]

Azef's grim and reticent manners, although clearly unattractive, did not put his comrades on guard, and the fact that he was hardly an idealist did not cause them to see him as a fraud. Perhaps his coldness merely gave them a sense of foreboding about the man who seemed to have become involved in the struggle against the tsarist government not as a matter of conscience, but as a result of a strictly logical prediction that the old regime was bound to capitulate to the forces of progress. Hence, without doubting the sincerity of Azef's radical convictions, they perceived him as a somewhat alien character in their midst.[54]

Azef could not have been oblivious of this, and he sought to eliminate the distance between himself and his comrades by outright pretense. He gradually learned the value of inflammatory slogans and enticing political clichés, and while he never succeeded in conquering his audience with exceptional oratorical powers, he had apparently realized by this time that a small dose of revolutionary ardor in his rare speeches would suffice to modify his image as detached pragmatist. He probably also sought to compensate for his lack of personal warmth by going to special pains to present himself as a thoughtful and caring comrade who was deeply concerned about his friends—something he would trouble himself with throughout his life among the radicals.[55] For someone as self-centered as Azef, it must not have been easy to feign personal involvement in the lives of others. His new role required great attention and skill, but, paradoxically, precisely because of his profound egocentricity, he could at least play it at no emotional cost, without sentimental investments and affectionate sacrifices that would have been most difficult for him to make.

By this time, Azef could not have been entirely unaware of the pretense in his behavior and, simultaneously, of his far from trivial gift for deceit. Indeed, this awareness (still rather vague perhaps) might have even spurred him on to perfect his skill for subterfuge and to master the art of duplicity. For the time being, however, he was still a promising amateur, exercising his increasing proficiency in cunning against his young comrades, who surely wanted to see Azef as a friend and promptly allowed themselves to be swayed by his simulation of affection.

Meanwhile, revolutionary treatises and pamphlets could not save Azef from immediate practical urgencies. After he finally received his secondary school diploma, he was no longer able to rely on his father's support and had to find suitable employment. He quickly realized that his education provided him with few career opportunities. At best, he could count on occasional employment, and for the next couple of years he drifted from one job to another, partly, it seems, as a result of his desire for instant rewards without substantial effort. He struggled to support himself with occasional private lessons and by performing tedious clerical tasks. For a while he worked as a chronicler for a tiny local newspaper, the *Don Bee (Donskaia pchela)*. Among the journalistic small-fry, nicknamed "hard-labor convict-reporters" for their round-the-clock citywide hunt for news stories, Azef unsuccessfully competed with more experienced correspondents, even the best of whom subsisted on the miserable salary of thirty-five rubles a month. Eventually he became a traveling sales representative,[56] but none of these jobs could provide him with either sufficient financial resources for the present or bright prospects for much-desired material prosperity in years to come. Downcast and uncertain as to what to do next, Azef had little choice but to resist his mounting melancholy and endure with patience what he hoped would be a period of only temporary difficulties, always keeping his eyes open for a sudden opportunity to improve his lot. But no miracle happened, and this cheerless truth made it increasingly clear to Azef that a university degree was his only chance. He lacked the financial resources to undertake further studies, and the gloomy thought that he had reached a dead end most likely intensified his despondency, bitterness, and disaffection, bringing him closer to other disenchanted and frustrated outcasts among his revolutionary-minded associates.

At the same time, stormy clouds were gathering over their small radical circle. While playing their rather innocent revolutionary games, which amounted primarily to reading and circulating antigovernment literature, in their hearts the young rebels could hardly consider themselves dangerous subversives and a real threat to the tsarist regime, regardless of all attempts on their part to dramatize the significance of their underground activities. Local police officials, however, were of a different opinion. Unwilling to tolerate any organized opposition, no matter how insignificant it might have appeared, and inclined to attribute more importance to the tiny revolutionary cell than even its own members did, the authorities were determined to do away with the group by swift arrests.

For the radical upstarts, full of youthful bravado and remarkable nonchalance toward the risks associated with subversive activity, the news that the police had disbanded their secret circle came as a sudden shock, and, for all his caution, Azef was caught off guard. Yet, as soon as he learned early in 1892 that a number of his acquaintances had been taken into custody, his natural shrewdness suggested that he, too, was under suspicion and might soon share the fate of his apprehended comrades.[57] The very thought that he would have to undergo arrest, interrogation, and probably the tribulations of prison or exile submerged him in agony.[58] Azef was certainly unprepared to bear the onerous consequences of his half-hearted involvement in radical politics and dreamed only of removing himself from imminent danger, of finding a safe place to hide, of disappearing without a trace. There is little doubt that the feverish dread of prosecution and the urge to escape completely overshadowed and rendered irrelevant his avowed allegiance to the radical group. This rather flimsy and translucent allegiance from the start had been self-seeking and contingent upon Azef's inner pains and anxieties being soothed by the collective. Now that the collective was no more, and since his fear of punishment caused more anguish than ever before, Azef for the first time resolved to take his destiny in his own hands: he would save himself from arrest by fleeing abroad.

Azef's determination to go to the West was not entirely panic-based or new. For some time he had been contemplating the idea of leaving Russia for the sake of seeking a higher education, which he considered a major prerequisite for a "better life," and which, as a poor Jew, he was denied in his own country.[59] The greatest obstacle to realizing this dream was lack of money, and before the police scare all prospects of going abroad were in the realm of fantasy. Now, at this important turning point in his life, when his freedom was at stake, Azef made up his mind to raise the sum required for his trip no matter what the odds were. Instead of waiting around to be arrested, he did not waste any time and took the very first opportunity fate presented to him. As a traveling salesman he had received a consignment of butter from a merchant, which he sold for 800 rubles. With that money in the spring of 1892 he fled abroad.[60]

Arguably the emotion driving Azef to thievery was lacerating consternation, complemented by the lack of self-value that had highlighted his younger years and easily reconciled him to stealing. After all, a person endowed with stout self-respect as a conscientious human being would be greatly troubled by the inability to reconcile a favorable perception of his own personality with behavior that by any ethical norms is classified as unequivocally criminal. Typically, such a self-respecting individual would prefer to pursue the arduous course of solving immediate practical difficulties rather than invite a lifetime of trouble by compromising himself with a facile yet iniquitous solution, potentially damaging for his sense of self-worth. In committing this crime, Azef, on the other hand, acted very much in accordance with his already low self-expectations. Tragically, throughout his life his approach to any situation would "reflect the image of himself he buil[t] in his earliest years,"[61] an image that reflected insecurity and self-loathing.

As the train to Karlsruhe, Germany, crossed the Russian imperial border, a nervous young passenger, portly and looking older than his true age, could sigh with relief: he had fooled the police and no longer dreaded retribution for his political or commercial machinations. In addition, the sizeable packet of banknotes in his billfold, evoking a novel and sweet feeling of security, seemed to be solid assurance of the beginning of a new life. Yet overjoyed, complacent, and suddenly tranquil as he was, leisurely admiring the well-groomed scenery of the Junkerland, this man carried with him to the West the severe emotional afflictions of his youth. Among these, the truly pernicious one was his incurable fear. By the time he left Russia, his deeply ingrained anxieties no longer needed to be concretely defined; regardless of objective circumstances, which might or might not require circumspection, Evno Azef would always remain a frightened soul, a danger to himself, and, consequently, to anyone destined to cross his path.

2

Yet Another Way to Sell Your Soul

When our actions do not,
Our fears do make us traitors.
　　—William Shakespeare, *Macbeth*

Fortune seems to have remained with Azef during his first months in Germany. Soon after his arrival at Karlsruhe,[1] he entered the Polytechnicum and immersed himself in the intricacies of mechanical engineering. He also succeeded in revitalizing his connections with several Rostov acquaintances, and through them established ties with other members of the small colony of Russian students in Karlsruhe. So as not to appear the odd man out among the politically minded émigré majority, he became a member of a Social Democratic circle, where he built a reputation as a "most moderate" Marxist and an opponent of extremist tactics.[2]

Azef's immutable dilemma of poverty soon caught up with him, however. The stolen 800 rubles—a substantial sum at the time—had been sufficient to cover his travel and initial settling expenses, but it was not long before he faced financial hardship again. He was hardly in a position to expect help from home, and because of his still rudimentary command of the German language, he found only sporadic employment opportunities. Azef shared a cheap and poorly heated fourth-floor apartment at 30 Wertherstrasse with a fellow named Kozin, also from Rostov-on-Don, and impressed those who knew him at the time as a man "literally suffering from hunger and cold."[3]

True, his situation differed little from the plight of most other Russian students abroad, who were poorly clothed and often exhibited early signs of consumption on their pale faces and unhealthily burning cheeks. Chronically short of funds, they were perpetually concocting fanciful schemes for raising money, and were driven by their empty stomachs to the streets of foreign cities on the lookout for a lucky chance to make a bit of cash. But Azef refused to find consolation in the fact that there were hundreds of similarly destitute young men and women. He had no desire to endure his difficulties stoically until his engineering degree could provide him a comfortable living.[4] Stoicism had never been his strong suit, despite the routine economic deprivations of his childhood and early youth. Perhaps precisely because of his chronic neediness, Azef attached exaggerated importance to material comforts and never took them for granted, in contrast to many individuals who enjoy casual access to luxuries from childhood and place little value on them. Azef's eagerness to compensate for the misfortunes of his past was easily transformed into self-indulgence, and he resented and feared a spartan way of life.[5] Every new day that drove Azef closer to financial catastrophe became a stinging reminder that somehow he had to find a permanent source of income, and do so urgently before extreme poverty could interfere with his studies at the Polytechnicum and jeopardize his prospects for the future. While his fellow students embarked on a rugged course of hard work and self-denial in order to survive the depressing times, obtrusive thoughts about poverty gradually became Azef's haunting fixation.

Then, quite suddenly, he had a brainstorm, a stunning idea that might have been precipitated by a conversation with a certain Meierovich, a fellow-student in Karlsruhe. Meierovich was said to have told Azef that the Russian secret police paid salaries to its informers in the revolutionary milieu.[6] Eureka! The fainthearted, confused, and vacillating Azef, whose mind must have been running desperately in circles for a painless solution, knew what to do. He would send a letter to the Police Department in St. Petersburg, indicating his willingness to share the secrets of the radicals abroad with the imperial authorities. How easily he would then be able to avoid eternal deprivation. It would only take a few reports containing trifling information about the high-minded rubbish discussed in revolutionary student circles in Karlsruhe, information that Azef probably sincerely believed had absolutely no political weight or implication.

Psychologically, Azef doubtlessly needed to minimize the significance of the step he was about to take, but probably not because of a guilty conscience. An opportunist par excellence, he most likely did not torment himself with ethical dilemmas. Despite his familiarity with revolutionary doctrine, he never was a true believer. Since his relations with his comrades emanated from purely selfish needs, the thought of betraying their trust was unlikely to repulse Azef. He had already crossed a moral Rubicon in financing his escape from Rostov; and trading revolutionary secrets for money could hardly offend his sense of self-perception more severely than his earlier thievery, which had left Azef with a single intellectual retreat—the niche of cynicism.

Even though his concern seems to have laid outside the realm of ethics, as soon as Azef felt disentangled from his financial deadlock by his resolution to contact the police, he no doubt became susceptible to a new agonizing thought that threatened to undermine his will: what if someone found out? His reputation would be ruined beyond redemption; he would be ostracized by the entire émigré community; and perhaps his former friends would even take unpleasant action against him—the radicals had been known to avenge themselves on unmasked police spies and informers.

So as not to permit anxiety to divert him from his chosen course, Azef might have taken comfort in his own prudence and superior intellect, which had rescued him from major troubles in the past. As is often the case with a cynic, determined to rely exclusively upon rational calculation untempered by ethereal motives and passions, he did not seem to have much regard for his comrades' intellectual powers. Perhaps their minds indeed were rendered less effective by an array of ethical, aesthetic, and spiritual modulations. Balancing his understandable nervousness with a shield of cultivated arrogance, Azef was conceivably able to stake his future on his own superior intellectual discretion, which would surely enable him to keep the gullible students ignorant of his dealings with the police.

Azef's plan, like his earlier theft, can be seen as another shortcut taken by someone who could not boast of courage or self-confidence. Rather, his behavior contributes to the image of him as an apprehensive man, overwhelmed by a difficult situation and anxious to rid himself at once of his immediate problems at the expense of others. Imagining his tenure as a secret informer to be a fleeting adventure would surely have given him great solace. The last thing Azef probably wanted at this point was to turn into a professional police agent; his transient encounter with the Russian authorities was to be only a passing flirtation, he might have reassured himself, a liaison of convenience, from which he could safely withdraw as soon as he felt more secure financially. He finally made up his mind, oblivious to the forbidding consequences the decision would have for his entire life.

"I have the honor to inform the Gendarmerie," Azef wrote in his first letter to the police on 6 April 1893, "that there exists a group of socialist workers in Rostov-on-Don." There followed a list of names and a few facts intended to serve as proof for the Rostov authorities that the volunteer informer was indeed in possession of indispensable intelligence data.[7]

The officials in Rostov-on-Don were in no hurry to employ a new agent, however; apparently, they had ample experience with various shady individuals in dire need of funds who claimed to be in a position to assist the government against the revolutionaries. In reality many of these willing informers had no contacts and absolutely nothing new to reveal about the radicals. The police officials had sufficient reason to suspect that Azef was another of these useless frauds, especially because in his initial communication he failed to reveal his name.[8] As if anticipating such hesitation on the part of the local authorities, and already impatient with the delay, four days after sending his initial letter to the Rostov Gendarmerie, Azef dispatched another nameless offer, very similar in content, this time directly to the head of the Police Department in St. Petersburg. Azef was eager to persuade "His Excellency" that he might be useful in the government's efforts to fight revolutionary activity in Russia and abroad.

The police could easily identify their anonymous correspondent, for they knew the names of several students from Rostov living in Karlsruhe and could easily trace the author of the letter by his "characteristic slightly childish handwriting."[9] After receiving the requested information from Rostov-on-Don, the head of the political investigation section of the Police Department, G. K. Semiakin, called Azef by his true name in his May 31 reply to the prospective informer and, with a tint of sarcasm, asked him to confirm his mailing address.[10] For Azef, this unpropitious debut served a twofold purpose. The first was educational, as he immediately realized that he lacked the experience to play games with the tsarist police and that he had to be more cautious if he was to win their trust in the future. At the same time, by exposing himself to the Rostov officials, Azef gave them the opportunity to present a report to the Police Department summarizing his personal credentials, which the St. Petersburg authorities found most satisfactory for a prospective secret informer. They judged Evno Azef to be an "intelligent and clever intriguer; . . . in close touch with the young Jewish students living abroad," and stated that "he could thus be of real use as an agent. It can also be assumed that his covetousness and his present state of need will make him zealous in his duty." This recommendation decided Azef's fate, along with the fact that the price he had so boldly asked for his services was "delightfully low." Accordingly, on 10 June 1893, an assistant to the minister of the interior formally authorized Azef's employment, marking the inauguration of the secret agent's brilliant police career.[11]

With the first government payment, which the newly recruited informer received promptly at the end of June, came the long-awaited, albeit minimal, financial assuagement; regular checks from St. Petersburg would at least ward off the worst afflictions of poverty and keep Azef afloat until better times. In addition, he could look forward to promised annual bonuses every New Year. As far as his acquaintances could tell, however, his lifestyle underwent no visible transformation. Azef took special pains to conceal his abruptly acquired security, pretending to be permanently troubled by his miserable circumstances. He continued to send one financial aid appeal after another to every possible charitable organization abroad, never neglecting to show these supplication letters to his comrades under the pretext of seeking their help in correcting his broken German. Azef spent his police salary discreetly and maintained the image of a poverty-stricken émigré student to the end of his university course abroad.[12]

With his financial dilemma resolved, he now devoted a great deal of time to his studies at the Polytechnicum, gradually developing a strong preference for electrodynamics at the expense of his major field of mechanics. This interest led him to transfer in 1896 to Darmstadt, where he pursued a course in electrical engineering at one of the best technical colleges in Germany. The move facilitated his acquaintance with wider radical student circles outside the tiny colony in Karlsruhe, and allowed him gradually to broaden his contacts in the Russian émigré community at large. To accommodate the needs of the Police Department, Azef had already started on this process as early as 1893, when, encouraged by his official superiors, he took several trips in Germany and Switzerland to attend a number of more important revolutionary gatherings, including several that convened in Zurich in August of that year. Almost immediately Azef managed to impress many oldhand radicals and to establish himself in their eyes as a potential revolutionary leader.[13] Simultaneously—and again in conformity with the wishes of his police superiors, who were understandably most concerned with practical revolutionary efforts—he changed his ideological position, from a very moderate theoretical Marxism to an extremist and "fervid terrorist" orientation.[14]

Significantly, Azef underwent this transformation painlessly, without intellectual or moral ferment. Never having developed true radical principles of his own, he easily adapted his views to the new requirements of his police service. Since it was the Russian extremists, whether inside the empire or beyond its borders, who particularly alarmed tsarist security officials, Azef now sought to build his reputation as a man of action, presenting himself as a devotee of radical populism.

As early as 1893, a veteran-*narodnik* Sharl' Rapoport (An-skii) recommended him to the revolutionary Populist Vladimir Burtsev: "Here is a major force *(krupnaia sila);* here is an interesting person—young, energetic; he is ours."[15] (In retrospect, Burtsev must have appreciated the irony of his first encounter with the man whose life, by association, would secure his own name a place in history.) In 1894 Azef joined the Union of Russian Socialist Revolutionaries Abroad, recently founded in Berne by the revolutionary guru Khaim Zhitlovskii and his wife, and before long he began to feature himself as a convinced advocate of terrorist tactics.[16]

No doubt he took his police duties seriously, placing himself in the best position to provide the Police Department with the most germane reports, and assiduously polishing his presentation in accordance with police needs. His dispatches to the Police Department were hardly literary masterpieces and were not always grammatical.[17] His early letters even elicited a peevish comment from a high-ranking officer to the effect that Azef ought to "make more sense," so that it would at least be possible to understand whether he was referring to a man or a woman. However, already in 1896 a security official praised his reports as "impressive in their meticulousness and complete absence of verbosity."[18] Not only did Azef make every effort to keep his superiors informed about the activities of certain well-known advocates of extremist tactics among the émigrés,[19] he even demonstrated a certain gift for prediction, inviting his police superiors to pay special attention to a number of young and as yet undistinguished revolutionaries who, like Mikhail Karpovich and Vladimir Zenzinov, would soon build their reputation as terrorists.[20] At the same time, while claiming to champion radical practices, Azef did not expose himself to the genuine risks associated with them; as long as he remained abroad, where there was no major political organization capable of sponsoring wide-scale terrorist activity inside the Russian Empire, he was exempt from actual involvement and out of physical danger.

No wonder Azef was in no hurry to return to Russia after he finally received his engineering diploma in the spring of 1899.[21] Instead, he went job hunting in Germany, and soon succeeded in acquiring a position as an engineer with the firm of Schukert in Frankfurt-am-Main. Gone were Azef's days of poverty and hardship, for his new employment provided him with a comfortable living, while his police salary, now increased to one hundred rubles each month[22] plus an additional bonus at Easter and the New Year, was sufficient to satisfy his growing penchant for bourgeois extravagances.

Azef's police superiors had ample reason to be grateful to their agent, who supplied them with accurate information about the revolutionaries abroad and their contacts in Russia. Azef had already gained enough experience in his secret trade to feel confident of his ability to divert any suspicion; moreover, he obviously enjoyed the irony of his steadily escalating prestige in the radical émigré circles. Nonetheless, he was presumably still vulnerable to sporadic attacks of anxiety, the enthralling spasms of panic that would momentarily immobilize him as he faced his chronic fear that sooner or later every spy is unmasked. After all, he could not be entirely blasé about those evanescent rumors regarding his possible association with the tsarist police back in 1893—uncorroborated gossip that led nowhere, yet caused some of his acquaintances to follow him with leery looks.[23]

As he strove to overcome his weakness during these moments of panic and hysterical confusion, Azef could have extracted certain indirect psychological benefits from his dangerous situation. Indeed, his hazardous position might have brought "the relief of releasing unexpressed tensions"[24] by serving as a tangible surrogate for his perpetual state of inner anxiety, which constituted an intrinsic, rather than a situation-based condition. By taking advantage of a chance to rationalize his fear as a normal and legitimate emotional response to an objective threat, Azef could reassure himself with equally objective evidence—all pointing to the solidity of his position. He could judge, for example, that his recurrent election as chairman at student gatherings and the exceptional respect shown him even by radical émigré patriarchs indicated that he had an outstanding revolutionary career ahead of him, were he to choose that path. In all truth, Azef had no cause to complain about his almost risk-free police employment—at least until mid-1899, when he received orders from St. Petersburg to return to Russia.[25]

By the turn of the new century tsarist authorities were obviously alarmed by the revival of terrorist sentiments. There had been a twenty-year interlude of relative, if deceptive, tranquility following the fateful day of 1 March 1881, when a member of the notorious People's Will (*Narodnaia volia*) party detonated the bomb that claimed the life of Tsar Alexander II. But for all its preoccupation with quelling the opposition, the government of Alexander III had clearly failed to kill the spirit of revolution in Russia. From his first days on the throne, Nicholas II, who succeeded his father in 1894, was nicknamed "Nicholas the Last," serving as a painful reminder to the authorities that the revolutionaries had not renounced their intent to overthrow the tsarist regime.

The police were equally concerned about the growing number of underground groups operating throughout the empire, a sign that the radicals had not given up their efforts to reestablish a consolidated party even after more than ten years of disorganization following the dissolution of the People's Will. Although during the 1880s and early 1890s the police had been fairly successful in keeping the radicals disunited, in the last decade of the nineteenth century the revolutionaries made persistent attempts to join their forces into formidable political organizations founded on revised ideological principles and newly formulated tactics.[26] The government's struggle against radicalism consequently centered around two essential concerns: to prevent the opponents of autocracy from uniting into new revolutionary parties, and to forestall a repetition of the People's Will terrorist campaign and—most important—the March 1881 outrage. Azef's orders upon his return to Russia would reflect these two general objectives: he was to extend his connections to a wider radical milieu and especially aim at forming ties with larger groups of terrorist orientation.

By 1899, Azef's police superiors probably understood their agent well enough to suspect that his first reaction to the new assignment would be reluctance and fearful hesitation, since any unanticipated change would evoke resistance in an apprehensive personality. They sought to present their demand as an enticing opportunity that Azef could hardly refuse. Although he was no longer a poor student, prepared to render his services for minimal compensation, his correspondence with the Police Department reveals his avidity for money. In fact, it was a rare letter that omitted mention of pay, either in the form of acknowledgment of its prompt receipt or as a reminder to his employers to send it without delay, since, supposedly, he was always low on funds.[27] Accordingly, the police chiefs in St. Petersburg guaranteed Azef a significant raise in his salary if he would accommodate their need to put him to work in Russia. They also promised him assistance in finding a remunerative post as an engineer in a prestigious firm, which was a tempting proposition for Azef, who apparently had become quickly disgruntled with the daily tedium of his job at Schukert and, after only two months in Frankfurt, had switched to a temporary job at an electric company in Berlin.[28]

With his propensity to consider every possible outcome of every new situation, never underestimating even a trifling factor, Azef was concerned that if he refused the new terms of his police employment, the authorities would terminate it and stop their payments. In the new situation, however, financial loss was most likely not his major cause for apprehension. He probably could not help worrying (possibly having been adroitly, if subtly, baited by the police to do so) about what would happen if the government became incensed enough at his insubordination to diminish or even curtail their efforts to conceal his role as a spy, leaving him on his own to face the revolutionaries.

Azef probably already felt trapped at this early stage of his police career. The tsarist security forces had at their disposal sufficient means to ruin their spy, and his own distrustful and spiteful nature was prone to a nervous foreboding that his secret employers were capable of using compromising evidence against him in a reprisal, were he to antagonize them by defiance. This apprehension, cultivated into a new torrent of anxiety, from then on would keep Azef outwardly docile and permanently entangled in the dilemma of retaining both the favor of his superiors and the freedom of his own action. On this particular occasion, however, he chose to conform, and communicated to St. Petersburg his consent to return to Russia.[29]

In the summer of 1899, Azef set out for Moscow. By this time, he was a family man, although his young wife Liubov' (Liuba) and their four-year-old son Leonid did not accompany him in this somewhat reluctant journey back to his motherland.[30] Azef had met Liubov' Grigor'evna Menkina in April 1895 in Darmstadt. She was struggling to make a living as a seamstress in a small sewing shop, but had never given up her dream of enrolling in a university in Switzerland.[31] This rather ordinary, provincial Jewish girl was an archetypal representative of the female émigré student who had been denied access to higher education in Russia and therefore sought to pursue university studies abroad. Away from home, these young women shared all the poverty-related hardships of the male students and, like them, customarily gave the expected tribute to radical politics.

Liubov' Menkina was by no means an original thinker; in fact, she was not a thinker at all and even gave the impression of being a simpleton.[32] At the same time, she longed to associate herself with a cause that would elevate her from petty bourgeois routine and give her life intellectual meaning and moral justification. Soon after she finally made it to Switzerland and entered the University of Berne, she became acquainted with members of a small radical colony of expatriates from Russia. Under the influence of her new friends in Berne, she accepted revolutionary principles as her own, and having done so, simply took them for granted, never wavering in her commitment to them.

For Azef, who during the period of his courtship—very brief and apparently short of being romantic—already enjoyed a reputation as a "leading personality," the task of impressing this innocent idealist was not a difficult one, his unattractive physical appearance notwithstanding. This girl, who apparently never had had any intimate friends, was dazzled and flattered by the attentions of such a prominent revolutionary. A few of his letters, "full of ... deep sorrow" for the hardships of the common people and "at the same time of the ardor of a fighter burning with the fire of idealism,"[33] were enough to conquer her heart. She considered some aspects of his personality and lifestyle odd and unappealing; thus, Liubov' was vexed by the fact that whenever she would visit his apartment, she would find him either preparing a beefsteak or sleeping—even in the daytime.[34] Still, she was the last person to suspect him of having connections with the tsarist police, and it did not take Azef long to decide that he was unlikely to find a better candidate for his wife.

"A small woman with short hair and light freckles," Liubov' could not boast of stunning beauty,[35] nor was she particularly clever or talented; indeed, she appears to have been rather colorless and languid. She was, however, unquestionably loyal, trusting, and—equally important for someone with Azef's character—perfectly undemanding. The young woman was modest in her tastes and did not have expensive habits, which would have placed onerous demands on Azef's wallet and compelled him to overcome his closefisted selfishness.[36] Not that Azef had any intentions of spoiling her; indeed, Liubov' later remembered that from the beginning of their relationship he was neglectful and even insolent.[37] Yet she respected her husband's growing importance in the antigovernment movement; she also recognized (and accepted with endless forbearance) that his increasingly active involvement in radical politics would require his undivided attention, relegating all private or family matters to the background of his life. To tolerate such a marriage was to make a sacrifice that would become part of Liubov's struggle to liberate herself from the bonds of middle-class conventions; it would also be her personal contribution to the revolutionary cause, which required every free-spirited female to emulate the proverbial devotion of the Decembrists' wives, those beautiful and noble women who had followed their rebellious husbands to Siberian exile after 1825.

Liubov' Menkina, too, was prepared for the role of lifelong companion to a revolutionary leader. She rarely made claims on Azef's time; she dared not complain about his frequent and prolonged "business trips"; and she did her best to spare him from burdensome chores and distractions. Even before they were married, Liubov' was upset and insulted upon noticing how carefully Azef concealed from her everything related to his past, and the little she knew about her husband's troubled family she had found out only by chance. He was also extremely circumspect in making sure that she would not get hold of his correspondence. Usually she did not protest, and her occasional and feeble attempts to express her resentment only led to quarrels and fights, during which Azef would brusquely dismiss her complaints: "Oh, leave me alone! What the hell do you know!"[38]

Wishing to make the best of their relationship, she gradually learned to overlook any odious personality traits that might have dimmed the illusory image she had built for herself and to accept with unassuming gratitude every sign of affection that Azef offered her, despite the lingering trace of condescension or possessive aggressiveness.[39] Perhaps nothing is more revealing in this regard than the information Azef's brother Vladimir related to Liubov' about the fact that in his youth Azef had stolen money from his employer.[40] She, thus, found out about Azef's theft long before his exposure, which meant that for years she blocked from her consciousness an ugly incident that could irrevocably mar her husband's image.

Despite her marked inattentiveness and self-deception, and all her tolerance notwithstanding, Liubov' was puzzled by certain "astounding sides" to Azef. "I felt," she subsequently revealed, "that while he was a revolutionary, there was a great deal in him that did not go together with being a revolutionary. . . . When his tongue would occasionally untie, and he would become more outspoken, he would depict the whole peasantry as near idiots, capable for nothing; the same with workers." He would say that "in general, the Russian person was not individualistic, was good for nothing, and so on." "Why do you work for the revolution then?" Liubov' would ask, only to hear his usual dismissal: "Oh, you don't understand anything!"[41] For all her meekness then, it was not easy for Liubov' to bear her husband's tactless treatment, particularly his rudeness, which increased, since it did not encounter any serious deterrents. "Sometimes I had to listen to him saying terrible things to me," she would later complain, "so terrible that I simply could not stomach them."[42]

Pretending had already become second nature for Azef, but he still needed to take special care while posing as a devoted, if perhaps somewhat patriarchal, husband before the admiring young woman, who was unimposing, yet subtly solicited attention. He might have appreciated his wife's generosity, but he clearly did not love her; this perpetually fearful man, a habitual liar who would do anything to avoid closeness, lest his true nature be discovered, simply could not love anyone. It has long been a truism that "love and fear can hardly exist together,"[43] and Azef's anxious insecurity left no room for the great risks intrinsic in a genuine emotional attachment.[44]

Azef could not respect his wife either. Anyone who was gullible enough not to perceive his true self and who did not possess any manipulative skills, had little chance of winning his high regard. Liubov' remembered how much her husband "mistreated his brother Vladimir," who admired Evno for his superior intellect, but was seen by him as only "a fool."[45] Azef's attitude toward his wife was similar. She struck people as a plain and self-conscious woman—which she was indeed, largely as a result of her husband's constant daunting, which often took the form of reprimands against her for not knowing how to comport herself properly.[46] Even if we were to believe Menkina's highly questionable retrospective avowal that she never considered Azef extraordinary clever,[47] by always taking everything he said at face value she implicitly subjugated her intellect to his, and consequently fell into the same category of people whom Azef invariably treated with arrogance and derision—as fools.

Liubov' was certainly gullible, not doubting his words even in situations where anyone else would most assuredly have demanded explanations. "I must say," she later remembered, "that at the time I could be told anything, and I would believe it."[48] Azef's marriage to a rather dull girl, naïve (not to say silly) thus had as little to do with respect as it did with love: it was but a tribute to middle-class propriety and expectations, which, interestingly, he carried even into the revolutionary milieu. Liubov's role in this marriage was that of a victim, exploited not only for her husband's daily comfort but also in order to build him a reputation as a family man and so ward off any suspicion as to his true interests and inclinations.

To delineate Azef's personal preferences and tastes is to venture into the swampy ground of unmitigated vulgarity. A man of narrow intellectual interests, he was a veritable philistine whose perception of a "good life" was strictly materialistic and presupposed physical pleasure and entertainment of quite an unrefined variety.[49] Although he did make feeble attempts to convince his intellectual revolutionary acquaintances that he was very interested in philosophy,[50] there is absolutely no evidence to substantiate the claim that he "had superior knowledge of N. K. Mikhailovsky" and "read E. Kant in the original."[51] People who were close to Azef noted that "in general, he did not like to read" and certainly kept away from books on sociopolitical themes.[52] When he did on occasion read fiction, he consistently seemed to avoid the masterpieces of literature, casting aside powerful and profound literary works for the sake of poorly written shallow novels and stories. In music, art, and theater his taste was stale and truly provincial, betraying a proclivity for melodramatic sentimentality.[53] Azef relished lachrymose motifs, which "might have dazed him as a flute would entrance a snake";[54] he also enjoyed sugary romantic plots, but preferred live entertainment in cabarets, music halls, and restaurants, where female dancers and divas offered the garish diversion that soon became his favorite pastime.[55] This was "Azef's heaven ... genuine, veritable paradise": surrounded by flamboyant music, extravagant dresses, bare shoulders, and excessive perfumes, Azef could be satisfied, carefree, and almost mindless of the tormenting anxieties of his fraudulent life.[56]

"Verses are in disharmony with fear";[57] these words of Ovid may well be extended to a notion broader than this specific reference to poetry. Indeed, there was something intractable in Azef's avoidance of any form of entertainment that required intellectual involvement and emotional keenness. He could have felt instinctively that these might disturb his deeply enshrined sense of identity, lead to introspection, and direct his attention to the perils of his personal situation, illuminating the dark corners of his soul and intensifying his self-hatred and fear. It was as though he was hearing an inner voice warning him: "Don't peek behind the painted veil of appearance, don't lift it, or else you'll realize that it merely serves to hide our essential identity of anxiety, fear, and questioning ignorance ... and you'll come once more face to face with yourself, old man."[58] Fear dictated and shaped Azef's taste, narrowing it down to the nightclub as a nirvana of safety and contentment.[59]

Refined taste and appreciation of exquisite beauty are said to contribute to the individual's dexterity in discerning and shielding himself against not only aesthetic, but also emotional and moral depravation. A person with cultivated, delicate judgment is typically less susceptible to any variant of bawdiness, including the most insipid stereotypes, fads, or temptations.[60] Azef, who was hardly ennobled by a penchant for the genteel or the sublime, provides a reverse example of this dictum. His desires and tastes—frankly more vulgar than those of a plebeian—attested remarkably to a grievous indigence of what some high-brow judges have designated as "inner culture." This aesthetic and cultural paucity presumably further debased Azef's already less-than-regal inclinations and demeanor; indeed, it might even have served to reinforce the characteristic coarseness that so dominated his emotional makeup.

Just as he intuitively molded his choices in entertainment to accommodate a compulsion to overpower his uncomfortable thoughts with the clangor of a floorshow, so his other habits and preferences also appear to have been formed by a need to soothe his relentlessly troubled ego. For Azef, the objects he owned were symbols of his enhanced status and, consequently, of psychological tranquility. Azef considered things beautiful and valuable only insofar as they embellished his self-image. In accordance with conventional bourgeois taste (and probably also to compensate for physical homeliness), the nouveau riche Azef attributed great significance to conspicuously expensive clothes and accessories, sumptuous meals accompanied by high-priced wines, and luxurious hotel accommodations.[61] Among these extravagances (which Azef skillfully camouflaged by an apparent puritanical disinterest in any pleasures of the flesh, and which he had no trouble justifying on occasion as convenient conspiratorial devices), women were always a special priority.

The man who in conversations with his radical comrades always posed as an abstemious moralizer, and almost naïvely defended family values against promiscuity; the man who would insist on expelling a veteran activist from the Party of Socialist Revolutionaries for having contracted syphilis; the man who in many eyes therefore was an example of austere ethics[62]—was a secret womanizer and adulterer. For his affairs, he chose women just the opposite of his plain, modestly dressed, and unassuming wife, who throughout her life retained the habits of a poor student.[63] In fact, Azef's preference is best described by the corny limerick:

> Queenie was a blonde, and her age stood still,
> And she danced twice a day in vaudeville . . .

Attracted to everything flashy, spectacular, and lascivious, he was enticed by the excessive makeup, flagrant clothes, and less-than-innocent manners of his incidental acquaintances from a cluster of cabaret singers and actresses. Some of these charmers with their dazzling looks and dubious reputations might have done honor to Rubens's canvases, and for Azef, who was looking for diversion rather than intellectual or emotional intimacy, they were ideal companions in his secret night life. On the other hand, it did not take long for him to realize that, like all the other objects serving to satisfy his needs, these women, whether claiming to be respectable entertainers, playing the role of concubine, or frankly selling their bodies, had to be paid for with cash allowances and valuable gifts.[64] When it came to racy nocturnal amusements, Azef tended to be less than frugal; quite fastidious in his choice of brothels, for example, he settled only for the very best, expenses notwithstanding.[65]

Always avid for extra cash, Azef gambled occasionally, and gradually developed a strong, yet well-controlled, passion for cards and the roulette wheel—a passion that might have served partly as an outlet for inner tensions by providing a situation of spurious risk.[66] However, as much as he loved the sight of gold coins rolling across the green surface of the casino tables, he was too calculating to rely on chance to provide him with steady financial resources. Burdened by the responsibility of providing for his family, this man of dissolute instincts and behavior was in the lamentable position of having to sustain a reputation as an exemplary husband and father. Upon his arrival in Moscow, he thus had no choice but to plunge himself fully into the whirlpool of his secret triple life: the clandestine revolutionary milieu, the secret police work, and the furtive night life.

As a Jew, Azef could legally reside in Moscow only after passing graduation exams at a technical college or by securing a position as an engineer at a local company. Due to his failure to follow the rules for studying in absentia, he was not allowed to take the diploma examinations at the Electrotechnical Institute, to which he had submitted a petition letter. He tried to use his contacts in the Police Department to force the institute's administration to reconsider his case, but by March 1900 he had achieved nothing and instead accepted employment as an engineer at the General Electrical Company, earning a salary of 175 rubles per month.[67]

Menkina later described what she denigrated as a dull and "terribly bourgeois" routine in their tiny Moscow apartment located on a sidestreet off Vozdvizhenka. There were hired servants and Azef went off to work every morning. As far as she was concerned, this was hardly the lifestyle of revolutionaries and therefore it was psychologically difficult and depressing for Liubov'— an idealist turned housewife.[68] Azef, on the other hand, showed no signs of discomfort, although his heart clearly was not with his job. His carelessness and negligence, his frequent absences, his tendency to dismiss orders and suggestions from the company's administration abruptly, and his generally indolent way of handling himself at work[69] all suggest that by this time the expectation that he could obtain money easily and without a steady effort was well ingrained.[70] This assumption, in turn, precluded success in the field of engineering.

Azef's mind was not on a professional career, for as soon as he arrived in Moscow he found himself entangled in the life of the local revolutionary community as part of police efforts to paralyze its activity. In accordance with his instructions, Azef quickly formed a growing circle of new acquaintances. As early as 1899 he used an exceptionally flattering letter of recommendation from the Zhitlovskiis to make the acquaintance and quickly win the trust of Andrei Argunov, who, along with a number of like-minded colleagues, had recently founded the clandestine Northern Union of Socialist Revolutionaries. Late in 1900, Argunov also launched the group's newspaper, *Revolutionary Russia (Revoliutsionnaia Rossiia)*, whose first two issues were published by an underground press in Finland, and then he began entertaining plans to unify radical socialist forces across the Russian Empire.[71] The leaders of the Union steadily gained support among other radical groups and isolated revolutionaries, and immediately attracted the special attention of Azef's new police superior in Moscow, the distinguished head of that city's Okhrana section, Sergei Zubatov.

In the late 1890s, the secret police could be relatively certain of success in preventing the unification of the various independent clandestine groups inside the Russian Empire. The authorities sought to eliminate them one by one but they tended to reemerge under new names and leadership shortly after mass arrests. Given the small size of these groups and their comparatively inexperienced membership, the authorities, while becoming increasingly keen on recruiting informants among the revolutionaries, also relied extensively on a tactic known in police jargon as "external surveillance" (*vneshnee* or *naruzhnoe nabliudenie*), involving special agents called *filery* who followed the radicals everywhere they went. Information supplied by the *filery* was a major supplementary means of uncovering the entire network of revolutionary contacts. The authorities could then strike at the very center of the revolutionary circle itself. It was sufficient for the police to arrest the leaders of a tiny organization in order to render it nonexistent, causing the rest of its membership to abandon underground activities and either to disperse throughout the country or to emigrate.

With each abortive attempt to create a powerful political party inside Russia, more and more participants in revolutionary circles became aware of the futility of their efforts. By the turn of the new century, an increasing number of well-known revolutionaries and extra-legal politicians, having armed themselves with the support and confidence of their associates in antigovernment circles, emigrated abroad and busied themselves with the process of setting up new major organizations with headquarters in western Europe, away from the watchful eyes of the Russian secret police. This was exactly the policy that Azef advocated first as a sympathizer and then as a member of the Northern Union. In his relations with its leadership, he was extremely circumspect about not eliciting their suspicions by any display of overt curiosity about the secret affairs of the group, but when his help was requested, he always tried to be of assistance. He thus quickly established a reputation as "a cautious and prudent but not cowardly man, whose advice might prove useful on practical questions, and his counsel was more and more frequently sought."[72] Among other suggestions, the revolutionaries took seriously his police-inspired skepticism concerning the formation of a large unified organization inside Russia.

Zubatov's policies aimed to carry this message to the radicals. His immediate goal was to do away with the Union's underground press, without, however, endangering Azef's position in the organization. The plan was to let the radicals know that the underground printing house was under constant police surveillance and about to be raided, thus forcing them to transfer it out of Finland without delay. With detectives literally "hanging on their heels," the revolutionaries speedily disassembled the press and moved it in pieces to a secluded house in the forest outside the city of Tomsk in Siberia. Zubatov did not need to worry about losing track of the equipment; Azef promptly informed him about its whereabouts, and the local police busied themselves with keeping its operations under close surveillance. Then, in September 1901, just before the revolutionaries were ready to print the third issue of *Revolutionary Russia*, Zubatov gave his last order to the Tomsk police: they were to raid the underground press and arrest its personnel.[73]

This devastating and seemingly inexplicable fiasco confirmed the Union leaders' suspicions that the Okhrana was fully aware of their operations and that they were about to be arrested. Anxious to save the nucleus of the organization, Argunov and his associates finally arrived at the desperate solution of transferring its headquarters abroad immediately. Next, they decided on the spur of the moment that, under the circumstances, the person best equipped to represent the organization outside Russia was none other than Azef, whose association with the radicals they assumed was unknown to the police. Additionally, Argunov argued later, Azef "wholeheartedly shared our sorrow. It might have been his own grief. His attitude changed. From a passive collaborator he became an active member of our 'Union,'"[74] who from the day of the Tomsk disaster urged his comrades to leave Russia.[75] It also appeared to be a convenient coincidence that Azef (having, of course, obtained prior directives from Zubatov) informed Argunov of his intention to travel abroad on personal business, offering his services for arranging all revolutionary affairs there. The last opportunity could not be lost, and, as Argunov explained in his account, "like a dying man, we entrusted everything to Aseff. . . . We told him all our passwords, all our connections . . . the names and addresses of our associates, and we recommended him warmly to all our friends. He was to arrive abroad . . . enjoying our full confidence as the representative of the 'Union,'"[76] which, according to the plan, was soon to merge with other socialist revolutionary groups into one all-Russian organization.

Zubatov and other high-ranking Okhrana officials were then fully informed about this revolutionary blueprint, as well as of the fact that prominent figures in the radical camp were leaving Russia to take part in negotiations aiming at the unification of all the socialist revolutionary groups scattered throughout the empire. Remarkably, this not only failed to alarm official circles, but, on the contrary, caused them to feel relief at having gotten rid of the troublemakers at home. The authorities seem to have even encouraged radicals to leave Russia by sometimes replacing their sentences of internal exile (and occasionally even imprisonment) with exile abroad.[77] They also issued foreign passports freely, as, for example, in the case of Mariia Seliuk, a notable member of the Union whose role as Azef's assistant in the forthcoming negotiations in Europe was known to the authorities, but who nonetheless easily obtained permission to emigrate.[78] At the same time, the police wished to keep an eye on radicals beyond the Russian borders. Azef seemed to be an ideal choice for this job; he was now a man of considerable revolutionary reputation, and entrusted with a mission crucial to the radical cause. Therefore, in accordance with the official plan to place an agent at the very heart of the all-Russian organization, at the end of November 1901, Azef again left Russia to take part in the formation of what would soon be known as the Party of Socialists Revolutionaries.[79]

By early 1902, two months of negotiations successfully concluded with a general agreement among revolutionary leaders in Berne and Paris stating the SR Party's program and tactics, and an entirely new phase began for the newly organized opposition. SR leaders in emigration directed revolutionary activities from outside the Russian Empire, while increasing numbers of rank-and-file members inside Russia were being organized into cohesive local groups and cells that were accountable at least in theory to the central party command abroad. This new arrangement made matters exceedingly difficult for the police: the previously successful practice of external surveillance led to disorganization among the rank-and-file members of local SR revolutionary cells, but now the central PSR leadership remained almost entirely beyond the reach of official sanctions.[80] The authorities' old techniques of combatting the revolutionaries thus were no longer effective in destroying the radicals' headquarters, thereby eliminating the ideological and financial sources of the organized opposition. The only remaining solution was enhanced "internal surveillance" (*vnutrennee nabliudenie*), which would depend primarily on the use of secret police agents among the revolutionaries to keep track of all top-level planning and decision-making regarding general PSR affairs, and particularly the terrorist undertakings that were held in much regard by the party's leadership as its key tactic.[81] At this point, the police chiefs in St. Petersburg, realizing that their policy of ignoring the perils of organized antigovernment parties in the West had proved a major political blunder, invested all their hopes in Azef, their main agent among the SRs, who from the group's earliest days had played a prominent role in this newly formed party.

From Azef's perspective, the authorities chose the best way of showing their appreciation for his services: at the time of his trip abroad, they increased his salary dramatically, from 150 to 500 rubles per month. It was an imperative long-term investment for them, with profits beginning to show almost immediately. By July 1902, Azef's position in the PSR was so notable that his police superiors felt obliged to bring his case to the attention of Interior Minister Viacheslav von Plehve. The timing was essential: only three months earlier, on April 2, SR Stepan Balmashev, dressed in the uniform of an army aide-de-camp, presented himself at the Mariinskii Palace in St. Petersburg, saluted Plehve's predecessor, Interior Minister Dmitrii Sipiagin, and, while handing him an "urgent message" in a sealed envelope, fired two lethal point-blank shots at the minister. The letter contained the party's sentence to the official dignitary: "You are condemned to death. Organization."[82] This fateful episode was still perturbingly fresh in Plehve's memory. Yet, in an interview with a *Matin* reporter, he vouched with unruffled aplomb: "My security is impeccable. An assassination attempt against me may be accomplished only by accident."[83] Plehve's confidence seemed justified; his defense scheme indeed appeared flawless. Contrary to the Police Department's general regulations for secret agents that prohibited their close personal involvement in radical activities, Plehve would order Azef to penetrate the party's center and its Combat Organization—a specially organized terrorist unit meant to serve as the SR's primary tool in a projected campaign of terror in Russia's capitals.[84]

3

Terrorist-Neophyte, 1902–1905

> If a man is not afraid of what is really frightening, the most terrifying occurs.
> —Lao-Tzu[1]

Azef gradually became intimate with the PSR's most prominent personalities: the young and brilliant Viktor Chernov, the party's theoretician and foremost ideologist; Mikhail Gots, the ailing survivor of a lengthy hard-labor term in Siberia and the SRs' chief organizer and practical mind; the gray-haired and portly, yet still-buoyant, Ekaterina Breshko-Breshkovskaia (otherwise known as Babushka or "grandmother of the revolution"), a revered Populist agitator who had decades of experience in stirring protest among the peasants and had served time in tsarist penal institutions; and, finally, the astute, sardonic, and emphatically acrid Grigorii Gershuni, whom Sergei Zubatov had given the befitting nickname, "an artist of terror."[2] All the PSR leaders considered political assassinations expedient. Chernov labored away on formulating a lucid theoretical justification of the tactics; Gots was working out a functional way of carrying out the combat work; Babushka "whipped up the enthusiasm" for the SR terrorist campaign; and Gershuni set out to demonstrate the practical relevance of a contemporary cliché that was very much in vogue in radical circles: "One does not talk about terror, one does it."[3] In 1902 Gershuni founded the Combat Organization and became its renowned leader or, in Chernov's words, "its dictator in a true sense of the word."[4]

The "tiger of the Revolution," as the radicals nicknamed Gershuni,[5] never resorted to arms personally; he was the one who looked for and recruited potential *boeviki,* selected them for special combat operations, and incited terrorist acts. When everything was ready for a final strike against a designated target, Gershuni personally escorted the terrorists to the site of the projected assassination in order to urge them on and to thwart any last-minute doubts.[6] His decision to subject himself to the risk of being caught in the vicinity of a terrorist act had nothing to do with bravado, although some of his comrades noted his ostentatious vanity and proclivity for self-advertising and melodrama, which was suitable "for a yellow-press novel."[7] Gershuni's determination to remain with the *boeviki* was entirely practical, however: the preselected terrorists were often struck by fear or remorse moments before their scheduled attack and could be coaxed into action only by Gershuni's "hypnotic influence on people, who completely succumbed to his iron will."[8] According to a former Okhrana officer who had come to know him well, "clever, cunning" Gershuni

> possessed an incredible gift to take hold of . . . the inexperienced, easily carried-away youth. . . . His hypnotizing eyes and especially persuasive speech subjugated those he spoke to and made them his ardent admirers. A person on whom Gershuni began working would soon totally submit to his will and become an unquestioning executor of his orders. . . . There is something satanic in this pressure and influence of Gershuni on his victims.

His fellow revolutionaries also referred to Gershuni as a "soul-hunter," whose demeanor evoked the image of a Mephistopheles, with piercing "eyes that penetrated one's soul and . . . an ironical smile on his face."[9]

The Combat Organization under Gershuni was small; its membership never exceeded fifteen people, and Gershuni played the role of central coordinator. He was the terrorists' only link to the party's Central Committee and the only one who knew all the members of the combat unit. Even Pavel Kraft and Mikhail Mel'nikov, Gershuni's closest associates in Russia, were kept in the dark about some of his enterprises. "Improviser by nature, Gershuni developed plans which required instantaneous realization rather than prolonged and steadfast preparation for completion."[10] Thus, Gershuni contrived to use Interior Minister Dmitrii Sipiagin's funeral to stage two more assassination attempts. According to the plan, artillery officer Evgenii Grigor'ev, whom Gershuni had recently recruited for terrorist ventures, was to open fire at the Procurator of the Holy Synod, Konstantin Pobedonostsev. In the ensuing panic, Grigor'ev's fiancée, Iuliia Iurkovskaia, dressed as a male gymnasium student, was to try to kill the St. Petersburg governor, General Kleigels. The scheme miscarried, however: at the last moment Grigor'ev took pity on the elderly procurator and could not force himself to pull the trigger, thus precluding both attempts.[11]

On 29 July 1902 another of Gershuni's protégés tried his luck: a twenty-six-year-old woodworker, Foma Kochura (Kochurenko), using bullets doused in strychnine, took a shot at the governor of Kharkov,

Prince I. M. Obolenskii, as he was leaving the theater in the Tivoli Gardens. The terrorist missed his target but wounded the city's chief of police, who had the misfortune to have been nearby.[12] On 6 March 1903, Gershuni sanctioned another attempt organized by local radicals—against the governor of Ufa, N. M. Bogdanovich. This time the terrorist chief could celebrate an outright triumph: after he killed the governor, the SR Egor Dulebov managed to escape.

Given the relative success of the Combat Organization, one might expect the Police Department officials to have garnered reasonable grievances against Azef—at first glance a less than dutiful agent at the PSR center. Nicolaevsky wishes us to believe that although "to all appearances Aseff worked with great zeal for the police" in that period, filling his letters to the Department with names and facts, "this was only on the surface. In reality, his double game dates from this time, and he begins to conceal a large mound of important information," particularly "everything that had bearing upon Gershuni's terrorist activities."[13]

Azef's dexterous display of revolutionary zeal leaves a superficial impression that at this stage of his party career he was fully preoccupied with subversive activity—and terrorism. There was no question of anyone suspecting him of dealing with the tsarist police; on the contrary, a later testimony of Azef's wife is very revealing: "If I ever really loved him, it was in this very period," following Sipiagin's assassination in 1902. He seemed to be consumed by the revolutionary flame, and that was why, Liubov' confessed, she had "liked him very much then."[14] Nothing could be more facile (and befitting) for the spy to feign undivided loyalty to the radical cause by expressing increasing enthusiasm for terrorist warfare at the time. Yet, all fiery verbosity notwithstanding, in practice, quite in accordance with his compelling instinct for self-preservation, Azef refused to get too close to terrain where things really might have gotten hot.

Indeed, although the Police Department had insisted that Azef establish closer ties with the newly formed Combat Organization, he clearly sought to eschew the assignment. He could not entirely evade involvement with terrorist practices, of course, since, in order to provide the police with valuable information, he had to show interest in every sphere of the party's work. Still, the SRs confirmed that Azef "in fact took quite a small part in combat affairs" at the time of Gershuni's leadership. During the initial period of his police employment, until May 1903, he was quite successful in abstaining from intimate involvement with any of the SR combat undertakings. Consequently, he could provide the Police Department very little in the way of concrete or detailed information about the terrorists.[15]

Azef lived abroad much of the time: the birth of his second son, Valentin, in 1902 provided Azef (who always maintained the veneer of a devoted family man) with a plausible excuse to stay away from Russia, where all the action took place.[16] The authorities could thus hardly expect him to supply them with details about Gershuni's exploits. As a result of later investigating Azef's behavior, however, the revolutionaries came to believe that he did try "to send Gershuni to the gallows"—a fact also confirmed by police evidence.[17]

As early as 1901—even before the Combat Organization inaugurated its campaign—the spy informed the security organs about the "primary importance of terrorists Gershuni and Gots." After his first encounter with the *boeviki* chief, and appreciating his salience as a terrorist, Azef immediately alerted the Police Department about the hazard "this gentleman" represented.[18] The spy also reported promptly on the terrorist leader as soon as he showed up in France or Switzerland, extracting a certain pleasure from subverting Gershuni's efforts so as to punish him for "bragging too much."[19] Following the assassination of Sipiagin in 1902, Azef again provided the police with information about the organizer of the terrorist conspiracy, and also with the first clues about the identities of Gershuni's associates Kraft and Mel'nikov. Thus, the authorities could establish strict surveillance and take initial steps to eliminate this combat group.[20]

At the same time, due to Azef, Grigor'ev, Iurkovskaia, and several other members of the so-called "combat military organization" of St. Petersburg were arrested after a failed attempt to assassinate Pobedonostsev.[21] Azef knew nothing about Gershuni's hastily contrived plan to induct Kochura for the terrorist act against Obolenskii, but during the period from the summer of 1902 to the spring of 1903, primarily as a result of Azef's efforts, the authorities were able to prevent the first attempt on the life of Interior Minister Plehve.[22]

Azef evidently did not provide his police superiors with information that might have prevented the assassination of the Ufa governor, as he did not know anything concrete about Gershuni's preparations for Dulebov's attempt.[23] On the other hand, there is evidence to believe that the Police Department had known from its source—which at the time could only have been Azef—about Gershuni's involvement with the local *boeviki* in Ufa prior to Bogdanovich's assassination, and the terrorists owed their success to the fact that the police failed to act quickly enough in making preventive arrests.[24]

The authorities thus had no reason to complain about Azef's service at this time; he acknowledged his "active role in the Socialist Revolutionary Party" and provided information that invariably proved helpful for the investigation. Any missing clues about the Combat Organization remained obscure for the secret agent because of Gershuni's circumspect leadership.[25] Moreover, contrary to the accepted assumption that in the early part of Azef's service his police superiors did not make serious attempts to subject their agent to strict control,[26] there is much evidence to show that through direct surveillance the police chiefs were well aware of Azef's activities, making it impossible for him to misrepresent his position in the party or to conceal important information, if he had chosen to do so.[27]

Although it appears that the Police Department had received some clues as to Gershuni's whereabouts, Azef's information was most likely not a direct cause of the terrorist's arrest. According to Gershuni himself, after the attack on Bogdanovich, he left Ufa for Saratov and then vacillated, not sure whether to proceed to Smolensk or Kiev. He finally decided to go to Kiev, where a local informer betrayed him to the police.[28] On 13 May 1903, Gershuni was apprehended at a train station just outside of Kiev. The gendarmes then took him to the Peter and Paul Fortress in St. Petersburg. He had been chained and did not miss an opportunity for a mawkish theatrical performance that subsequently earned him much prestige: in the presence of several police officers, he kissed the irons as a symbolic gesture, full of ambiguous but ostensibly profound meaning.[29] In February 1904, Gershuni was tried by a military court, which sentenced him to death; thereupon, Nicholas II reduced his punishment to a life term at hard labor.[30]

Its leader's capture terminated the initial active period of the Combat Organization, which then had to replace its arrested cadres, including Gershuni's main associate, Mikhail Mel'nikov, and adapt itself to new leadership. If the SR version of the story is to be trusted, in June 1903 the Central Committee, acting on Gershuni's prior suggestion, named Azef to be his replacement. From "January of 1904, Azef stood at the head of the extended Combat Organization," and—according to the party's official line—was involved in every detail of the undertakings it planned and executed both in Russia and abroad, but for personal reasons he communicated only selected information to the police.[31] As it turns out, however, this interpretation of Azef's duties in the terrorist unit is clearly an exaggeration of his true role, which was limited to that of a representative of the Central Committee in the Combat Organization and certainly not that of its commander. As a result of their subsequent endeavor to demonstrate Azef's double game by amplifying his role in the Combat Organization, in their official statements the SR leaders neglected even to mention the name of Boris Savinkov, the true taskmaster and architect behind all central terrorist ventures of the party from mid-1903.[32]

A fascinating character indeed, Savinkov would best be described by a metaphor: he was a taut violin string, incessantly straining and vibrating, sustaining the subtle motif of its life to the end, always at risk of either losing itself in a sea of irking, foreign tones, or of making a lethal effort and breaking at a fatally high pitch. Among an impressive repertoire of eccentricities, the dominant theme at the core of his identity was an insatiable search for freedom—a tantalizing mirage, variously shaped and rather nebulously contoured at times, but primarily taking the form of an exalted desire for deliverance from mundane, conventional bourgeois existence. To succumb to such monotonous routine, as far as he was concerned, was to reduce life to a parody, to embrace ersatz life. This is why the son of a judge in Warsaw and endowed with the numerous advantages of his social status, Savinkov espoused revolution. A product of the Silver Age, he was an archetypal decadent and aesthete; he wrote novels, short stories, and poems—not entirely without talent.[33] Utterly egocentric, Savinkov perceived himself as the alpha and omega of the world around him, with his passions and idiosyncrasies playing the central role, very much as prescribed by the cultural vogue of the epoch. This intense individualist was hardly in need of any strict maxim, including a revolutionary tenet. He was spurred on his tenacious, if labyrinth-like, course toward emancipation exclusively by esoteric intellectual and emotional incentives.

He embraced the revolution, judging it to be compatible with his personal struggle of the free spirit against the philistine world. Some who knew Savinkov intimately suggested that he showed signs of being both a conceited person "of a cheap Nietzschean type" and a man with "a religious core *(sterzhen')*, a longing for God."[34] In no way, however, was he prevented from regarding traditional ethical canons as platitudes and discarding them as mere truisms, negating conventional morality for the sake of the individual's uninhibited search for "pure Beauty." In fact, for this individualist turned SR even an order from the party's Central Committee was frequently a dead letter. Almost proud of his apostasy, he justified his position: "In my 'heresies' I see an attempt, perhaps a feeble one . . . at *revolutionizing the spirit*, a struggle against that side of the person's self which, as I noticed, is unfree and deeply conservative even in the most emancipated people."[35] In the lifelong course of his voracious quest for liberation, Savinkov was known to tunnel deeply into a desolate lifestyle, wasting time in countless cafes, at horse races, and casinos, seeking diversion in women and surreal tranquility in alcohol, opiates, and morphine, and dipping superficially into occultism[36]—only to resurface on the political scene, where he continued his crusade for freedom as part of his search for inner fulfillment.

Savinkov had become a convinced terrorist long before he met Azef; in fact, he emigrated abroad in the hope of locating and joining the SR Combat Organization.[37] At the end of July 1903, Savinkov made a pilgrimage to Gots, who was then residing in Geneva and serving as the acting chief of the Combat Organization.[38] Although he declared an irrevocable desire to apply himself to terrorism, in his typically audacious manner Savinkov never concealed his profound indifference to socialist dogma and indeed to any theoretical issue, including the inherent purpose of the antigovernment struggle: the liberation of the workers and peasants. Contrary to what would be expected of a revolutionary, the most critical factor in shaping his behavior was not the plight of the toiling masses, but the inflated ego of this "thrill-seeking adventurer" and freedom fighter.[39] Nevertheless, in considering Savinkov as a candidate for the head of the party's central terrorist detachment, the SR leaders were impressed with his enormous vigor and energy, "probably sufficient for a thousand average human lives." His sybaritism did not prevent him from demonstrating "cold self-control next to almost insane courage,"[40] fortitude, perseverance, and unaffected integrity. Whatever Savinkov's faults, he was not a coward or a weakling—something that he would prove time and again throughout his turbulent life.

Savinkov's personality was thus entirely unlike Azef's, whose character would hardly have made him capable of leading the *boeviki* into action, even if he so wished. Throughout his life Azef's constant and most important priority was to elude the fear of getting hurt—physically and financially, as well as emotionally. And even though this very fear paradoxically had driven him to his dangerous affiliation with the revolutionaries and the police, in every situation he was forced to deal with as part of his life-threatening involvement with political espionage, Azef sought first of all to minimize the risks to his personal well-being.

In his desperate attempts to protect himself from any genuine or imaginary threats, Azef naturally avoided situations that might have exposed him to firsthand violence and physical jeopardy. The fear of violence also likely made him averse to immediate exposure to gore, which rendered it impossible for Azef to take personal part in terrorist acts. His obvious deficiency in physical fitness and his loathing for strenuous activity were also detrimental. In spite of his propensity for self-indulgence, Savinkov, the epicurean and bon vivant, obviously made a better candidate for the head of the Combat Organization: unlike Azef, he would never have allowed his life to be shaped by a dependence on physical contentment and an incapacity to bear even transient discomforts.

Savinkov's appearance was also everything Azef's was not. A handsome man, he had an animated and nervous face marked by gentility, with eyes that sometimes seemed sad and sometimes cold, almost cruel. He was slender and quick to the point of appearing impulsive, yet graceful in his movements. His elegant clothes, his urbane, amusing, and slightly ironic conversation, his refined, uninhibited manners all contributed to his image as a veritable dandy, a European gentleman, and an intellectual. Moreover, unlike Azef, Savinkov had a rare talent that enabled him to charm people and to evoke their sympathy and interest,[41] impressing and attracting many with his intelligence, his vivacious and sardonic flair, and especially with his enthusiasm and determination. Vera Figner, "the Venus of the Revolution," considered Savinkov the most brilliant person she had ever met.[42] Soon after having invested him with responsibility for the party's combat cadres, Gots, feeling an almost fatherly tenderness, called Savinkov "my Benjamin"; at the same time, realizing that Savinkov was living a life that was destroying him from within, the veteran-revolutionary dubbed his young friend "the fractured Stradivarius" (*nadlomlennaia skripka Stradivariusa*).[43]

The terrorists, too, easily accepted Savinkov as their leader. Convinced that he was chosen—by God, the Spirit, Fate, or some other Power—for great deeds, he effortlessly projected this image onto others, be they his acquaintances in the literary elite circles, such as Aleksei Remizov and Maksimilian Voloshin, or his comrades the *boeviki*.[44] He did so partly on account of his self-reliance and savoir faire: "If there are no followers, he remains alone, but does not give up."[45] Grateful for his self-possession, the combatants especially appreciated his integrity, depicting Savinkov as "a wonderful flower, brought here from God knows where. All his activity was marked by certain peculiar individualistic qualities: he was involved in the struggle as if *he were personally* insulted, as if his honor of a noble person were disgraced. And he struggled in such a way that could be an example to all of us."[46]

The Combat Organization under Savinkov thus inherited certain psychological qualities of its leader—foremost of which was his independence. The terrorist detachment operated almost entirely autonomously from the rest of the party and its leadership. Even though the Central Committee had the right to determine the general extent of central terrorist activity and to draw up a list of potential assassination targets, this was as much as the SR civilian leadership could interfere with the life of its main combat unit. The party leaders had absolutely no idea what was going on inside the Combat Organization. They did not even know all of its members, who were accepted as *boeviki* without the prior approval or even notification of the Central Committee.

Nor was the SR leadership familiar with any immediate plans or the details of terrorist operations.[47]

A number of prominent party members could not shut their eyes to the fact that the terrorists quickly adopted an unequivocally arrogant perception of themselves as the only "true bearers of Russia's revolutionary cross," that they developed a closed group mentality and values, often in contradiction of the mother organization's official ideology, and that their solidarity, based on sharing the many dangers of their clandestine life, took precedence over any obligation of loyalty to the PSR.[48] Rather than trying to eliminate a party within a party, the SR leaders justified their nonintervention with their desire to avoid subjecting the terrorists—glorified as a result of their initial successes—to additional danger by making their secrets available to a large number of insurgents who were not directly involved in combat ventures. For their part, aloof from the rest of the party, "the combatants preferred to deal with it always as a unified whole," expressing—usually via Azef—the opinion of an entire interest group rather than the opinions of individuals.[49]

Azef thus functioned as the overseer of central terrorist undertakings for the Central Committee. In his capacity as a link between the party's leadership and the *boeviki*, he was clearly an outstanding figure among the terrorists, many of whom were prepared to recognize his authority initially not so much because he was a member of the Central Committee, but due to the general understanding (fostered by Azef himself) that "Ivan Nikolaevich" was a close friend of their idol and suffering martyr—Gershuni.[50] However, unlike Gershuni, who was always present when his men executed a terrorist act, personally directing the operations, Azef left all aspects of practical preparation for the political assassinations to Savinkov. Azef "took the position of a ship's captain, and I—that of the main officer," Savinkov later recapped on the division of duties within the Combat Organization: "It was I who had direct contacts with all the comrades; it was I who had close relations with them. . . . He, if I may put it this way, did not leave his cabin, but gave orders through me, leading the organization through me."[51] This description could serve as a postscript to what the police authorities thought about the true identity of the terrorists' leader. Leonid Rataev, head of the secret police's foreign operations and Azef's main contact after Zubatov's dismissal from the Okhrana in the latter part of 1903, confirmed that in 1904, Pavel Ivanovich (Savinkov's alias) definitely stood at the head of the Combat Organization.[52]

Savinkov—and not Azef—restructured the Combat Organization after it was ravaged by the 1903 arrests, and he recruited new combat-

ants. One of them was twenty-five-year-old Egor Sazonov (Abel, or—
in Russian—Avel'), who had been exiled to the Iakutsk region for his
role in a revolutionary organization in Ufa and, having escaped
abroad, decided to become a terrorist. Like Savinkov, Sazonov initially contacted Gots, declaring his wish to join the Combat Organization, as did another newcomer, Maximilian Shveitser, a highly valued expert in chemical engineering, and several other radicals.[53]
Savinkov's school friend, twenty-eight-year-old Ivan Kaliaev ("the
Poet") did not need a formal initiation process. Formerly a moderate
Social Democrat, this man, dainty, painfully shy, and manifestly
beyond earthly concerns, in 1901 decided to kill the governor of Ekaterinoslav, Count Keller, who had resorted to draconian measures in
suppressing peasant disturbances in the province. Although he did not
accomplish the assassination, Kaliaev, in his own words, "realized
himself as a terrorist." In 1903 he went abroad and found Savinkov,
who persuaded Gots to admit the Poet to the Combat Organization
against the advice of Azef, who pronounced Kaliaev "quite strange."
Savinkov also recruited another childhood friend, Boris Moiseenko
(Opanas), who joined the *boeviki* in July 1904, along with Aleksei
Pokotilov.[54] In Pokotilov's case, however, Savinkov's competence
betrayed him: the former university student from Kiev, who had
approached the terrorist leader in early 1901 for assistance in his plans
to assassinate Minister of Education N. P. Bogolepov, turned out to be
a heavy drinker, fond of wild carousing,[55] which was bound to interfere with his duties as an explosives manufacturer. Savinkov's choice
of another bombmaker was much better for his purposes: the young
Dora Brilliant—fragile-looking and so strikingly beautiful that people
in the street would follow her to take another look at her sorrowful
Jewish face with its enormous and very dark eyes. She had taken part
in student disturbances and gone into exile in Poltava, where she met
Breshko-Breshkovskaia and Gershuni, whose influence turned her
into a convinced SR. Her dream was to become a *boevik*, and in 1904
she joined the Combat Organization.[56]

Azef rarely took part in the recruitment process, and when he did,
his involvement was strangely reminiscent of sabotage. Far from inspir-
ing or provoking the candidates for terrorist activity, he tried to talk them
out of it, always attempting to persuade a potential terrorist to try his
hand at nonviolent party work first to see whether this would not be a
better personal alternative. His fellow SRs would note in surprise how
extremely strict Azef was in selecting the terrorists, turning candidates
down "in case of a slightest doubt." Thus, he refused to admit SRs Bella
Lapina and Zinaida Konopliannikova into the Combat Organization

despite their persistent pleas, and to justify his decision declared that both of them were too impulsive and lacked self-restraint.[57] This tendency was in marked contrast to Gershuni's penchant for eagerly seizing every opportunity to attract to the Combat Organization "anyone who happened to volunteer as an implacable combatant" and even twisting the arm of a revolutionary novice to go through with a planned assassination.[58] Azef could in no way be accused of instigating political violence: all the members of the Combat Organization were staunch radicals with substantial revolutionary records; all of them embraced terror as mature adults—on their own accord and in full consciousness.[59]

Having recruited his terrorist crew, Savinkov began to work out new methods of terrorist warfare, emphasizing detailed planning and careful surveillance of assassination targets—again in contrast to Gershuni's hastily improvised strikes. For surveillance purposes, the terrorists pretended to be horse drivers, peddlers, couriers, and newspaper distributors, spending long hours on the streets of the capitals in order to ascertain the intended victim's movements and work out the most opportune plan for attack. In Gershuni's days *boeviki* typically used revolvers as primary assassination weapons, even though their chief realized that combat work required more sophisticated technical means. For his part, Savinkov decided to switch to homemade bombs and explosive devices, which, although most costly and liable to claim innocent victims, would undoubtedly be more effective, dramatically increasing the chances for the terrorists' successes.

Lacking scientific expertise, Savinkov left it to Azef—the engineer—to explain in technical detail to the rest of the SR leadership the obvious advantages of using dynamite explosives, which eventually came to be a standard practice of the Combat Organization. The spy immediately seized the opportunity to reaffirm his prestige in the eyes of the Central Committee members, all of whom had only a very vague understanding of the technicalities of explosives manufacturing and utilization. He discussed the advantages of the "dynamite technique," not forgetting to fill his lectures with heavy specialized jargon. While the rank-and-file SRs, invested with the perilous job of bomb making, proceeded to establish their laboratories in Russia and abroad, Azef, without becoming involved in many details, pretended to coordinate the entire process of explosive manufacturing for the party. It was not difficult to instill the awe of the "infernal machine" into the uninitiated and to impress such vastly impractical people as Chernov, who quickly became convinced that "without exaggeration ... the resolution of the question about the new practice of using dynamite belongs to Azef."[60]

Azef's role as the originator of innovative assassination techniques was very much inflated, however. In fact, he initiated no methods that had not been used in the 1870s, even prior to the terrorist campaign by the People's Will. These methods, ironically, largely emulated certain practices of the *filery*—tailing or persistent surveillance.[61] In any case, equipped with new cadres and weapons Savinkov set out to discharge a new wave of central terror. He did not waste time selecting the main target for his campaign: long ago the assassination of the hated Interior Minister Plehve had become "the question of honor" for the PSR.

Azef meanwhile altered his tactic of dealing with the tsarist officials. As early as the end of 1903 he had begun to conceal information from his police superiors, choosing not to notify the authorities about some of his less important connections among the revolutionaries for fear of being compromised.[62] Rather than immediately accusing him of double dealing, however, we should perhaps consider that his new position as the Central Committee representative in the Combat Organization was in and of itself an extenuating circumstance that helps to explain his modified behavior.

Indeed, his singular status in the party and among the combatants was both demanding and dangerous, for while his police superiors now had every reason to expect detailed reports on the combatants, they had to use the information Azef provided with great care in order to prevent the terrorists from suspecting him of treachery. In dealing with the authorities, Azef did not conceal his real concern for his safety, and his fears seem to have been well justified: his police superiors demonstrated little regard for protecting their agent and often utilized their newly acquired facts about the terrorists in a most indiscreet manner. Azef expressed many grievances about the way the police handled his information, and on numerous occasions complained that the authorities rushed ahead with arrests without considering that their actions would place him in serious danger and jeopardize his position among the revolutionaries.[63] To make matters worse, in 1903, his Moscow "control" Zubatov, as a result of some confrontations with Azef, purposely made arrests without consulting his agent, thus causing some of Azef's comrades "to look askance at him."[64]

Azef's concerns at this time were undoubtedly intensified by the fact that for the first time since he was a student in Germany, rumors began to circulate about his police connections. He was also extremely worried by the fact that certain secret documents, some of them containing information provided by him, disappeared from the Police Department and made their way to the revolutionaries, causing him to suspect that there was a traitor in police headquarters.[65] Thus, unable to trust his personal safety to the police, the master spy designed a strategy that allowed him to continue his service and simultaneously minimize its risks.

His plan consisted of two parts. He began first of all to limit his reports to very general facts, and instead of supplying the authorities with direct and detailed information on participants in assassination plots and their proposed actions, he now tended to provide only vague descriptions of the combatants, leaving it to the police to establish surveillance and thus determine the direction and extent of the terrorists' criminal activities. He would disclose just enough information to allow them to pursue their targets without compromising him in the eyes of the revolutionaries.[66] If the information provided proved inadequate for the successful establishment of surveillance, the second part of Azef's strategy called for him to use every means at his disposal to sabotage a prospective terrorist attack. Azef's new approach to his police duties worked perfectly for many months,[67] until Savinkov and his associates were ready to reveal to the world the reason for their presence in St. Petersburg.

On the morning of 15 July 1904, Viacheslav von Plehve's carriage speeded along Izmailovskii Prospekt in the direction of the railroad station. Punctual as usual, the interior minister was on his way to the tsar's residence in Peterhof to present his regular report. Several Okhrana agents on bicycles followed Plehve as guards. The carriage dashed along, street policemen stood at attention, cab drivers hastened to move their horses out of the way, and passersby twisted their heads to get a better look at the powerful dignitary. Three terrorists from Savinkov's group started their fatal stride toward the speeding carriage, walking calmly, keeping intervals between one another— each carrying a twelve-pound bomb.

Close to the bridge over Obvodnyi Canal, a man dressed in a railway worker's uniform, with a package under his arm, suddenly stepped off the sidewalk and took a few steps toward the carriage. When he was right next to it, the man lifted his arm and cast the package inside the carriage. In a huge blast, Plehve's impetuous confidence in the thoroughness of his security "blew up along with the bomb,"[68] which shattered his carriage to pieces. The interior minister was killed instantly, as was the driver and the horses. Terrorist Egor Sazonov, thrown off his feet by an Okhrana bicycler, was wounded.[69]

Following the assassination, the radicals received sympathy rather than scorn from the general public; not only revolutionaries, but also people who could never be suspected of left-wing leanings failed to shed tears over Plehve's death. "In all truth, no one felt sorry for him," as "he had always quelled even the most innocent initiative of the society."[70] "Not a word of remorse was spoken" about Plehve's demise from any quarter; on the contrary, "it was hard not to feel happy" about the reactionary minister finding his end[71] in the hands of the omnipresent terrorists, whose victory was convincing evidence of the imminent and "irrepressible strikes of the Combat Organization."[72] The PSR as a whole suddenly gained unsurpassed recognition, enjoying—as always at times of triumph—an unprecedented upswing in new membership and a cascade of financial donations that overflowed the treasuries of the party and the Combat Organization. The SR civilians revered the *boeviki* as revolutionary heroes who had won fame and glory for their party, and in everyone's opinion, the place of greatest honor among the terrorists belonged to Azef.

On 15 July, Azef was in Warsaw; he was walking down one of the main streets with the revolutionary Praskoviia Ivanovskaia when "newsboys came running toward them shouting" out newspaper headlines: "'Bomb thrown at Plehve!' ... 'Plehve Assassinated!'" Azef's initial reaction to the death of the interior minister was certainly not that of a man who expected the news. Ivanovskaia remembered that "he suddenly complained of feeling faint and went limp, letting his arms drop loosely by his sides."[73] Nor was it the reaction of a triumphant avenger who had finally fulfilled his haunting dream of slaying his mortal enemy. Azef's response to Plehve's assassination revealed his feeling of defeat, impotence, and confusion as to what to do next. Among other emotions, anxiety must have reigned supreme. How would he explain his failure to frustrate the terrorists' attack to the Police Department?

"Present fears [a]re less than horrible imaginings,"[74] so Shakespeare consoles, but at the moment Azef was most likely not in the mood for taking solace from classical literature. It must have taken him some effort to regain self-control, to cast away his habitual misgivings about his status with the police, and comfort himself with the fact that his incompetent superiors were responsible for Plehve's death, since they had proven themselves unable to interpret and act on the information they had received from their agent. On the other hand, such a paroxysm of panic might have had an almost ameliorating emotional effect on Azef. This was one of the very rare moments—Ivanovskaia interpreted it as the naturally strong reaction of a gentle soul to his own involvement in bloodshed—when he could stop pretending, allow free rein to his feelings, and express his fear-ridden self without inhibition. Would it be a far-fetched conjecture that Azef in fact needed such periodic psychological release so that moments later he would be able to get a grip on himself and reassume his role? Indeed, in personalities such as Azef's, "under conditions of prolonged stress . . . a temporary exhaustion" and debilitation could be "followed by restored or even increased functional capacity."[75] Thus, on 15 July 1904, having recovered his ability to assess the burdensome situation, the spy knew how he could turn his predicament into his advantage.

Without waiting for Savinkov, as had been agreed, he hurried abroad to reap the fruit of the terrorists' success.[76] Adroitly amplifying his role at Savinkov's expense, Azef grabbed the opportunity to boost his reputation in the radical camp by acknowledging what so many jubilant—and credulous—comrades were all too willing to attribute to him—that he was the one who had masterminded Plehve's assassination. His position in the SR Central Committee rendered his efforts at self-promotion highly effective, and his prestige reached new and unrivaled heights even among revolutionaries like Ekaterina Breshko-Breshkovskaia, who had never been among Azef's fans. Having learned about the terrorist act in the capital, the Grandmother now approached Azef, bowed to the ground, and kissed him in the presence of numerous other SRs, as if apologizing for her past reservations and thanking him for the glorious deed of killing the tyrant. When another revolutionary veteran, Mark Natanson, who had been intuitively repelled by Azef and hesitated to treat him as a comrade, shared his doubts about Azef with Gots soon after Plehve's assassination, the party leader was emphatic in his praise, affirming with tears in his eyes: "You can believe him as much as you believe me."[77] Whenever someone would venture a misgiving about Azef, the SRs remembered: "And what about Plehve?"[78] When the ill-omened Savinkov, true champion of SR terror, finally made it to Europe, it was too late for him to try to collect the tribute that was rightfully his. Although he too was greeted with much accolade for his role in the sensational political assassination, the *boevik* leader found himself hopelessly overshadowed by Azef's inflated figure, undeservedly adorned with the laurels of the terrorist hero.

Years later, of course, it was precisely the assassination of Plehve that became the trump card in the hands of the revolutionaries in their attempts to compromise the government by demonstrating that its spy was guilty of staging terrorist acts and thus acting as a double agent. Contrary to many early assertions of the SRs that Azef was much less involved in the Plehve affair than was commonly supposed,[79] he subsequently was alleged to have been the primary organizer of this assassination, not only because he had supposedly come up with the idea of using revolutionaries dressed as cab drivers and street peddlers for surveillance purposes, but because—the SRs claimed—he had been preoccupied personally with such minute details of the terrorists' work as their clandestine contacts, safe apartments, and directions for secret meetings. "In a word," insisted Chernov, "everything that was planned and everything that was carried out was due to Azef first and foremost."[80] Finally, according to another leading SR, Vladimir Zenzinov, Azef literally "put the bomb in Sazonov's hand."[81]

Azef did not deny directly having taken part in developing the broad plans of the Combat Organization against Plehve or in helping the combatants to work out the general strategy, yet long after his exposure he was entirely justified in observing:

> Nobody wondered that the head of such a serious organization was a rather strange character: he is never close to the organization, he is not interested in it, he disappears under various pretexts, he does not go to cities where he himself schedules appointments, and it is only possible to meet him by accident. . . . Does it not occur to anybody that it is more accurate to suppose that it was Savinkov who stood at the head of the organization, [a man] who never left it [and] who shared its joys and sorrows.[82]

Savinkov's description of the Combat Organization in this period inadvertently confirms Azef's assertion. The depiction underscores that the *boeviki* were emotionally and spiritually bonded together as "friends" and even "brothers," connected to one another by the "strongest ties"—all, "with an exception of Azef."[83] Even though after Plehve's assassination Savinkov always publicly yielded the glory of the leader among the combatants to Azef, he later confirmed privately that Azef "in fact, did not participate" in the attempt against Plehve or in any other terrorist ventures during this period. It was hardly surprising, then, that a revolutionary and would-be terrorist remembered: "As strange as it may seem, I did not know that it was Azef who led the Combat Organization, even though I had permanent contacts with [revolutionary] veterans and, in general, with people who were close to the party. . . . For some reason it appeared to me . . . that Savinkov played a role no smaller" than that of Azef at the time.[84] By 1910, having gone through great pains to find incriminating evidence against the spy, Burtsev had but to recognize in private discussions with the SRs that Azef's self-made reputation as the people's avenger who had slain the hated interior minister with the help of his obedient combatants, "was unjustified."[85]

Unlike Savinkov, the on-site commander of the terrorists, Azef was frequently absent from St. Petersburg during the preparations for the attack against Plehve[86] and could hardly supply the police with specific details about the terrorists' operations, even if he had decided to risk his position by focusing on the particulars. This notwithstanding, an analysis of Azef's reports to the Police Department leaves little room for doubt as to the sincerity of his attempts to prevent Plehve's assassination by providing his police superiors with sufficient information to nullify the efforts of the terrorists, never neglecting to preserve his personal safety, of course. Even during the initial stages of the combatants' plot against Plehve, Azef had already indicated that Sazonov was "preparing something extremely important."[87] The police were thus able to establish surveillance on Sazonov as early as December 1903.[88]

All participants in the hunt for Plehve gathered in St. Petersburg in February 1904, and during this period Azef was already giving descriptions of the terrorists in his daily reports to Rataev, who, appreciative of his agent's efforts, once made a confession to him: "More than anything in the world I am afraid of compromising you and losing your services" as a result.[89] The reports concentrated in particular on Kaliaev and Shveitser, although Azef claimed not to have known their true names. At the same time, in accordance with his two-sided policy, Azef invented numerous pretexts to delay the act, calling for patience and caution, and finally yielding only to unanimous pressure from the terrorists. He agreed to proceed with the assassination attempt on 18 March.[90]

This attempt turned out to be a failure. Prior to the attack, Azef had informed Police Department director Aleksei Lopukhin of the expected disposition of the terrorists,[91] and on the designated day there were so many Okhrana agents patrolling the streets near the proposed scene of the crime that one of the participants felt encircled and ran away, thus jeopardizing the entire scheme. On the other hand, this incident provided an excellent illustration of what may justifiably be seen as police incompetence, potentially perilous for the informant, since the authorities lost the opportunity to eliminate the entire terrorist organization. Azef's reports had made the physical appearances of the combatants familiar to the surveillance agents and detectives, and yet not a single terrorist was arrested for possession of a bomb on 18 March.[92] Savinkov himself was puzzled as to why the participants of this operation were not apprehended, especially since Kaliaev, who stood in front of Plehve's house for nearly an hour, unquestionably attracted attention, and Pokotilov carried two bombs that were distinctly noticeable in his coat pockets.[93] In any case, having been fortunate to escape detention, Savinkov and his crew resumed their preparatory efforts, waiting for an opportune moment for the fatal strike.

Azef in the meantime continued to provide the police with other significant, if fragmentary and indirect, clues on the activities of the Combat Organization directed against Plehve. Early in April 1904 the spy's report informed the director of the Police Department that the PSR Central Committee had instructed Sazonov to proceed with the organization of an act against the interior minister, and had designated a sum of seven thousand rubles for this purpose.[94] Approximately two months later, on 11 June 1904, Azef revealed that the person who had been killed several days earlier in an explosion while manufacturing home-made bombs in a Northern Hotel room in St. Petersburg was Aleksei Pokotilov,[95] whose accomplices resided in Odessa and Poltava, and that he had been producing the explosive devices, "probably for an attempt against . . . Plehve." Azef immediately proceeded to Odessa, from where he reported on 19 June that the assassination of Plehve was being postponed—but only until new bombs could be prepared.[96]

He then left the country. To disclose any other information about the Combat Organization's activities would have meant an additional risk for Azef, who obviously deemed the police capable of acting on his clues. These clues, admittedly rather vague at times, were in combination more than adequate for the establishment of surveillance.[97] His police superiors acknowledged that Azef "certainly provided enough information to prevent the assassination";[98] they therefore could not hold him responsible for the fact that the indolent authorities in St. Petersburg failed to save the minister's life by prompt action on or before 15 July: "They had not even had the sense to vary von Plehve's timetable or to guard his carriage from the front as well as from behind!"[99]

Without any question, "it was not in Azef's interest to assassinate Plehve";[100] the risk of evoking the wrath of the Police Department, whose officers could easily have doubted Azef's loyalty and held him accountable for negligence or withholding information about preparations for the murder, certainly was not worth the status he may have acquired in the PSR as a result. Any cautious person would have to have a grave incentive to play this dangerous game, not to mention Azef, perpetually fearful as he was and hardly eager to increase the perils of his entanglement with the two rivaling camps.

Most contemporaries—and many future historians—still opted to acquiesce to the SR's subsequent allegation that Azef was reluctant to prevent the 15 July attack of the Combat Organization. Seeking to explain his seemingly illogical behavior, they claimed that Azef wished to settle personal scores with Plehve because, in line with all radical and liberal public opinion in Russia and abroad, he considered the interior minister to have been the chief instigator of the ghastly Jewish pogrom in the city of Kishinev in April 1903.[101]

Azef, however, had done much to help the authorities prevent terrorist operations against Plehve not only before the pogrom—in late 1902 to early 1903—but also at least once after the Kishinev massacre. Indeed, the second assassination attempt against Plehve was planned by Serafima Klitchoglu's circle at the end of 1903, but owing to Azef's timely interference, the group was destroyed by police action in January 1904.[102] In addition, according to Rataev, even though Azef may have been outraged by anti-Jewish violence and indeed may initially have held Plehve responsible for it, he finally became convinced that all of the accusations that the authorities had deliberately staged the pogrom were "obvious and absurd nonsense." "No government in the world can ever or under any circumstances profit from disturbances and riots, no matter where they came from and against whom they were directed, since the spontaneous rebellious power, which today allegedly serves the interests of the government, tomorrow may turn into a dangerous weapon directed against that very same government."[103]

It is more than unlikely that Azef, driven by his Jewish identity and a desire to avenge the suffering of all the victims of antisemitic violence, purposely allowed the terrorists to kill Plehve. Contrary to a prevailing opinion, Azef had no great attachment to his Jewish heritage, as he felt little esteem or fondness for any integral fragments of his troubled personality. Indeed, a fellow revolutionary who worked closely with him in 1905 noted in surprise that Azef never revealed a trace of Jewish nationalism.[104] On a deeper level, he might have longed to rescind his Jewish origins, which had given him nothing but humiliation and misery; if anything, the stigma of poverty was undoubtedly associated in his mind with his Jewish background.[105] According to a Moscow rabbi, Ia. Maze, Azef's neighbor in 1901, he "bitterly derided the customs, traditions, [and] religion of his people." For example, responding to his father-in-law's pleas to circumcise his grandson so as to observe the Jewish law, Azef ridiculed the ritual as sheer stupidity.[106] Whether it involved negating or merely neglecting his religious or cultural identity, Azef was fully prepared to renounce his Jewishness for convenience's sake. His wife remembered how, prior to his return to Russia from Germany in 1899, he announced to her one day that he had been baptized. Feeling very strongly against conversion, Menkina was stunned by the news and by Azef's explanation: "Of course this is nonsense, but just in case . . . I am going to Moscow, you know, and as a Jew, I do not have the right to reside there." This attitude filled Menkina with indignation, and seeing how vexed she was by his cynicism, Azef suddenly roared with laughter and said: "How can you always believe whatever I tell you?" To the end, Menkina did not know whether her husband had in fact converted to Christianity, as appears very probable.[107]

For the next six months after Plehve's assassination, while living away from Russia, Azef continued to provide the Police Department with services that varied in significance. Being involved with general PSR activities abroad in 1904–05 allowed the agent, for instance, to apply himself effectively against the growing movement within the PSR in favor of so-called agrarian and factory terrorism. Otherwise known as "economic terror," this particular brand of revolutionary extremism involved attacks on landlords and their property in the countryside, including the use of such traditional forms of violence as arson—or in peasant jargon, the "red rooster" *(krasnyi petukh)*—and attacks against the owners of industrial establishments in the cities.[108] The suitability of economic terror produced an intense controversy in the SR circles in emigration, and during their heated debates "Azef assumed a totally irreconcilable stand with regard to this movement," declaring categorically that its adherents had nothing to do with the SRs and therefore "ought to be thrown out of the party."[109]

Living abroad also rendered it easy for Azef to provide the authorities with information about noncombat party events. Thus, in 1904 he supplied his police superiors with important information about the international socialist congress in Amsterdam and about the Paris conference of all Russian revolutionary and oppositionist groups, whose main purpose was to formulate a general antigovernment program of action to be implemented jointly by various enemies of Nicholas II. Azef was present at both of these gatherings as a respected representative of the PSR, and his detailed reports to St. Petersburg included the important revolutionary documents that had originated at these conventions.[110]

The spy's police superiors could be certain that he was not involved in the affairs of the terrorist band at this time, and not merely because Azef himself assured them of the fact. Another convincing proof was that other police agents operating within the PSR, including Zinaida Zhuchenko, an unquestionably loyal and long-standing informer close to the party center, did not mention Azef's role in the Combat Organization.[111] When police agent Nikolai Tatarov betrayed the entire membership of the Combat Organization to the authorities in February 1905, he did not mention a word about Azef.[112] Savinkov, too, felt that the combatants had "nothing to do with him."[113] Thus, Azef was by this time of limited usefulness for illuminating terrorist affairs inside Russia, although he most likely reported whatever he knew.[114] Busy with SR activities abroad, however, he was not able to supply the Police Department with any intricate details of the Combat Organization's next project—a plan against the tsar's uncle, the governor-general of Moscow, Grand Duke Sergei Aleksandrovich.[115]

The assassination of the Grand Duke in Moscow on 4 February 1905—a direct strike against the imperial family—provided the second most important piece of evidence in support of the revolutionaries' thesis that Azef was a double agent, since the security police allegedly knew nothing about the preparations for this terrorist act performed under Azef's leadership.[116] As in the case of Plehve's assassination, however, there is little reason to accept this claim without serious modifications[117] because Azef apparently played no direct role in this undertaking. Under the sole leadership of Savinkov, the Moscow contingent of the Combat Organization then included three other persons: Kaliaev, Moiseenko, and Dora Brilliant, who usually was in charge of preparing the dynamite.[118] Echoed by the other *boeviki*, Savinkov denied Azef's involvement in the arrangements for the attack against the Grand Duke, and in private conversations and memoirs, he made no attempt to attribute any responsibility for the Moscow assassination to Azef,[119] who had not set foot on Russian soil since July 1904 and had lived in Paris and Geneva for the entire six-month preparation period.[120]

Azef did know about the terrorists' preliminary and very general plans, and had he chosen to provide the police with timely information, the authorities probably could have had Savinkov and his combat crew arrested in the very early stage of their preparations for the assassination, perhaps as they were crossing the Russian border. Yet, here one essential point must be considered: only very few people were informed about the terrorists' return to Russia, and Azef's rushed report would undoubtedly have led to serious suspicion against him. Acutely conscious of this danger, Azef waited for a better chance to notify his police chiefs about the prospective terrorist venture in Moscow, meanwhile sabotaging the work of the Combat Organization by ignoring Savinkov's request for money.[121]

As time went on, however, it became much more difficult for Azef to betray the SRs to the police, for all participants in the Combat Organization used false passports and lived under different names that were, in truth, unknown to Azef.[122] He did, however, know how to find the terrorists' leader,[123] and that was exactly what he reported to the police, outlining Savinkov's role in the Combat Organization.[124] According to the 1906 testimony of police defector Mikhail Bakai, the authorities were indeed informed of the fact that Savinkov was among the terrorists preparing an assassination in Moscow, and immediately after the Grand Duke's assassination, the Police Department circulated telegrams enjoining its officers to arrest the terrorist leader at once under any circumstances.

The fact that after the terrorists had arrived in Moscow, Azef reported whatever he could find out from abroad is also clear from additional evidence. Bakai claimed to have been informed by the head of the city's external surveillance operations, D. V. Popov, that, anticipating an attempt against the Grand Duke, the Moscow Okhrana had stationed the *filery* along his daily route, thus attempting, albeit unsuccessfully, to prevent Kaliaev's attack.[125] Finally, Aleksei Lopukhin later asserted that as director of the Police Department he had insisted on the immediate arrest of the *boeviki* in Moscow, but that his superiors preferred to keep the terrorists under constant surveillance and to allow them to continue their preparations for an attack against the Grand Duke, hoping to liquidate the Combat Organization right before it was ready to strike.[126]

On 4 February, the Grand Duke, who, despite all pleas from those in his entourage refused to take precautions and alter his daily schedule, left the Kremlin's Nikolaevskii Palace as usual at 2:30 in the afternoon. As his carriage approached the Nikol'skii Gates, Kaliaev, dressed as a worker wearing high boots and a sheepskin hat and carrying a bundle wrapped in a scarf, suddenly ran up to it—coming so close that he could see the Grand Duke's face become instantly aghast and bewildered. A moment later the terrorist hurled his homemade bomb, which exploded with a thunder that was heard even in remote corners of Moscow, causing people to think an earthquake had taken place. At the site of the attack, "there lay a shapeless heap . . . of small fragments of the carriage, of clothes, and of a mutilated body . . . [with] no head. Of the other segments, it was only possible to distinguish an arm and part of a leg."

The bomb that killed the Grand Duke also severely injured his coachman, as well as the terrorist himself.[127] His wounds notwithstanding, Kaliaev, seeking to employ his arrest for the benefit of revolution, continuously screamed while being taken away: "Down with the tsar, down with the government!"[128] Inside the palace, Grand Duchess Elizaveta Fedorovna, upon hearing the tremendous explosion, cried: "It's Sergei!" and ran out to the square, where she dropped on her knees and began to gather the scattered bloody pieces of her husband's body.[129] According to an eyewitness, a large crowd quickly gathered at the scene of the terrorist act; the people stared at the remains of the Grand Duke's body, but no one removed his hat in respect. A spectator said: "Good job, boys! No passerby even scratched; no need to harm people for nothing." A jester in the crowd touched with his boot the scattered bits

of what used to be the Grand Duke's head and, apparently not overly shaken by the gory scene, ruminated out loud: "Brothers, and they
said that he had no brains!"—a comment repeated by cheeky wise-
crackers over and over again as a joke amidst the "universal jubilation"
in Moscow.[130]

In the eyes of the public, the Grand Duke, like the late interior minister, was an incorrigible reactionary, and his title as well as his close
relations with Nicholas II had additional symbolic value: he was the
first member of the Russian royal family to have been killed since 1881.
His assassination confirmed that the spectacular victory against Plehve
had not been a mere fluke for the SRs. Thus, as the second major terrorist success brought a new wave of widespread recognition for the
PSR, it also solidified Azef's personal position in the party to the highest degree. For just as after the attack against Plehve, Azef usurped the
lion's share of the glory as terrorist hero, affirming before the activists
in the high SR circles abroad that he, rather than Savinkov, was the mas-
termind behind the new sensational assassination.[131]

It would seem that Azef's task as a charlatan would have been complicated by the fact that, in contrast to his machinations in St. Petersburg during the campaign against Plehve, he had stayed in Paris and
Geneva during the whole time that Savinkov's group was preparing
for its fatal strike against the Grand Duke in Moscow. Yet, precisely
because he was in a position to represent the terrorists abroad while
Savinkov remained far away, still playing cat-and-mouse with the
Russian police, Azef easily sustained the legend about his firsthand
contribution to the Combat Organization's stupendous success. His
prestige reached its apogee at this time. So as not to allow his reputation to wane, Azef now made a scintillating psychological move: he
mentioned in conversations with several leading revolutionaries that
the next logical objective of the Combat Organization was to kill the
tsar himself. Nothing was impossible when Azef took the reins in his
hands, thought the awestricken SRs, and wished him Godspeed.

Figure 1. Evno Azef's childhood drawings.

Figure 2. Young Azef
with acquaintances.
Photo probably
from 1890s.

Figure 3. Sergei Vasil'evich
Zubatov, head of Moscow
section of the Okhrana and
one of Azef's police superiors.

Figure 4. Azef as a young man. Photo probably from early 1900s.

Figure 5. Viktor Mikhailovich Chernov, one of the organizers and leaders of the PSR. Main ideologue of the party and the author of its program.

Figure 6. Ekaterina Breshko-Breshkovskaia ("Babushka," or "Grandmother of the Russian Revolution"). A long-standing revolutionary and an active member of the PSR.

Figure 7. Mikhail Rafailovich Gots, a lifelong revolutionary and one of the organizers of the SR movement. Leading member of the PSR.

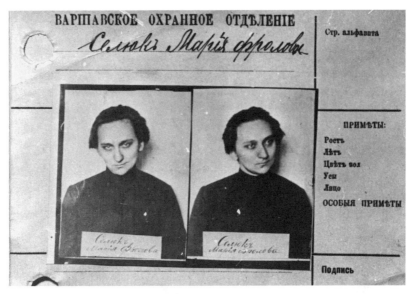

Figure 8. Maria F. Seliuk, member of the Northern Union of Socialist Revolutionaries and of the SR party, actively involved in its terrorist tactics. Photo taken in the Warsaw section of the Okhrana.

Figure 9. Petr Vladimirovich Karpovich, member of the SR Combat Organization, assassinated N. P. Bogolepov, the Russian Minister of Education, in 1901.

Figure 10. Grigorii Andreevich Gershuni, founder and first leader of the Combat Organization of the PSR.

Figure 11. Boris Viktorovich Savinkov, head of the Combat Organization after Gershuni's arrest in 1903.

Figure 12. Viacheslav von Plehve, Interior Minister of Russia and victim of the SR plot in July 1904.

Figure 13. Egor Sazonov, member of the SR Combat Organization, assassinated Interior Minister von Plehve.

Figure 14. Grand Duke Sergei Aleksandrovich Romanov, governor-general of Moscow and uncle of Tsar Nicholas II, fell victim to SR terrorism in February 1905.

Figure 15. Ivan Kaliaev ("Poet"), member of the Combat Organization responsible for the death of Grand Duke Sergei Aleksandrovich.

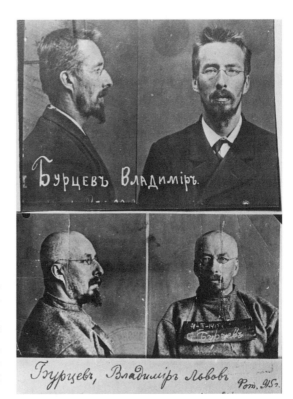

Figure 16. Vladimir L'ivovich Burtsev was nicknamed "Sherlock Holmes of the Russian Revolution" for his role in unmasking Azef in 1908.

Бурцевъ Владиміръ.

Бурцевъ, Владиміръ Львовъ

Figure 17. Aleksei Aleksandrovich Lopukhin, Director of the Police Department between May 1902 and March 1905. In 1908 radicals forced him to reveal Azef's police connections.

Figure 18. Azef in the last period of his police career.

Figure 19. Azef, the unmasked police informer. Photo appeared in Russian and international press after the outbreak of the spy scandal in 1909.

4

Terrorist-Virtuoso, 1905–1908

The combatants deem Azef to be a very brave person. They say of him that he has the fearlessness of fear, that he does not even know what fear is.

—From the Findings of the Judicial-Investigatory Committee on the Azef Affair[1]

In the fall of 1905 news spread of the Imperial Manifesto of 17 October, which guaranteed basic civil liberties to all Russian citizens and granted legislative powers to the State Duma. The event marked the commencement of a new parliamentary order in Russia. Many SRs took the tsar's concession for what it indeed was—a sign of weakness, and celebrated it as a partial victory of the revolutionary movement. Among them, "no one was more cheerful and satisfied than Azef," who resided in Geneva at the time, and in conversations with the PSR leaders clearly indicated his wish to retire as a terrorist.[2] "This is the finale of terror—period, the end," he repeated with unconcealed delight; "it is necessary to declare that the party terminates its terrorist activity" for the sake of a constitutional course.[3] Amidst heated debates in the leading spheres of the party as to whether to proceed with terrorist activities after the promulgation of the October Manifesto, Azef "was an ardent advocate of peaceful means," promoting his views—quite temperate and "hardly more left-wing than those of a moderate liberal"[4]—so zealously that his comrades surmised him to have fallen into the trap of "believing in the Duma and government's goodwill."[5] It was at this point that his revolutionary colleagues christened him "the liberal with a bomb."[6] Far from being abashed by criticism from the radicals, Azef admitted frankly that indeed he was "only a fellow-traveler of the party"; as soon as the constitutional order was established in Russia, he would turn into a consistent "legalist and evolutionist."[7]

Azef insisted further that terror as a tactic was entirely inappropriate in the new political situation and at least for the time being must stop.
Despite violent protests on the part of Savinkov and the rest of the combatants, he then categorically proclaimed the need to dissolve the Combat Organization. The October Manifesto was a perfect chance for him
to get out of his deadly game without losing face or invoking suspicions. Yet, habitually painstaking as far as his cover was concerned, he
pretended to have given in to the terrorists' demands by agreeing to
one last assassination plan—an attack against the governor-general of
St. Petersburg, Dmitrii Trepov. This concession was but a cagey step
aimed at self-protection: as soon as Azef arrived in Russia, he "changed
his mind"[8] and cancelled the operation.[9]

Azef's success in deluding the radicals may in part be attributed to
his tendency to stay as superficially close to the truth as possible, and
never to conceal his views, even when they were entirely contradictory to the mainstream thinking of the PSR. In this way, Azef inevitably
projected the image of an individual who had a mind of his own and
would not dodge from defending his independent opinion even when
it was at odds with the orthodox party line and spirit. For the sake of
his reputation as a veracious nonconformist, he was prepared to show
that he was a stranger to the party in ideological matters, to which he
never failed to show deep-seated indifference.

In late December 1905 the First Congress of the PSR convened in
the Finnish town of Imatra. During this important gathering where the
SRs adopted the official party program, Azef's negative attitude,
according to one of his comrades, was surprisingly conspicuous: "He
usually had the physiognomy of a very bored person; he would show
up, listen, barely paying attention, and then he would take his leave. . . .
All in all, this was the attitude of a person who did not care in the least,
who was not at all interested in any questions" being discussed. As it
was during other SR caucuses, his role at the congress was minimal,
"if only because . . . he always kept silent."[10] Chernov concurred,
asserting that "Azef played no role in working out the party program"
and made no contribution to SR theory.[11] Savinkov did "not remember ever talking seriously about programmatic questions with Azef:
this never happened." He later purported that it was "meaningless to
talk about Azef's ideological influence; it was zero."[12]

Given what we know about Azef, there is no evidence whatsoever
confirming the declaration that "Azef was . . . well versed in theoretical
questions" or, more generally, that "the extent of his intellectual interests
was very broad" and "his stalwart impetus for intellectual improvement
impressed the *boeviki*."[13] Conversely, many of his comrades noted how

uninformed and "unenlightened" Azef was.[14] Mariia Seliuk, who had known Azef since the early days of his career as a revolutionary, argued strongly against other comrades who considered Azef "a dimwit and ignoramus." She claimed that in his youth he had seemed to be "well-read" and showed "interest in theoretical questions"; yet, she admitted that "later this interest apparently disappeared altogether. . . ."[15] The sole argument in support of Azef's penetrating ideological awareness was his incidental 1901 speech on Populist thinker Nikolai Mikhailovskii—his only theoretical comment that his comrades found worth remembering and referring to time and time again after his exposure.[16]

Azef did not fool himself about the gap in his philosophical erudition and did well not to try to convince his comrades of his adequate knowledge of socialist theory. He instead demonstrated his scorn for any sort of theorizing with bravado—something that the SR leaders respectfully accepted as the natural attitude of a military commander, alienated from civilian mentality by his life of constant risk and danger. Accustomed to Azef's uselessness as an ideologue, most SRs welcomed any of his trite theoretical observations, to which they assigned an inflated value.[17] Some revolutionaries, however, showed better judgment. Ekaterina Breshko-Breshkovskaia once said of him: "Azef does not care about peasants or socialism. He has no need for socialism."[18] Indeed, since Azef considered socialism to be merely an "ornament" for Russia, another leading SR, Il'ia Rubanovich, argued, albeit in retrospect, that such an approach suited only a "non-socialist" who had no business being on the Central Committee of a socialist party.[19] In 1905–06, Azef nevertheless not only remained among the highest SR leadership, but also retained his unmatched prestige as the most accomplished leader of the Combat Organization, despite the fact that the terrorist team proved to be a complete failure in the final period of his career.

Cases of Azef's assistance to the police in thwarting terrorist acts are too numerous to list. Among the most serious ones was the impeded assassination of Petr Durnovo, who was Russian interior minister from October 1905 to April 1906. The authorities were able to obstruct an SR attack against him largely due to Azef's timely information. They were able to preclude attempts against the mayor of Moscow, Medem; Minister of Justice M. G. Akimov; General Georgii Min and Colonel Riman, who had played a leading role in suppressing the Moscow uprising in December 1905. Azef also enabled the police to establish close surveillance of the terrorists, forcing them to postpone temporarily an attempt on the life of the governor of St. Petersburg, V. F. von der Launits, as well as to abandon their efforts to assassinate Petr Stolypin.[20]

While receiving generous praise and equally generous financial reward from his police superiors, Azef somehow had to vindicate his leadership in the eyes of his subordinates among the terrorists, who gradually began to show anxiety and needed an explanation for the persistent lack of success in any of their undertakings. Azef was fully aware of the combatants' antipathy to the PSR's civilian leadership, and in dealing with them, resorted to a hackneyed scapegoat device by shifting the blame for the Combat Organization's inefficiency from its members to the party's Central Committee. Knowing exactly what the combatants preferred to hear and what they would most likely accept as the absolute truth, he argued that civilians in the party did not trust the *boeviki* enough[21] and were inhibiting their operations by constant incompetent intrusions from the center.

Savinkov remembered that Azef invariably presented Central Committee members in a negative light in his conversations with the terrorists, who did not know every party leader personally and therefore tended to accept Azef's characterizations of their personalities at face value.[22] Azef's knowledge of people was largely circumscribed by a proclivity to discern his own inadequacies in others in whom these weaknesses were often much less striking. One might also surmise that as a slave to the darker, cryptic side of his personality Azef was bound to remain the victim of the need to project his own inadequacies and inner impairments onto others. This need caused him to be constantly conscious of the weaknesses and imperfections of those around him. In a case where the combatants avidly waited for any information about the party leaders' foibles, Azef's ability to discredit the SR high command proved to be to his great benefit.

Savinkov remarked that occasionally Azef's characterizations "really grated upon the ears" *(priamo-taki rezalo ukho)*, miffing one's senses *(korobilo)*, as was the case when Azef talked about Chernov, depicting him as "a talented and intelligent man, but a regular liar."[23] Responding to Savinkov's aggravated protest, Azef referred to some trivial matter that supposedly qualified Chernov as a person who was inconsistent in his assertions.[24] Typically, the negative traits to which Azef carefully directed the combatants' attention were mild shortcomings rather than deadly sins, but by propelling people to consider such nebulously elucidated imperfections as "lack of experience," "pretentiousness that leads to difficulties," or simply "certain sides that may puzzle,"[25] Azef often achieved a triple objective. By detracting from the personality of a party leader, Azef gained esteem in his listener's eyes by the contrast, if only implicitly suggested. Also, by being confidential, he profited by obtaining additional trust and eliciting a certain dependence from the ingenuous person listening to him—as if their conversation had turned them into accomplices, implicated in something vaguely secret, about which no one else should know. Finally, another goal of his constant intrigue may be described as "preventive treatment." By bolstering tensions between the Central Committee and the *boeviki*—tensions that existed autonomously from Azef's efforts yet were constantly stirred up thanks to his instigation—Azef gradually established a position from which he could manipulate each side by presenting himself as the only person who was tolerant and tactful enough to sustain the loose contacts between the intractable rank-and-file members of the Combat Organization and the "civilian generals." By occasionally setting one against the other, without either knowing that a third party had come between them, he hoped to preclude any possibility that the party leaders and the terrorists would ever get together behind his back, compare information, and perhaps catch him in a lie.[26]

In the meantime, Azef's relationship with the Police Department underwent a marked change. As a result of a major reorganization of the secret police, in August 1905 his immediate supervisor, Leonid Rataev, was forced to retire from his position. Azef's new "control" was to be Petr Rachkovskii, the head of the Political Section of the Police Department.[27] From their first meeting on 8 August, when the master spy "divulged important information, including leads about Boris Savinkov,"[28] Azef was understandably anxious. He knew that he could trust Rataev to remain circumspect in protecting his agent, but he was not at all sure that Rachkovskii would be as discreet. The following month confirmed his worst fears. In September 1905 a confused member of the SR committee in St. Petersburg showed him an unsigned letter brought to him by a veiled lady. Taking the letter from the comrade's shaking hands, Azef read: "Comrades, the Party is in danger of a pogrom" due to the efforts of two secret police collaborators in the PSR, a certain T— and "the engineer Azief."[29] Always on the alert for this sort of bombshell, Azef controlled an immediate spasm of panic, explaining in a matter-of-fact manner, with poise and total composure: "T—, that can only be Tatarov. And the engineer Azief, that must be myself." He immediately departed, leaving the comrade in a state of astonishment. Not that Azef could pretend nonchalance for a long time; according to a witness, he later had an hysterical breakdown and threatened to commit suicide because his honor was besmirched by an anonymous accuser.[30]

After he recovered from the initial shock, Azef was able to assess the risk involved in his association with Rachkovskii, who had implanted another secret agent in the PSR Central Committee and had protected his main informant so poorly. Azef continued to provide the police with occasional information about the terrorists' projects—information that was of vital importance at times; for example, when the extremists planned to demolish several of St. Petersburg's bridges, blow up the headquarters of the Okhrana, destroy electric wires and telephone lines, or kidnap the prime minister, Count Sergei Witte. None of these ventures materialized because, according to Savinkov, "the security was so tight, as if the police had been alerted beforehand."[31] The police certainly acted at least in part on information provided by their best agent among the SRs. They were also able to seize two dynamite factories that Savinkov had set up in the capital, capturing several terrorists, among them Dora Brilliant.[32] Yet, until Azef could be entirely confident that his Police Department superiors would exercise the utmost prudence in dealing with their employee, he clearly resolved to protect his own life by carefully selecting the information that he supplied to the authorities.

In the period following what came to be known as the "Petersburg letter" incident and the subsequent investigation and execution of Nikolai Tatarov by the SRs on 22 March 1906,[33] an episode occurred, whose consequences might have led the police authorities to suspect Azef of being less than loyal to the government cause. Living in Moscow in the spring of 1906, he knew about the preparations for an assassination attempt against the city's governor-general, Admiral Fedor Dubasov, but he did not warn the Police Department. The Combat Organization was free to make its move, and so Azef's superior, Rachkovskii, blamed him for the wounding of Dubasov on 23 April 1906.[34]

It must be remembered, first of all, that most of the planning for this attack took place during a hiatus in Azef's career as an agent, during a period when Rachkovskii, Azef's only Police Department link at the time, neglected all communication with his spy. He provided Azef with no instructions and did not pay him for five months, leaving him with no contacts at police headquarters to whom he could have reported, had he wished to do so.[35] The spy was painfully conscious of the fact that although the "Petersburg letter" did not lead to a formal investigation of his case, it left a manifestly negative impression on some party members. Azef was therefore unwilling to make new contacts among the authorities or to approach directly any unfamiliar official from the Police Department with information that, if used indiscreetly, might have contributed to SR suspicions.

Azef did find indirect ways to provide the Moscow Okhrana office with some clues about the Combat Organization without notifying his superiors in St. Petersburg. According to Savinkov, by early spring the police in that city had become aware of the terrorists' plans to kill

Dubasov; they knew enough details to have been able to establish strict surveillance just prior to the day that had been designated for assassination. The police obviously tried to scare the *boeviki* away by demonstrating that they were entirely aware of the combatants' plans and were determined to liquidate their conspiracy if the terrorists proceeded with their venture. Forced to call off the act at the last minute, Savinkov felt fortunate to have evaded arrest and ordered his associates to flee to Finland.[36]

Immediately after their escape, some classified information leaked to the press, and an article appeared in the conservative newspaper, *New Time (Novoe vremia)*, that described "a band of miscreants" and incidentally mentioned the correct time and place of the would-be assassination.[37] According to a member of the Combat Organization, Valentina Popova, the police knew details that "could only have been provided by a person standing close to the organization or even one of its members."[38] Savinkov, too, immediately suspected treason and rushed to share his suspicions with none other than Azef himself, who easily convinced the gullible terrorist chief that he should put the article out of his mind as purely "coincidental."[39] To ward off any misgivings on the part of other members of the combat crew, Azef, while never forgetting to stress that the venture against Dubasov was proving to be simply too difficult, yielded to the terrorists' determination to try their luck against the governor-general one more time. According to the new plan, the assassination was to take place on 23 April, when the terrorists expected Dubasov to show up at a church ceremony in the Kremlin. Azef insisted on this attempt being the last one,[40] while obviously nourishing the intention never to let it take place.

Azef's attention was meanwhile diverted by a different problem, however: in February 1906 the terrorist Petr Rutenberg (Martyn) revealed to the party's Central Committee stunning news about his friend, the revolutionary priest Georgii Gapon. Gapon, a charismatic proletarian organizer, had led the workers in a fatal procession to the Winter Palace to present a petition to Nicholas II on 9 January 1905. On that fateful day known as "Bloody Sunday," he had barely escaped the fate of the numerous victims of military execution, but several months later, the famous hero of revolutionary politics, who enjoyed stupendous popularity at home and abroad, contacted SR Rutenberg and confessed his ties with the tsarist secret police. Moreover, Gapon offered to pay his friend, who had marched beside him to the Winter Palace and had saved his life by leading him to safety when the government troops began shooting at the crowd, one hundred thousand rubles if he betrayed the Combat Organization to Rachkovskii. The SR high command, which had established collaboration with Gapon, was flabbergasted by the news and immediately sanctioned his execution, commissioning Rutenberg to carry out the death sentence on the traitor. To make Gapon's police ties evident to his followers, the Central Committee decided that Rutenberg must kill Gapon together with his primary police contact Rachkovskii during one of their secret meetings.[41]

Acting with the Central Committee's sanction, Rutenberg pretended to consider Gapon's proposition, insisting on a rendezvous with Rachkovskii—a meeting that would provide the revolutionary an opportunity to kill both intended victims. However, as time passed, and Rachkovskii proved too prudent to meet the revolutionary on his terms, Rutenberg grew increasingly impatient and finally decided to get rid of Gapon alone, thus partially violating the Central Committee's order.[42]

On 28 March 1906 he lured Gapon to a deserted house near the Finnish border, supposedly to conclude the negotiations about the betrayal of the Combat Organization. Several workers were hidden in a room adjacent to the one where Gapon was urging Rutenberg to backstab his comrades. Convinced of Gapon's treachery, the workers rushed out of their hiding places, placed a rope around his neck and hanged him on a hallstand.[43]

The SR leaders were concerned about the anticipated negative reaction of the masses, with whom they believed Gapon was still extremely popular; given the shady circumstances of his execution, they feared that the workers would suspect that he had been killed as a result of party rivalry and petty intrigues. To get themselves out of the awkward situation, the Central Committee used the fact that Gapon had been murdered without Rachkovskii, against its orders, as a reason not to recognize the assassination as a party act. The person who paid for the evasiveness of the SR leadership was Rutenberg, who suddenly found himself transformed in the eyes of the public from a revolutionary vigilante to a common criminal suspected of murdering Gapon on his own initiative out of private motives. For months Rutenberg persistently demanded an official party statement confirming that he had been ordered to assassinate Gapon by the Central Committee, but the SR leaders were equally persistent in dismissing his claims.[44] Then, in desperation, Rutenberg announced that it was Azef, in his capacity as a Central Committee member, who had implicitly permitted him to proceed with the plot against Gapon alone, in the event that it proved impossible to assassinate Rachkovskii as well.

Rutenberg did not initially blame Azef for his secret role in the Gapon affair. Immediately after the execution, the terrorist did not deny that he had killed Gapon alone on his own initiative.[45] Only in 1909, after Azef's exposure as a police agent, did Rutenberg begin to accuse him of having provoked Gapon's murder, making use of the fact that Azef could no longer disprove any charges.[46] In fact, the master spy had no personal stakes in having Gapon killed at a risk to his position in the PSR Central Committee; and as far as Rachkovskii was concerned, in March 1906 none other than Azef himself had warned Rachkovskii about the danger of the prospective assassination by Rutenberg.[47]

Azef was the one who broke the news to the police about Gapon's murder and then informed the authorities about the secret house in Finland where the priest's body could be found.[48] These reports were made after the spy had resumed his relations with St. Petersburg, which he did under the most bizarre circumstances.

On 15 April 1906 two undercover detectives seized Azef on the street of the Russian capital after his meeting with a terrorist disguised as a cab driver and, ignoring his furious protests, took him to the secret police headquarters located on the bank of the Moika, in the famous house where Pushkin died. There, the Okhrana director, Gerasimov, personally interrogated Azef, spurning his official identity papers that were issued to "engineer Anton Cherkas." Instead, the head of the Okhrana made it clear that he had no doubt he was talking to one of the secret police agents.[49] As Azef continued to deny any association with the police world, Gerasimov ordered his detectives to lock the detainee up in a prison cell, where he was to remain until he chose to demonstrate better judgment. A few anguished hours in confinement did the trick; clearly, he had no other alternative but to reveal his true identity to the top Okhrana official. Azef asked to see Gerasimov again. He was willing to be frank, he submitted, but only in the presence of his former chief Rachkovskii.

They did not have to wait long before the top-level Police Department officer presented himself in Gerasimov's office, greeting Azef in a perfectly friendly manner. Exasperated by his prison experience, Azef responded in the most offensive and vulgar "language of horse-cab drivers (*izvozchiki*),"[50] and in a tirade of "choice abuse" and curses he fervently attacked his stunned police superior for deserting him, "refusing to reply to his letters, cutting off his salary, ignoring his requests for interviews, . . . abandoning him to the 'mercies of fate,'" and finally allowing him to be jailed. Is this how Rachkovskii showed gratitude for the fact that his agent had just saved his life by informing him about Rutenberg's plot?

Rachkovskii was undoubtedly taken aback by Azef's vehement onslaught. He did not dispute any of the spy's allegations and was

obviously embarrassed by such an overt revelation of his professional ineptitude. Even Gerasimov "felt a twinge of conscience" about the
Police Department's mistreatment of its agent, who had every reason
to be indignant.[51] Turning his humiliation into victory, Azef restored
his relations with the St. Petersburg secret security. The three men
agreed that Azef would report directly to Gerasimov, who would be his
main police contact from then on.

Azef was anxious to demonstrate his goodwill to the supportive
Okhrana chief and began a new phase of his police career by reporting important information about the Combat Organization, divulging
the plots against Interior Minister Durnovo, General Min, and Colonel
Riman. But he still hesitated to notify the authorities of the terrorists'
renewed preparation for Admiral Dubasov's assassination. He could
not be expected to trust Rachkovskii again; nor was he initially inclined
to rely for his safety on his new chief, Gerasimov, who clearly had to
win the agent's trust before he could count on his unequivocal sincerity. While this behavior does not contribute to Azef's image as an
informant who was selflessly devoted to police service, several factors
must be considered before he can be proclaimed a traitor to the government cause and a double agent.

First, as always, it was Savinkov, not Azef, who assumed the leading role in organizing the final action against Dubasov.[52] The only reason why the Central Committee of the PSR later thought otherwise was
that its members relied exclusively on Azef's description of the terrorists' success, and his acceptance of the credit, without considering it
necessary to question any of the combatants themselves.[53] In reality,
however, Azef did not play any role in the immediate preparations for
the act. Just as in the past, he took such an indirect part in the affairs
of the Combat Organization at this period that, according to one female
boevik, she saw Azef only one time, in February 1906—six months after
she had been accepted in the terrorist band.[54] During March and most of
April, he stayed in Helsingfors and did not show up in Moscow even
once, leaving it to Savinkov to plan the prospective assassination. Azef
persistently warned that it would not succeed.

To prove himself right, he relied on the second aspect of his game
against the terrorists, which involved active sabotage. Thus, Azef made
an attempt to undermine the assassination scheme by resigning from
the Combat Organization. "I am weary," he suddenly declared to
Savinkov during one of their meetings in January 1906; "I fear I cannot work anymore. Think of it: I have been in this work ever since the
days of Gershuni. I am entitled to rest. . . . I am convinced, nothing will
come of all this new work of ours. . . . It's a lot of nonsense. I have

decided to quit."[55] Behind Savinkov's back he also did everything he could to convince the rank-and-file *boeviki* that their usual methods of terrorist warfare were obsolete, and that it was necessary to terminate all operations of the Combat Organization for the time being in order to develop new combat techniques.[56]

Azef's ever-present fear of eliciting suspicion prevented him from abandoning the terrorists. In principle, he acquiesced to Savinkov's protests and appeals to remain in the Combat Organization, but continuously abstained from any close participation in the preparations against Dubasov. Yet, Savinkov insisted that Azef return to Russia from Finland, to which the spy agreed with obvious reluctance.[57] He was certainly not in any hurry to reunite with the terrorists, arriving in Moscow only on the eve of the 23 April attempt—just in time for a rendezvous with the *boeviki* to discuss the next day's attack.[58]

All evidence suggests that when Azef finally came to Moscow, he did so with the unequivocal intention of sabotaging this terrorist act. Most likely, the secret agent expected to be able to prevent the assassination at the last moment, as he had done occasionally in the past. A couple of months prior to the campaign against Dubasov, in early 1906, the frustrated *boeviki*, realizing that their old terrorist methods remained fruitless despite their persistent efforts, decided on a terminal step: they would hide explosive devices under their clothes, make their way into Stolypin's house, and blow themselves up together with the hated prime minister. During initial discussions Azef pretended to be in favor of this desperate attempt, most likely thinking that the terrorists would in fact never go ahead with it. But when it became clear that the *boeviki* were determined to proceed with their plan, Azef began to show signs of wavering and then categorically declared to the terrorists that he would accede to the fatal attack on one condition only: he himself would take part in the attempt and die among other combatants.[59] No doubt, he knew perfectly well that his comrades would never agree to such a sacrifice and merely found a convenient excuse to sabotage what would have been a sensational and bloody feat using "live explosives." It is more than likely that Azef counted on a similar chance to prevent the terrorist act in late April 1906 without evoking the SRs' distrust. When he could no longer hope that the *boeviki* would rescind the attack on the 23rd, he sought to sabotage it at the last moment, even at the risk of arousing resentment and suspicion.

To begin with, he—the alleged leader of the plot—simply failed to show up for the combatants' final meeting dedicated to settling the last details prior to the assassination. Contrary to Azef's expectations, however, Savinkov sanctioned the attack.[60] Still, Azef was relatively sure that nothing would come of it: he was well aware that one of the terrorists, the one who, according to the plan, was to wait for Dubasov near the Kremlin and cast the fatal bomb, did not have an explosive device with him.[61] Even before Azef was exposed as a police spy, Savinkov considered his behavior on this occasion "negligent to the point of malfeasance."[62] Savinkov later asserted in a private conversation that, save for the attempt against Dubasov, Azef did not in fact participate closely in any of the Combat Organization ventures in the period from mid-1903 to mid-1906. As for the case of Dubasov, Savinkov added, Azef "should have been tried" by the revolutionary tribunal "for his role."[63] One of the combatants, Valentina Popova, later confirmed that Azef's scheme had aimed to sabotage the terrorist act in Moscow.[64]

The fact that the assassination attempt turned out to be partially successful was contrary to Azef's intentions and strictly accidental. Seeing that Dubasov's carriage had safely left the Kremlin, *boevik* Boris Vnorovskii, dressed in the uniform of a naval officer and stationed nearby, decided to take the initiative—after all, the other members of the Combat Organization had concluded that their final effort to kill the governor-general had failed. Acting on the spur of the moment, Vnorovskii charged ahead, caught up with Dubasov near his house on Tverskaia Street, and suddenly cast a bomb—disguised in a lovely box of candies adorned with a fancy ribbon—that wounded the admiral and killed his adjutant along with the terrorist.[65]

The act against Dubasov remains a rather shadowy episode in Azef's career as a secret agent; yet this assassination attempt hardly proves that the police agent converted to, or played on the side of, the terrorists during the temporary break in his police service. The SR leaders made that claim subsequently, notwithstanding the opinion of many of their party colleagues, who had to acknowledge that even in the period of Azef's short-term inactivity as a police agent, he had been obstructing their efforts. Interior Minister Durnovo, they said, "was not killed only because Azef did not want this" to happen.[66]

The wounding of Dubasov was Azef's only faux pas in the latter part of his police service. Not a single successful central SR terrorist act had occurred since he resumed his secret employment in the spring of 1906.[67] Yet, the credit for the security force's impressive stand against the radicals must be attributed not only to Azef but to the policies of his new Okhrana superiors, and particularly to Gerasimov, whose main goal as the Okhrana director was "to create a well-established apparatus of the so-called secret internal surveillance in the revolutionary ranks." In his words, "the internal life of the revolutionary organizations operating in the underground was a really special world, absolutely inaccessible to those who did not belong to these organizations." He therefore had "no choice but to rebut the clandestine conspiracy with his own counterintelligence," that is, his "trusted agents, who pretended to be revolutionaries," discovering the radicals' plans, and reporting them to their Okhrana headquarters.[68] Appreciating Azef's past and potential services, Gerasimov placed utmost value on his spy in the PSR—enough to allow him at least in part to assert his own conditions for police employment.[69]

Gerasimov did impose strict controls on his agent, even to the point of partial surveillance,[70] but this measure turned out to be largely beside the point, for it did not take long for Azef to comprehend that his new chief was, as even his adversaries conceded, "the most courageous ... and intelligent police official of his time."[71] The spy therefore chose not to conceal from this perceptive and experienced officer the fact that he usually knew more than he reported, explaining that his constant fear of exposure required him to be very selective in determining what information could be revealed to the police without arousing the suspicions of the terrorists. At the same time, he promised to do all he could to disable the radicals. Although anxious to enlist Azef in his fight against the radicals. Gerasimov realized that in order to insure productive and mutually profitable cooperation, each side had to respect the interests of the other. Accordingly, he respected Azef's desire to take precautions against exposure. Unlike other police officials who, in Azef's words, were ready to sacrifice him to "the bullets of the revolutionaries," the head of the St. Petersburg Okhrana concluded that as long as the agent provided adequate material for the prevention of terrorist acts, he was entitled to protect himself by not disclosing information that, in case of indiscreet use by the police, could endanger his position among the revolutionaries. Gerasimov agreed that it was the duty of the police to make the best possible use of the sometimes indirect and scanty clues an agent provided in order to establish surveillance and determine the details of any revolutionary plot along with the names of all its participants. In the long run it did not benefit the investigation to demand every bit of information at the agent's disposal; that amounted to asking for his imminent exposure.[72]

In consultation with Azef and with Stolypin's approval, Gerasimov devised an elaborate plan to disorganize the SR Combat Organization. He disagreed with Zubatov's method of identifying all the members of a radical cell and annihilating them "in one blow," contending that "since every liquidation of a revolutionary organization also meant the exposure of the agent who operated within it, the result was a net loss to the secret police."[73] Therefore, if he could rely on a competent agent among the radicals, Gerasimov would try for as long as possible not to take the revolutionaries into custody—an approach upon which Azef always insisted, perpetually dreading careless arrests that could easily arouse the suspicions against him. Acting on Azef's information, the authorities were to keep the terrorists under constant control and to paralyze all efforts of the Combat Organization systematically, hoping eventually to convince the SRs that central terror was for the time being absolutely infeasible and futile. While permitting the revolutionaries to go on with their preliminary preparations for assassinations, the police would persistently place unexpected and unavoidable obstacles in the way of any terrorist undertaking. The *filery* would establish undisguised surveillance of the combatants, who would be allowed to sense the police's presence at each step of the way, no matter what course of action they took.[74]

The results of this approach could be seen almost immediately: the terrorists were exhausted by their continuous and seemingly inexplicable failures, which to most of them appeared not the consequence of treason but merely a series of unhappy coincidences. They gradually began to despair, feeling that even their preliminary attempts at getting close to their targets were destined to fail.[75] Incidentally, this was exactly what Azef had predicted to Savinkov in the spring of 1906, when he declared that he was tired and convinced that nothing would come out of their new terrorist campaign. As life seemed to be proving him right, even Savinkov, usually an ardent advocate of central terror, became inclined to concur with Azef. For his part, the spy was careful to make it evident that it was Savinkov and not himself who now appeared as the chief spokesman for the cessation of combat operations, allowing Azef to camouflage his own role in trying to sabotage the SR terrorist campaign.[76]

After much hesitation the PSR Central Committee agreed to acknowledge the breakdown of central terror. When it finally did so in November 1906, disillusioned by the incessant failures of what the terrorists consider to have been repeatedly "unlucky" attempts to stage assassination attacks against Stolypin during the summer and fall, it wearily honored Azef's demands for a much-needed rest and relieved him of his responsibilities in the Combat Organization. Savinkov resigned along with Azef, who made certain that the initiative for their joint resignation had come from his comrade.[77] He also made sure that Savinkov, in his repeated declarations aimed at explaining the failures of the terrorist campaign, blamed the Central Committee for the "absence of a friendly intent" toward the Combat Organization. In arguing with such bitterness and resentment—to the point of appearing to be "making a scandal"—Savinkov acted in good faith. He had been convinced by Azef's carefully phrased insinuations against several party leaders, particularly Chernov, whom the great manipulator had accused of being involved in scheming and secretly agitating against the terrorists.[78] Savinkov's behavior showed that he had "too much unswerving dignity and [too] little ability for intrigue"[79] to discern a political subterfuge. Oblivious of Azef's true motives, he behaved like "an honest fool" and "a pawn" in the hands of the government spy, who from his sheltered position behind Savinkov's back pressed the terrorist chief to invalidate the SR central terror.[80] The outcome of this tactic could not have served Azef's interests better: confronted with the resignation of their leaders in November, the rank-and-file members of the Combat Organization had only one option—to give up their plans and disperse. Thus, in late 1906 the central Combat Organization ceased to exist.[81]

Gerasimov and Azef could now celebrate a complete triumph—a bit prematurely, as it turned out. Around the same time, news reached revolutionary émigrés abroad that Grigorii Gershuni had escaped from the Akatui hard-labor prison and had managed to make it from Siberia to America. There he had begun a fund-raising campaign and acquired significant donations for the PSR, particularly its combat work. In early 1907 the legendary revolutionary hero returned to Europe. Even before he had had a chance to meet with other members of the Central Committee and familiarize himself with the internal situation of the party, Gershuni had a rendezvous with Azef for the purpose of arranging future collaboration in terrorist affairs. As a result of their meeting, the two men agreed to restore the Combat Organization under their joint leadership. As far as Savinkov was concerned, Azef did everything to discredit him in Gershuni's eyes, naturally doing so surreptitiously while pretending to remain friends. One recent episode in Savinkov's revolutionary career presented a perfect opportunity for Azef to undermine his status in Gershuni's eyes.

Right after the terrorists' success against Dubasov, in May 1906, Savinkov went to Sevastopol, where his goal was to organize an assassination attempt against Admiral G. N. Chukhnin, who had recently suppressed a Black Sea naval mutiny with great brutality. On 14 May the terrorist chief was arrested and mistakenly accused of having taken part in a plot against Lieutenant General V. S. Nepliuev, commander of the Sevastopol fortress, during a parade celebrating the Emperor's coronation day. Savinkov was tried by the Sevastopol military tribunal, which after the first session decided to postpone the case, giving the ter-

rorist a chance to escape on 16 July.[82] Now Azef intimated that
Savinkov's arrest had left a striking impact on the terrorist, who no
longer wished to risk his life, yet was too proud to resign from the
Combat Organization simply due to an unwillingness to subject himself to danger. Therefore, Azef explained, Savinkov had insisted on the
dissolution of the Combat Organization back in November 1906 so as
to give himself a legitimate reason to retire. Gershuni accepted Azef's
argument at face value, and did everything to convince other members
of the Central Committee from then on not to have any dealings with
Savinkov. Owing to the spy's fraudulent insinuations, Savinkov
emerged in Gershuni's eyes as an "immoral and completely depraved"
man, a person dodging his duty as a terrorist because he was afraid to
feel the rope on his neck again.[83] According to Natanson, who had firsthand knowledge of Gershuni's opinion of Savinkov, this was "one of
the most penetrating and thoroughly calculated of Azef's intrigues."[84]

Yet, his efforts to estrange Gershuni from Savinkov turned out to be
largely irrelevant. Gershuni's desire to return to the ranks notwithstanding, he was in no position to involve himself in terror; in 1907 he was
already very ill. His death in March 1908 left Azef as the sole leader of the
rejuvenated Combat Organization. Needless to say, he had no intention
of inaugurating a new wave of terrorist activity. His wife remembers that
in this period Azef showed signs of lethargy and often complained of
weariness. Declaring that he could no longer work in the field of terrorism, he would say: "What a life! How happy would I be to run away from
here! . . . I can take it no longer; I am tired."[85] Accordingly, during the
entire period of its existence in 1907–08, the Combat Organization under
his leadership did not carry out a single successful terrorist venture. Several of its members did make it to St. Petersburg, but one of them later
testified that whatever he and other terrorists were doing there "could not
be called [combat] work. . . . Everyone lived in his own realm, and no one
did anything." After a few months of this stalemate, the members of the
Combat Organization gave up and returned abroad.[86]

Although this period was unavailing for central terror, it was quite
a successful one for the various small SR terrorist units scattered
throughout the country. Their members continued to stage awe-inspir-
ing political assassinations. Among the most sensational terrorist acts,
members of the SR Northern Flying Combat Detachment, led by
Al'bert (Karl) Trauberg, killed Chief Military Procurator V. P. Pavlov
in the capital; another terrorist unit in St. Petersburg finally managed
to liquidate the city's governor, V. F. von der Launits; the Moscow
group executed Adjutant General Count Ignat'ev.[87] Azef had nothing
to do with any of these attacks, and technically, he was not responsi-

ble for helping the police to preclude combat ventures perpetrated by terrorists outside the Combat Organization. Yet, these independent assassination attempts did not leave him indifferent,[88] and whenever he was able to obstruct them without invoking the suspicions of the radicals, he did all he could to be of use to the government cause.[89] One thing Azef sought to do was to unify the terrorist forces under the auspices of the central Combat Organization in order to control the combatants and also be in the position to provide the Okhrana with more substantial information about their undertakings.

Even after the breakdown of the Combat Organization, Azef's reports helped the Okhrana to uncover at initial stages several terrorist plots in 1907 and in the early months of 1908. The most notable of these was a planned explosion in the State Council during one of its sessions. Only the SR Central Committee members knew that the prospective executor of this assault, a certain Kal'vino, was actually a revolutionary named Vsevolod Lebedintsev. As one of the party leaders, Azef was also aware of the identity of the person under this pseudonym, and it was he who shared this information with Gerasimov. At the time of Lebedintsev's arrest in Finland, the local authorities confiscated his notebook, and Burtsev was later able to retrieve it from them, immediately transferring it to the PSR Central Committee. Was it such a great surprise that from there the notebook mysteriously disappeared, reemerging in . . . the Okhrana headquarters in St. Petersburg?[90] Then, in early February 1908, following Azef's circumspect lead about *boevik* Anna Rasputina, the police struck a terrible blow against the terrorists in the capital. In a swift operation in St. Petersburg, it liquidated the Northern Flying Combat Detachment of the PSR, promptly arresting Karl Trauberg and his associates, who were armed with explosive devices and revolvers, en route to an assassination site where Grand Duke Nikolai Nikolaevich and Minister of Justice I. G. Shcheglovitov were to become the party's next victims.[91]

Even more important, Azef averted all attempts at regicide.[92] Acting on his information, in early 1907 the police were able to prevent an attack against the tsar organized by a terrorist squad in which the main perpetrators were former naval lieutenant Boris Nikitenko and the student B. S. Siniavskii (Purkin).[93] Significantly, the *boeviki* attributed the miscarriage of their ventures to the presence of a police informer in their ranks, with Azef naturally being the last person they would suspect.[94]

Owing to Azef, the authorities prevented two more attempts on the life of Nicholas II, whom the Central Committee had declared to be their primary target. Plans for the first of these acts against the tsar were designed in Finland by a group of combatants under the immediate leadership of veteran terrorist Mikhail Karpovich. He had recently escaped from Siberia where he was serving a twenty-year sentence at hard labor for the murder of the conservative Minister of Education, N. P. Bogolepov, in 1901. Due to Azef's information, the St. Petersburg Okhrana was aware of all the movements of the *boeviki*. Again, to insure his agent's safety, Gerasimov promised Azef to avoid arrests and simply warned the tsar against returning to the capital from his residences in Peterhof and Tsarskoye Selo when the terrorists were expected to show up in the capital. Similarly, it was only with Azef's help that the police were able to eliminate any possibility of the successful realization of a planned SR attempt on the tsar's life during the May 1908 visit of Edward VII of England to the Baltic port of Revel. This attempt was intended to undermine Russia's diplomatic efforts by convincing both the European public and the diplomats of the instability of Russia's domestic situation.[95]

In their subsequent efforts to demonstrate Azef's role as a double agent, the SRs claimed that in the summer and fall of 1908 he, along with Savinkov and Karpovich, made plans for another assassination attempt against Nicholas II and failed to notify the police of the proposed attack. The revolutionaries alleged that this enterprise—the only one Azef headed in 1907–08—did not materialize for a reason beyond the spy's control: Gerasim Avdeev, the sailor recruited by the SRs to shoot the tsar during a ceremonial review of the cruiser *Riurik* in Glasgow on 24 September 1908, lost his nerve at the last moment and did not pull the trigger.[96] Gerasimov later admitted that the police indeed had known nothing about the preparations for this act, but he was convinced that all the stories about Avdeev's plans to kill the tsar were "invented by the revolutionaries."[97]

For the sake of fairness, it should be considered that by May 1908, Azef had terminated his employment as a police informer, and so, no matter what his subsequent activities were, he was no longer obliged to report to Gerasimov and could under no circumstances qualify as a double agent.[98] Moreover, there is little reason to suppose that Azef was involved with detailed preparations for the attack, or "did everything in his power to bring this attempt to a successful conclusion."[99] Again, this seems to be a case of exaggeration of Azef's role after the fact. In the summer of 1908 he stayed in southern France and, according to independent police sources, was not among the SRs who took part in the planning of regicide or of any other terrorist ventures.[100]

This information is supported by Savinkov's testimony, from which it is evident that it was he, and especially Karpovich, who were the ones dealing closely with the sailor Avdeev.[101] Furthermore, even if there indeed was talk of assassinating the tsar on board the *Riurik,* it was only talk, since, as Savinkov admitted, neither he nor Azef nor Karpovich thought that Avdeev would actually go ahead with the act.[102] Savinkov also stated that throughout all their discussions of regicide, he was irritated by Azef's sluggishness and had a feeling that "whatever plan [was] suggested, Azef would have torn it apart no matter what."[103] Savinkov subsequently asserted that some aspects of Azef's behavior seemed bizarre even to his unsuspecting party comrades, who, of course, still took for granted his sincere devotion to the revolutionary cause. Azef had insisted on recruiting for terrorist purposes a ship servant who appeared to Savinkov and Karpovich as a highly unappealing character, and who, in the tsar's presence, was selected from the crew of seven hundred men to escort Nicholas II around the ship. Azef also visited the ship freely under the feeble pretense that he was an inspection engineer. Savinkov later declared with absolute firmness that "Azef would have never allowed this assassination to take place. . . . It was but a fictitious attempt." Azef's efforts were directed only toward "creating a grandiose fib."[104]

5

The Exposure

I do not know a more illustrious name in the Russian revolutionary movement than the name of Azef. His name and his activity are more splendid than those of Zheliabov, Sazonov, Gershuni, but under one condition: if he is an honest revolutionary.
—Vladimir Burtsev[1]

During the course of Azef's fifteen-year tenure as a police agent at the heart of the PSR, there were a number of occasions when the revolutionaries suspected him of police connections,[2] but for a variety of reasons he always managed to escape detection. In Germany in 1893 radical students simply did not get around to a serious investigation of fleeting local rumors regarding his association with the imperial authorities. In 1903, leftist writer N. A. Rubakin, a one-time member of the PSR, wrote a letter to Mikhail Gots in Geneva accusing Azef of being a police informer, but the irritated party leader cast it away as rubbish that was not worth looking into.[3] In the 1905 "Petersburg letter," an anonymous sympathizer, who later turned out to be police renegade Leonid Men'shchikov, provided compromising, if inconclusive, evidence to demonstrate that Azev and Nikolai Tatarov were government spies in the PSR.[4] While the SRs were perfectly willing to investigate the evidence against Tatarov, a newcomer to the PSR, no one thought of opening a case against Azef, the renowned executioner of Minister of the Interior Plehve and Grand Duke Sergei. "It was absolutely unthinkable for the SRs to recognize that the idol of the whole party was a *provocateur*."[5] Gots once mentioned the reports about Azef's involvement with the secret police to Georgii Plekhanov, a leader of the Russian Social Democrats; yet, the veteran revolutionary dismissed them with utter indifference: "They have said the same thing about myself and Lavrov."[6] In March 1906 when Tatarov, who was about to be found guilty of treason and killed by the SRs, informed Savinkov that the police spy within the PSR was "Tolstyi" (Azef), the terrorist chief discarded this assertion without the slightest reservation as Tatarov's desperate attempt to acquit himself at the expense of an innocent man.[7] By this time, however, the SR headquarters had received warnings from a number of other sources either directly or circuitously suggesting that the informant in the party might be Azef, and a few of his colleagues in the party were beginning to be irked by vague misgivings.[8]

Most comrades, especially those in the high spheres of the party, still considered him beyond suspicion, but from time to time his fellow revolutionaries noted in surprise how self-assured Azef was in his ability to outwit the police. He ostentatiously ignored even the most basic conspiratorial precautions, yet always emerged exceptionally "lucky" and he had avoided detention for many years.[9] Despite all his prestige, many SRs could not ignore the fact that Azef did not fit into the intelligentsia circles, and that he frequently revealed cultural lacunae, "crudeness and even cruelty." Although Azef always portrayed himself as a person who was barely making ends meet, many party members also noted his proclivity to indulge in extravagances and his "avariciousness . . . in money matters." Both tendencies were contrary to the spirit of selflessness and indifference to material interests prevalent among the SRs. Some revolutionaries also registered "the meagerness of his thought, the absence of emotional thrust. In a word, his entire . . . image did not elicit sympathy and distinguished him sharply and negatively from among his comrades."[10] Whereas many long-standing SRs were prepared to overlook these shortcomings, Azef's physical unattractiveness, coupled with his petty-bourgeois and rather blunt manners, repelled many of his newer acquaintances in the radical milieu, some of whom tended to think that the current high opinion of Azef's talents and revolutionary accomplishments was obviously exaggerated.[11]

Initial encounters were particularly difficult for Azef; they invariably left negative impressions on people, to the point of eliciting instinctive suspicions and causing him rather unpleasant moments. One professor at the Polytechnicum in Karlsruhe, upon meeting Azef as a young student, commented, "Ah, that spy."[12] Invited to evening tea at Viktor Chernov's house for the first time, Azef rang the bell expecting a warm welcome. The nanny of Chernov's children opened the door, and, taking one look at Azef, ran to the mistress of the house, anxious to warn Olga Chernov that "some police character wanted to see her." A few minutes later, Chernov's wife was laughing with her guests about the "funny mix-up," but in the merry crowd, "it was Azef himself who guffawed louder than anyone else, longer than anyone else. He throttled with paroxysms of laughter; he could not stop. His whole corpulent body swayed from side to side, he choked, and continued to laugh."[13] In a similar episode, a group of SR friends sat down to play cards. Suddenly, Vera Figner, a revolutionary veteran whom Anatole France nicknamed "Jeanne D'Arc of the Russian revoluton,"[14] walked into the room. Knowing how much this ascetic woman, who had spent twenty-three years in the dreadful Schlüsselburg Fortress, despised card playing and not wishing to offend her, the guests quickly hid the cards under the table. At that moment in awkwardness and confusion, Azef raised the tablecloth and burst out, "Look, Vera Nikolaevna, these people are playing cards while you are not looking!" Infuriated, Olga Chernov yelled: "Shame on you! You are a real provocateur!" You're right, the spy must have thought, hysterically laughing off the indictment. "'A provocateur, a provocateur!' he repeated between spasms of chortle."[15]

Throughout the year 1907—a period when many terrorist attacks of which Azef had no knowledge were successfully carried out, and every combat venture familiar to him ended as a fiasco—rumors about a traitor in the SR Central Committee became particularly intense. In early 1908 the police, obviously acting on precise information from an internal source in the PSR, succeeded in thoroughly liquidating Trauberg's Northern Flying Combat Detachment in St. Petersburg. This defeat caused many in the SR circles to demand an urgent investigation from the party's leadership. Especially determined to ascertain the spy's identity were members of the so-called Paris Group of Socialist Revolutionaries (*Parizhskaia gruppa sotsialistov-revoliutsionerov*), otherwise known as the Minority Initiative Group (*Gruppa initsiativnogo men'shinstva*), some of whom went so far as to accuse the Central Committee of negligence detrimental to the party's interests.[16]

Clouds were gathering over Azef's head, particularly after several remaining members of the Northern Combat Detachment not only attributed their failures to the presence of a police informer in the PSR, but also explicitly incriminated a certain Zhenya (diminitive of Evgenii, a Russian variant of Evno).[17] But Azef's prestige as a terrorist was so well established, and his position so prominent, that the party leaders, irritated with what seemed to them insipid and deleterious talk about a master spy in the PSR, dismissed all warnings as part of an elaborate government intrigue originated in the Police Department for the purpose of staining the reputation of a leading revolutionary, halting his activity, and slandering the entire party through him.

This attitude made the position of another accuser, Vladimir Burtsev, that much more difficult. Although not a formal member of the SR

Party, Burtsev was closely linked to it by virtue of his personal acquaintance with many of its leaders. In May 1908 he astonished his revolutionary colleagues in the SR Central Committee with a startling declaration. For months he had been on the trail of a police informer in the center of the PSR and finally he possessed enough evidence to announce the results: the person betraying the party for years was none other than Evno Azef.

Now that somebody—especially an outsider—had explicitly accused Azef of treason, members of the high PSR circles immediately cast aside any misgivings they may have had about his personality for the sake of defending the honor of an "innocent comrade." The SR leaders agreed almost unanimously that Azef was a man "who, thanks to his incredible talents [and] the immense services he has rendered to the party and the revolution, established himself above Gershuni and next to Zheliabov." "If Azef is a provocateur, we are all provocateurs," asserted the Central Committee members in unison, and some avowed: "if Azef were a provocateur, we would all have to put a bullet through our heads."[18] Not doubting for a moment that Azef was beyond suspicion, his colleagues in the PSR Central Committee faced only one dilemma created by Burtsev's outrageous claim: whether to treat this news as pure stupidity or as part of a preposterous police intrigue against Azef personally and the party as a whole.

There was, however, a small group of nonconformists among the SRs abroad who were prepared to support Burtsev against the Central Committee and demanded a formal investigation, "despite the absence of any 'hard' evidence against Azef."[19] The Central Committee acquiesced to this pressure, establishing a "Commission of Inquiry into the Rumors of Provocation within the Party." The result of its perfunctory investigation was predictable and very much in line with the opinion of the Central Committee: although evidence suggested that the party had indeed been infiltrated by a police agent, so far as Azef was concerned, "the rumors of provocation have been shown to be utterly without foundation."[20]

Burtsev refused to be satisfied with this impasse. During the August 1908 SR Conference in London, he circulated among the delegates his open letter to SR Aleksei Teplov, in which he reaffirmed his charges against Azef, opening the way for a public controversy. From that point on, speculations about a traitor in the party's center became "the topic of the day."[21] When all efforts to silence Burtsev had failed—he was not about to give up his Quixotic crusade and insisted on the accuracy of his allegations—the Central Committee members finally decided that they had had enough of this bullheaded, self-assured and misguided zealot who was degrading the entire SR movement.[22] In an effort to put an end to this embarrassing episode once and for all, they set out to hold a secret revolutionary court of honor at which they were determined to convict Burtsev of slander.[23] His desperate attempts to make them cast aside their a priori assumption of Azef's innocence by presenting one piece of presumably compromising evidence after another led only to steadily deteriorating relations between Burtsev and the SR leaders. They felt profound irritation and hostility toward the man who dared to insult one of the most renowned members of the party's Central Committee.[24]

Confident of the outcome of the trial, the SRs went so far as to consult Azef on this matter, allowing him to examine all the evidence accrued by the Commission of Inquiry. Having scrutinized these materials, Azef must have sighed with relief. Although he would be forced somehow to explain certain troublesome facts, the revolutionaries did not know anything that might have inculpated him unequivocally in their eyes. Nonetheless, Azef seemed somewhat flustered in those days, inducing his comrades' concern and sympathy; even those who had never been fond of Azef sought to comfort him and went out of their way to show him their absolute trust.[25] Speaking for all his revolutionary colleagues, Chernov portended: "Burtsev will be crushed. He will be compelled to repent before the court."[26] As the controversy assumed an increasingly scandalous character, some SRs went so far as to threaten to kill Burtsev unless he produced absolute proof of Azef's treachery.[27]

In this extreme situation, Burtsev realized that his public accusations seemed groundless and were based almost entirely on questionable information provided to him by former agents and police officers who had defected to the revolutionary camp as well as on his own intuition and imperfect deductions. His primary informant up to that point was Mikhail Bakai, a defector to the radical camp who had been fired from his position as a police official for incompetence and corruption.[28] Upon his arrival in Paris in 1907, Bakai put himself at Burtsev's disposal, declassifying Okhrana information and—on Burtsev's orders—trying to recruit some of his former colleagues in the police world for the revolutionary cause, doing so largely through threats and bribes. Simultaneously, he was writing his reminiscences and sensational articles for the press, full of fantastic stories about the secret work of the tsarist police, whom he presented as a gang of conspiring criminals.[29] As for information about Azef, he could provide Burtsev with only indirect evidence, dubious at best.[30] To secure his position at the court of honor, scheduled for the end of October 1908, Burtsev urgently sought to confirm his claims with a more credible government source.[31] What more could fortune offer than the oral testimony of the retired director of the Police Department, Aleksei Lopukhin.

On numerous occasions Burtsev subsequently described his arduous path toward the unmasking of Azef. It was a genuine drama, culminating with the extraction of the long-pursued compromising information from the retired police chief. Burtsev's public statements must be treated with the utmost caution, however, for in his numerous newspaper interviews and other public statements he was more than ready to allow his unverified assumptions, exaggerations, and blatant distortions of the evidence to pass as established truth.

According to Burtsev, he was perceptive enough to have distrusted Azef from the moment of their first enounter in 1893. Unlike all of his comrades, Burtsev claimed to have been struck by Azef's "rudeness, cruelty, cynicism" with regard to women, and also "his vulgarity in political matters," and had no desire to socialize with this "filthy and suspicious person."[32] Burtsev insisted that he retained this extreme antipathy toward Azef throughout the years, "always keeping him within eyesight."[33] In 1906 Burtsev started to pay closer attention to him, having allegedly become convinced that SR combat failures were the result of provocation. He began to analyze the internal situation in the PSR's highest spheres, and while none of the party leaders elicited his suspicions, when it came to Azef he had to stop and think twice. Burtsev maintained that he did not yet consider Azef a provocateur, but because of his "filthy personality," Burtsev deduced that Azef must be associating with similarly squalid characters, one of whom might turn out to be a spy.[34] Burtsev claimed to have started suspecting Azef himself in 1906, when he met Azef and his wife riding in an open carriage along the English Embankment in St. Petersburg without any fear of being spotted by the police.

Until September or October 1907 Burtsev did not say a word about his suspicions to anyone.[35] The first person he told was Karl Trauberg of the Northern Flying Combat Detachment, who alledgedly said—for reasons that Burtsev never chose to disclose—that he, too, "knew" or was "almost convinced" that Azef was a provocateur.[36] Thus, supported by the opinion of this prominent terrorist (who, incidentally, was executed in late 1907 and could neither confirm nor refute Burtsev's claims), the spy hunter proceeded to collect information against Azef, until he finally acquired a crucial piece of evidence from Lopukhin.

In Burtsev's account, while he was looking for additional evidence to justify his partly intuitive conviction that Azef was a police agent, he happened to run into Lopukhin on an express train from Cologne to Berlin. The two men were already acquainted: in his capacity as editor of *Byloe*, published in St. Petersburg in 1906–07, Burtsev had twice proposed that Lopukhin publish his memoirs in the journal—offers that Lopukhin categorically declined.[37] During their train encounter, Burtsev struck up a conversation with Lopukhin, and quickly turned the discussion from the neutral subjects of history and literature to the question that interested him most. Having impressed Lopukhin by his knowledge of the police world, which Burtsev was allegedly able to demonstrate primarily due to his association with Bakai, he proceeded to recount what he knew about a certain police agent—alias Raskin—who operated at the heart of the PSR, and whose true name Burtsev believed to be Azef.

In Burtsev's version of the events, Lopukhin merely listened at first, quickly perceiving that the spy Raskin had not only provided information to the authorities but had also personally initiated and carried out political assassinations, which made him a traitor to the government cause and a double agent. Unable to conceal his indignation and outrage, the former director of the Police Department in the end supposedly acceded to Burtsev's plea to reveal the identity of the criminal hiding behind the pseudonym, and informed him: "I know nobody by the name of Raskin, but I have seen the engineer, Ievno Aseff, several times."[38] For Burtsev, this statement provided a clear, if indirect, confirmation of his suspicions.

At the end of October 1908, Burtsev appeared before the SR court of honor, which initially convened at a private library on Rue Lhomond in Paris, from where the judges soon moved to Savinkov's apartment on Rue La Fontaine. This special judicial committee consisted of such prominent revolutionaries as German Lopatin, a veteran of the People's Will and former prisoner of the Schlüsselburg Fortress; the renowned anarchist leader Prince Petr Kropotkin; and the celebrated female freedom fighter, Vera Figner; as well as three representatives of the PSR—Mark Natanson, Boris Savinkov, and Viktor Chernov. None of the members would shake the hand of a "slanderer."[39] The wrath of Azef's associates in the Combat Organization undoubtedly made Burtsev even more uneasy, since the terrorists, who had learned about their chief's tribulations, did not hesitate to take Azef's side. Even in this dire situation Burtsev chose to keep his promise of absolute confidentiality to Lopukhin at least for the time being, concealing the main source of his information and evidently hoping to impress his judges with assorted circumstantial evidence against Azef before disclosing the most potent proof of his treachery. This approach proved to be an unqualified fiasco: the judicial committee dismissed all of his arguments as unsubstantiated. After the seventeenth session of the revolutionary court Figner said to Burtsev before departure: "You are an awful man; you have maligned a hero; the only thing left to you is to shoot yourself!" Not shaken, Burtsev replied: "I will, if it turns out that Azef is not a provocateur!"[40]

Then came the eighteenth and last meeting of the court, when the judges categorically rejected every one of Burtsev's allegations, which, in their eyes, centered mainly around questionable information from Bakai and other equally dubious sources. Only then, in a final attempt to defend his position, his honor, and perhaps his life, in what he perceived as a struggle "to the death,"[41] did Burtsev advance his last argument—informing the speechless judges of his conversation with Lopukhin and of the grievous secret extracted from him.[42]

Heavy silence fell upon the courtroom, only to be broken by an immediate emotional explosion. The conference suddenly shattered into bedlam: all were on their feet, shouting and gesticulating. The old Lopatin, chairman of the court, "walked over to Burtsev, put his gnarled hands on the journalist's shoulders, and looked into his eyes. 'Give me your word of honor as a revolutionary that you heard these words from Lopukhin.'. . . Burtsev began to answer, but Lopatin turned away, his eyes filled with tears. 'What's the use of talking?' he said hopelessly. 'It's all clear now!'"[43]

After the initial shock of Burtsev's announcement had subsided, the revolutionaries, astounded and perplexed, yet desperately trying to conceal their dismay from one another, resolved to remain calm and proceed one step at a time, so as not to make any impetuous decisions. Their first move was to acquit Burtsev of all charges of slander and attempts to harm the SR movement.[44] Although Chernov and Savinkov persisted in their vehement attempts to discredit the journalist's allegations, and the other judges were still inclined to suppose that Burtsev might have fallen victim to a police plot, the revolutionaries could not ignore Lopukhin's testimony. "One would be quite justified in killing [a spy] on such evidence," Lopatin said. Burtsev's trial thus turned into his partial triumph: at least the "presumption of Azef's innocence had vanished,"[45] and the judges confirmed their intention to go ahead with and intensify their investigatory efforts.

Prior to violating his pledge of confidentiality to Lopukhin during the last session of the revolutionary court of honor, Burtsev demanded from his judges that the information he was about to reveal be kept in complete secrecy, lest Azef find out prematurely about the main source of compromising information. The arbitrators promised not to divulge the sensational evidence, but one of them, most likely Chernov or Savinkov, failed to keep his word, and so it was not long before Azef found out that during Burtsev's trial the most serious evidence against him had been Lopukhin's statement. He also learned that the members of the judicial committee, now in consensus with Burtsev, had decided to contact Lopukhin again in order to demand a confirmation of the information he had provided, this time before a representative of the PSR Central Committee in the Russian capital. The commission to interrogate Lopukhin fell on SR Andrei Argunov, who was, ironically, one of the earliest, yet still unsuspecting, victims of Azef's police work.[46]

In a final effort to prevent his exposure, Azef immediately set out for St. Petersburg. He presented his SR colleagues with a shoddy excuse for his absence from Paris: he was allegedly going to Germany for about ten days to see an old party comrade. Disheartened, inundated with anxiety, yet trying his best to subdue the whirlwind within, Azef was on the verge of hysteria, for the first time in his life forsaking his circumspect and almost pedantic habit of leaving no trails and establishing indubitable alibi. "When God wishes to punish someone, He takes away his reason," the spy later explained his behavior to Aleksandr Gerasimov.[47] Once in the Russian capital, he hastened to meet with the Okhrana chief to tell him about Burtsev's conversation with Lopukhin, who, Azef was afraid, would soon be forced to repeat his testimony before the SRs. Having greeted Azef in his apartment on Bol'shaia Ital'ianskaia Street, Gerasimov dismissed the whole story as sheer nonsense: he had known Lopukhin for seven years and was convinced that he could never be a traitor or a state criminal. Burtsev was bluffing when he made reference to Lopukhin's name before the revolutionary tribunal and Azef ought to visit the retired police officer just to reassure himself that his needless panic was as ridiculous as Burtsev's deception.[48] Gerasimov's aplomb and composed manner were comforting to the man who wished for nothing more in the world than to regain the fading confidence of his SR colleagues. Casting aside his proverbial prudence, on the evening of 11 November 1908, Azef appeared at Lopukhin's apartment at 7 Tavricheskaia Street. He begged his former police chief to tell him the truth: did he say anything to Burtsev about their relationship, and if so, would he retract his words before the SRs and deny that they were acquainted?

This step, which eventually proved to be fatal for Azef, was to no avail. Lopukhin, although claiming that he had revealed nothing to Burtsev, coldly rejected Azef's pleas to save his life if approached by the SRs. Desperate, Azef then asked Lopukhin directly what he intended to do if the SRs were to demand his testimony against the spy in their Central Committee. He received silence for an answer.[49]

The next morning Azef was at Gerasimov's apartment again. Having heard his agent's account of his conversation with Lopukhin, Gerasimov, somewhat shaken in his conviction that the incident was trivial and did not require his serious attention, decided to take up the matter with Lopukhin personally. He promised Azef that he would talk to the retired police director and give him Azef's letter, in which the spy pleaded with Lopukhin to remember his flawless service and to save his life as he had previously saved Lopukhin's life when the radicals were determined to avenge the arrest of Gershuni in 1903. On 21 November, the head of the St. Petersburg Okhrana paid a visit to Lopukhin, imploring him to respect the interests of police security, reminding him of his oath of loyalty to the tsar, and appealing to his sense of compassion.[50] His attempt to help Azef proved as useless as was the spy's own bid: Lopukhin declared to Gerasimov that he "could and would do nothing for . . . that scoundrel." Little did Gerasimov know that Lopukhin could indeed do nothing for the secret agent by that time: three days earlier, on 18 November, the retired police chief had had a secret rendezvous with SR representative Argunov, whom he had informed about Azef's visit to his apartment.[51]

In essence, this was the end of the spy's grand game, but since Azef still stood firmly on the highest revolutionary pedestal in the eyes of the rank-and-file radicals, and "in the party . . . was trusted like nobody else but Gershuni,"[52] a number of SR leaders, including Chernov and Savinkov, were unprepared to convict Azef even after they had interrogated him and, by comparing information, established beyond all doubt that he had indeed been in St. Petersburg at the time of the alleged visit to Lopukhin, and not in Berlin as he claimed.[53] "If there were as much evidence against my own brother as there is against Azef, I would have shot him immediately," claimed Savinkov and added, "But I will never believe that Ivan is a provocateur."[54] Overwhelmed by the inevitable consequences of their findings, but still tenaciously clinging to the hope that it would all turn out to be a police trap, the SR leaders demanded a personal interview with Lopukhin. They also insisted upon a formal written statement from him.[55]

On 16 December 1908, Lopukhin came to London, and on the twenty-third of the month met with three representatives of the SR Central Committee—Chernov, Savinkov, and Argunov—in the Waldorf Hotel, to give his final testimony about Azef's November visit and his general activity as a police agent.[56] Since Azef could not provide an adequate explanation for his presence in Petersburg, there could be no more doubt as to the truth of Lopukhin's words, and before New Year's Day a group of SR leaders issued a secret death sentence against the exposed spy and established close surveillance of his apartment. Even so, Azef's prestige was so great and the discovery of his treason so scandalous that by a majority vote the members of the PSR high command, disarmed by the irrefutable evidence of Azef's guilt, yet still not entirely comprehending it, decided to give him one more chance to defend himself.

Around seven o'clock on the evening of 5 January 1909, Chernov, Savinkov, and Sukhovykh (a prominent *boevik* also known as Nikolai or Panov), paid a surprise visit to Azef's apartment at 243 Boulevard Raspail.[57] Greeting them, Azef "turned terribly yellow"; the SRs comported themselves unceremoniously and refused to shake his hand. Having followed him to his study, they overtly blocked the exit. The spy must have decided that the SRs would shoot him immediately, but Chernov declared: "We offer you a deal: tell us honestly about your relations with the police. We have no need to ruin your family."[58]

Relieved to find out that the revolutionaries were still prepared to talk, Azef vehemently protested the "disgusting suspicion," put on a melodramatic show, and insisted on being a guiltless victim of a fraudulent plot. The ace liar's swan song, devoid of solid arguments and evidently aspiring to elicit pity, was nebulous and unconvincing.[59] Nonetheless, the SRs, with all hopes of confirming their error shattered, yet still victims of what they would later describe as "collective hypnosis," again proved unable to take the decisive step. They gave him a few more hours—until twelve o'clock the next day—to reconsider their proposition. While there was more than a shadow of a doubt in their minds, the last thing they wanted was to deny their former comrade a chance to acquit himself—an opportunity that the spy promptly exploited amidst the general confusion, resolving to save himself by fleeing and changing his identity. He seemed to have sensed the SRs' vacillation, which spurred him to try his fate again. As soon as the revolutionaries departed, Azef left his apartment and vanished.[60]

For years the mystery remained as to why Lopukhin, a member of the most illustrious aristocratic circles in Russia, and formerly a leading government official, would agree to cooperate first with Burtsev, an outlaw and a political criminal with a prison term behind him, and then with the leaders of the subversive PSR. Burtsev's answer—generally accepted as the truth—emphasized that Lopukhin helped the SRs to expose Azef primarily since he wanted to prevent future cases of provocation, and because he was also outraged at having been fooled by his own agent, who had supposedly plotted with the terrorists against him and thus was directly responsible for the ruin of his career. This explanation, however, does not stand up to serious scrutiny.

Burtsev's story is undermined first of all by the fact that his encounter with Lopukhin could hardly have been accidental. Indeed, on a
number of occasions, at the risk of being inconsistent, Burtsev revealed
that he had gotten a general idea about Lopukhin's travel agenda in
Europe from his St. Petersburg contacts, and had waited for the retired
official in Cologne for days until he finally managed to catch him on
the train. For six long hours Lopukhin had no choice but to listen to
his uninvited travel companion, who was determined not to give up
until he had obtained the information he sought about Azef's police
connections.[61] All evidence considered, there is hardly any doubt that
"the meeting with Lopukhin on the train had been carefully contrived
by Burtsev," even though "he managed to give it the appearance of a
chance encounter."[62]

Many aspects of Lopukhin's personality and political career suggest
that the forty-four-year-old former dignitary "was far from an idealist" prepared to fight the evil of provocation even by collaborating
with the revolutionaries, an action for which he would certainly be
held responsible by the tsarist authorities.[63] His later statements notwithstanding, as the director of the Police Department he had fully
supported Zubatov's tactics of recruiting spies from inside radical
organizations and, to use revolutionary terminology, he "approved
the most outrageous methods of provocation."[64] Moreover, Lopukhin
was the one who had received Plehve's sanction to implant Azef at the
very center of the PSR—which made it impossible for the director of
the Police Department not to know about Azef's active role within the
party.[65] In all likelihood, Lopukhin was also well aware that Azef did
not disclose all information to which he had access by virtue of his
position in the PSR.[66]

Evidently, it was only much later that Lopukhin developed his
manifest "integrity" and formulated his rigid principles on the issue.[67]
But even supposing that he might indeed have repented and wished to
atone for his past wrongdoing by preventing what he suddenly realized to be his spy's provocation, it is unclear why he chose to turn to
the radicals.[68] Although he was no longer in state service, he still possessed sufficient contacts in the highest spheres of the imperial administration to have initiated an official investigation instead.

An official government investigation of the Azef affair would seemingly have provided Lopukhin more personal satisfaction. It could
have revealed major abuses by certain individuals in the 1908 administration against whom he held serious grudges dating from his forced
resignation during the 1905 revolution. In the midst of that crisis the
tsar had expressed dissatisfaction with the functioning of the Police

Department, which some officials, foremost of them Gerasimov, complained was a "caricature of a secret political police force." Lopukhin had been left with no alternative but to submit his resignation. As a result, he was the only former Police Department director who had not retained his salary after retirement and who had not been appointed a senator.

At the time of the 1905 upheaval he had also been involved in a dramatic personal conflict with Dmitrii Trepov, Governor-General of St. Petersburg. Upon hearing the news about the SRs' assassination of the Grand Duke Sergei Aleksandrovich, Trepov publicly called Lopukhin a murderer, holding him personally responsible for the death in the imperial family because of inadequate security precautions. Lopukhin also harbored profound hostility and contempt for Petr Rachkovskii. The revelation of his possible involvement with a double agent would undoubtedly have pleased Lopukhin greatly, as would any trouble that the exposure of an agent provocateur might have caused Gerasimov and Prime Minister Stolypin, a former classmate of Lopukhin's who was highly critical of his administrative talents.[69]

Perhaps it would be more justifiable to speculate about the rationale behind Lopukhin's actions (or, perhaps, the lack of such) if it were possible to determine why he agreed to engage in a conversation on the train with Burtsev in the first place. Much of this story remains obscured by mysterious circumstances, beginning with its precise timing. In his various descriptions of this meeting with Lopukhin, Burtsev is inconsistent about when exactly it took place, with the date ranging from as early as December 1904 to as late as September 1908.[70] On one occasion Burtsev revealed something that he would never disclose again, namely, the interesting fact that Lopukhin had agreed to unveil the spy's name not because of munificence, but as a result of blackmail. Allegedly, during their conversation on the train, Burtsev had threatened Lopukhin with the prospect of publishing certain compromising documents that the former police director would have hated to see on the pages of the journal *Byloe*.[71] This statement, made in the presence of several SRs, serves a dual purpose: it renders irrelevant and obliterates all subsequent references to the Burtsev-Lopukhin relationship as a harmonious accord; it also introduces for the first time the innuendo of criminal means that were employed to extract information from Lopukhin. In investigating this assumption, it is essential to consider crucial information that was overlooked by all subsequent analysts of Lopukhin's behavior—information that is indispensable for an understanding of his true motives.

In his unpublished memoirs A. S. Lopukhin, a cousin of Aleksei Lopukhin, relates a private conversation in which the tsarist police official describes why he betrayed his agent Azef to the revolutionaries. According to this account, during a trip abroad Aleksei Lopukhin received news that his daughter had been kidnapped in London. He immediately set out for England and was approached by Burtsev on the train. Burtsev made the pointed suggestion that Lopukhin give him the name of the police agent at the center of the PSR in exchange for the release of his daughter. Lopukhin named Azef, and a day later was reunited with the young lady at his London hotel.[72]

It is conceivable that the author of these reminiscences is not entirely accurate in detail and chronology. Nevertheless, his story is well supported by a police telegram from St. Petersburg, informing Okhrana representatives abroad that on 24 October 1907, Lopukhin's eighteen-year-old daughter, Varvara, had disappeared after leaving a theater with her English governess, a Miss Margaret (Margarita Ivanovna) Rossel (or Russell).[73] The director of the Police Department in the Russian capital, M. I. Trusevich, also wrote to his counterpart in London, Sir Henry, requesting his assistance in conducting an urgent investigation.[74] The story even appeared in the British press, producing a brief sensation.[75] As the governess clarified in a subsequent newspaper interview, several unknown individuals separated her from Lopukhin's daughter as they were leaving the London circus in a crowd, and pushed the young woman into a carriage. The kidnappers then took Varvara to a secluded apartment, where they kept her unharmed for several days until she received permission to return to her father. He had arrived in London only six hours earlier, evidently for the sole purpose of securing her release.[76]

The fact of the abduction of Lopukhin's daughter is thus hardly subject to doubt, although exactly who was behind this criminal exploit may always remain a riddle. While the leading SRs probably had nothing to do with it, it is reasonable to suspect certain independent advocates of terror in Burtsev's entourage, especially in consideration of the fact that Burtsev himself was a life-long proponent of terrorist action and as early as 1903 recommended kidnapping as a tactic to be used to achieve revolutionary goals.[77] This assumption is indirectly supported by a police source that indicates that Burtsev and a number of his followers, including a certain Iudelevskii, Krakov, and Kriuger, in 1907 formed a small conspiratorial group, the People's Will Group (*Narodovol'cheskaia gruppa*), for the purpose of planning "a grandiose terrorist act."[78] Varvara Lopukhina's kidnappers might also have been other lesser-known SRs, possibly members of the Paris Group, who were the first in Socialist Revolutionary circles to become determined to uncover the secret agent inside the PSR.[79] They were intent on eliminating the police spy by any means, and kidnapping and coercion were hardly the most reprehensible from the point of view of revolutionary ethics and party discipline. Indeed, according to Burtsev, a few SRs even suggested that he should quit his attempts to prevail upon the revolutionary tribunal: "Let us kill Azef and put an end to this business."[80]

Contrary to Burtsev's highly improbable account about his dealings with the retired police official, it appears that only as a result of this abduction did Lopukhin agree to disclose Azef's name to a well-known revolutionary. This evidence was likely not the final piece that Burtsev so desperately sought in order to expose the agent provocateur, but rather the very first and the only unambiguous fact lending substance to less definite clues against Azef. This more solid information served as the catalyst for the initiation of Burtsev's full-scale investigation.[81] An indirect justification for this hypothesis is the fact that at the time of his train conversation with Lopukhin, Burtsev's accusations against Azef were almost completely unsubstantiated. He was evidently unable to produce any documents or other clear evidence to demonstrate Azef's double role; nor was he able to enlighten Lopukhin as to many details of the terrorist attacks in which the alleged provocateur took part.[82] The former director of the Police Department could hardly have been so gullible as to believe unsupported claims about Azef's treacherous behavior presented by a man who during previous encounters had impressed Lopukhin as an "unstable enthusiast, calling himself a convinced *narodovolets*."[83] Equally significant is that Burtsev initiated his public campaign against Azef only in the early days of 1908[84]—a fact suggesting that he had obtained the first serious evidence against Azef not too long before, possibly at the end of October or the beginning of November 1907, during his conversation on the train with Lopukhin.

Lopukhin's disclosure of the name of the police informer among the SRs could not serve as the definitive exposure of Azef in their eyes. Since Lopukhin did not have any document or other unquestionable proof of Azef's contact with the Russian authorities with him at the time of his unexpected encounter with Burtsev, the revolutionaries could understandably have perceived his testimony simply as part of a ludicrous Police Department intrigue against Azef and the PSR.[85] Thus, even after the conversation with Lopukhin Burtsev had to obtain solid evidence that Azef was a spy, and during the following months the spy hunter did all he could to build a case against Azef.

It is only possible to speculate as to why Lopukhin chose to extend his cooperation to the SR leaders, although it is more than doubtful that this cooperation was strictly voluntary, as the revolutionaries persistently claimed, or that Lopukhin's motives were those of a disinterested seeker of truth.[86] From the beginning, Lopukhin preferred to remain inconspicuous rather than to publicize his conversation with Burtsev (and then with Argunov). If the former police chief had intended to defect to the revolutionary camp or to flush out the agent provocateur by means of a public scandal, his behavior most likely would have been different. Similarly, Lopukhin did not rush to provide Burtsev or the SRs with any other secrets of the police world that he possessed by virtue of his position prior to retirement; beyond the unmasking of Azef, he proved of little value to the revolutionaries.[87] Furthermore, Lopukhin was not at all eager to continue his relations with the radicals, evasively justifying his dealings with the SRs in St. Petersburg by "the pressure of fatal necessity."[88] In addition, in his conversation with Gerasimov in the capital, while warning that he would not conceal Azef's police role from the revolutionaries if they threatened him with a gun, Lopukhin promised: "I will not appear before a revolutionary tribunal. That is absolutely out of the question."[89]

Yet this is precisely what he did on 10 (23) December in a London hotel, even though he must have had little hope that the SR leaders would keep the meeting secret if forced by fellow party members to reveal their source of information about Azef.[90] Nor could he have doubted that upon his return to St. Petersburg he would be held accountable before the law for providing services to state criminals.[91] According to a police source, the SR Central Committee took measures to assure Lopukhin's continued collaboration.[92] The SRs did not feel the need to conceal their determination to "force ... and compel" Lopukhin's cooperation,[93] which he himself vaguely justified at the time by "common human judgement."[94]

After he had shown weakness before the terrorists and betrayed state secrets, Lopukhin probably became vulnerable to coercion and possibly blackmail by the revolutionaries. He attempted to rebut their pressure at certain points, for instance, when he declined Argunov's suggestion to set Azef up by inviting him for another discussion while allowing the revolutionary witnesses to hide in an adjacent room.[95] In general, however, the SRs could be relatively certain of Lopukhin's docile collaboration, for, in their words, he was at their mercy (*"on u nas v rukakh"*).[96]

Although Azef warned Lopukhin during their conversation on 11 November 1908 that the revolutionaries would not hesitate to resort to force to extract a statement from him,[97] Lopukhin, hoping to avoid appearing before a revolutionary tribunal, agreed to the SR demands to provide them a document that could be presented to the public as decisive evidence against Azef: a notarized duplicate of a letter Lopukhin had written on 21 November (the day of his meeting with Gerasimov) to Stolypin, with identical copies dispatched to the deputy minister of internal affairs, A. A. Makarov, and the director of the Police Department, M. I. Trusevich. In this letter Lopukhin described Azef's and Gerasimov's uninvited visits to his apartment and, protesting against such intrusions on his privacy, asked for protection against similar actions on the part of the secret police that may "endanger [his] personal security."[98]

Lopukhin very likely did not produce this letter voluntarily either. Instead, it might have been written at the suggestion or even under the direct pressure of the SRs. After the outbreak of the Azef affair, persistent rumors circulating in the Russian and foreign press had it that in November 1908 three prominent Socialist Revolutionaries "invaded Lopukhin's apartment, placed a revolver next to his chest, and demanded a clear, written, and substantiated answer to the question as to whether Azef was a agent of the Russian secret police. Unwillingly, Lopukhin rendered the demanded explanation."[99] Such journalistic conjectures were not confirmed by solid evidence; yet, we may be reminded that there is no smoke without fire.

In the first place, it is beyond doubt that Lopukhin did inform the revolutionaries of the content of this letter prior to sending it to the addressees. Lopukhin subsequently admitted to having shown his letters to two confidants whose names he refused to disclose, yet it was no secret that "Argunov read the letter in the original" right after it was written, most likely at the time of his second meeting with Lopukhin on 23 November.[100] It is equally noteworthy that although dated 21 November 1908, the letter was mailed to Stolypin, Makarov, and Trusevich on 24 November, the day after Lopukhin had left the capital for Moscow. Immediately before departure, he had given the letters to Argunov in unsealed envelopes, and there are indications that the person who delivered them may have been Vera Gots, widow of SR leader Mikhail Gots, who had come to St. Petersburg partly in connection with the Azef affair.[101]

At the beginning of the letter, Lopukhin announced in unambivalent terms that he had known Azef as a police agent in the years 1902–1905. As a former police official he was undoubtedly aware that strict precautions would be appropriate in the writing of such highly confidential matters, and yet he chose not to take them. The likelihood that the content of Lopukhin's letter was even dictated to him is suggested, finally, by its overly formal tone, which insinuates that the original was intended for a broader audience than Lopukhin's former classmate, with whom he had always been on a first-name basis.[102]

There is an indirect indication that Lopukhin's wife, Ekaterina Dmitrievna Lopukhina (née Princess Urusova), contributed to her husband's decision to cooperate with the radicals. According to an SR source, driven by "ethical motives," she threatened to go abroad and testify against Azef before the revolutionary court if her husband refused to collaborate with the SRs.[103] In a letter to Lopukhin dated 7 January 1909, Burtsev found it pertinent to state his regret for any problems he might unintentionally have caused for the former police chief by making their relationship public knowledge, and he expressed his sincere gratitude not only to Lopukhin personally but also to his wife.[104] It is highly unlikely, however, that Mme Lopukhina was determined to expose the alleged criminal activities of the Russian central administration even at the cost of her husband's imprisonment; it is more appropriate to suppose that the frightening experience with her daughter caused her to insist that Lopukhin yield to the revolutionaries.

The fact that Lopukhin proved so cooperative as to transmit to the PSR Central Committee a copy of a letter to the three highest officials in the Ministry of the Interior did not excuse him from an interrogation session with the revolutionaries in London, as he had hoped. How the SRs managed to obtain Lopukhin's agreement to a personal interview is unclear, but it is evident that he did not come merely because, as they subsequently claimed, "Burtsev wrote a letter to him, requesting that he come abroad for . . . interrogation."[105] According to Argunov, while still in St. Petersburg, Lopukhin agreed to meet with him and Savinkov in London, and perhaps it was again pressure from his wife, who accompanied him there in December 1908, that made Lopukhin decide to cooperate one more time.[106]

The fact that the radicals used coercion to force Lopukhin to supply them with evidence against Azef further discredits one of the main legends associated with the Azef affair—Burtsev's claim that Lopukhin helped to unmask the spy out of an altruistic love of truth. The threats against Lopukhin's family immediately transform the retired official from an ally of the radicals into their victim. Whatever the case, a copy of Lopukhin's letter to Stolypin soon appeared as a sensational lead story in newspapers throughout Europe. It was the only written document against Azef, and immediately opened the way for a major political scandal implicating the highest representatives of the Russian imperial government, foremost of them, the prime minister.[107]

6

The Public Scandal

Looking for the Guilty Head

> If a person has an ugly face, he can conceal it under a mask, but
> can he do the same with his character?
> —Voltaire[1]

If a sympathizer had to advise Aleksei Lopukhin about what to do
next to alleviate his predicament, he would perhaps have counseled
the retired official to stay abroad in order to avoid persecution by the
Russian government for having divulged an important state secret. Yet,
contrary to common sense, Lopukhin returned to Russia on 13 December 1908, no doubt expecting to suffer the consequences.[2] A month
later, on 18 January 1909, he was indeed arrested in St. Petersburg.[3]
Lopukhin was taken to Kresty Prison, where he was to be confined for
the duration of the official investigation.

Significantly, Lopukhin was not charged with abusing his former
official position by disclosing classified state information, or even with
giving assistance to an illegal organization. The former police chief
was accused of actual participation in a criminal association whose
manifest purpose was to destroy the existing socio-political order in
the Russian Empire by means of armed insurrection and terrorism. He
was not charged with malfeasance, but with a political crime. This
being the case, experts expected Lopukhin to be tried in the Court of
Appeal *(Sudebnaia palata)*—the standard court for considering crimes
against the state (the only exceptions being instances the tsar himself
considered important enough to be scrutinized by the Special Session
of the State Senate).

Given the extent of the ignominious publicity at home and abroad
created by the Azef affair and Lopukhin's arrest, Nicholas II indeed

considered the matter to be of primary significance for his administration's reputation. Accordingly, at the behest of Minister of Justice I. G. Shcheglovitov, on 23 February, the tsar ordered the transfer of Lopukhin's case to the highest court—the State Senate—for final judgment, following the completion of the preliminary investigation.[4] Wishing to put an end to the increasingly escalating and embarrassing revelations and to stop as quickly as possible all rumors about the felonious dealings of the state police, the tsar, while not giving a direct order, clearly indicated his desire that the preliminary investigation be completed without delay.

The investigators did not have to be given the hint twice: they did everything to expedite preparations for the trial, even to the point of neglecting certain formalities. They may also have judged that they ought to hurry the preliminary investigation because of Lopukhin's health. His relatives were allowed to visit him in prison twice a week, and by 25 February, newspapers reported that he was complaining of a severely deteriorating physical state and was even forced to consult a prison doctor. His request for bail was denied, however. At that point the investigators decided that their job was done—lest Lopukhin's health became so bad that he would not be able to stand trial. The plan was to get the sentence passed and close the embarrassing matter once and for all.[5]

Partly because Lopukhin did become seriously ill in prison, the Special Session of the State Senate dealing with his case opened in only two months, at 12:15 in the afternoon on 28 April 1909, in the building of the St. Petersburg District Court (*Okruzhnoi sud*), and under the chairmanship of Senator V. N. Varvarin. The trial was to be a public one—something that the newspapers acknowledged as an overt attempt on the part of the government to demonstrate that it did not intend to hide any "unpleasant revelations, expected at the trial."[6] Lopukhin chose a well-reputed attorney, Aleksandr Passover, to be his defense counselor.[7] On Passover's advise, Lopukhin pleaded not guilty.

The trial promised to be an event of major political significance, especially for the opposition, whose members expected the proceedings to reveal grievous wrongdoing on the part of the government and its security system. Newspapers screamed about the scandal and argued that "for Russia, the case of Lopukhin was what the Dreyfus case had been for France."[8] Journalists of leftist persuasion were busy preparing their audience for sensational disclosures: "This will be a trial not of Lopukhin, but of the entire bureaucratic police order, of the whole regime that watches over society, of everything illicit that is carried out by 'fully-empowered' central administrators, as well as by 'little officials' locally."[9]

Contrary to all expectations, the three-day trial of Aleksei Lopukhin was dull and tedious. During the first session, the judges reviewed the evidence and listened to several witnesses. On the next day, 29 April, after the investigatory part of the trial was considered complete, the prosecution and the defense attorneys made use of their chances to argue the case. The speech of the prosecution counselor, V. E. Korsak, which lasted approximately forty-five minutes, mainly delineated the facts already presented in the indictment. The prosecution rejected Lopukhin's claim that he had revealed Azef's name to Burtsev due to a "civil duty" to fight criminal activity: after all, the retired police director had exposed the alleged provocateur to the revolutionaries—in other words, to state criminals—and not to the government, thus providing the former with practical aid. As far as the prosecution was concerned, from the juridical point of view, Lopukhin's motives in helping the SRs did not matter as long as the fact was proven that he did provide this help. Accordingly, the prosecution demanded that the accused be convicted and punished as a formal member of an illegal antigovernment organization in accordance with Article 102, paragraphs 1 and 3, of the Criminal Code *(Ugolovnoe Ulozhenie).*[10]

The defense was equally trivial. Speaking so softly that it was at times impossible to discern his words, Lopukhin's attorney chose to concentrate on the general question of the role of the secret police. Without denying its importance for the state, Passover argued that the participation of secret agents in the central organs of those antigovernment organizations in which they serve as police spies invariably leads to provocation, since the agents cannot remain passive observers but are instead required to demonstrate their own initiative in order not to lose their standing in the criminal organization and consequently become useless to the authorities. By revealing Azef's true role, Lopukhin did a favor for the government, the defense council claimed, referring to the general opinion among revolutionary groups that the exposure of the spy in the SR Central Committee jeopardized the very existence of the Socialist Revolutionary Party. The judges should note, Passover argued finally, one significant consequence of Lopukhin's exposure of Azef: not one notable terrorist act had taken place during the last four months. While acknowledging that Lopukhin acted against "bureaucratic ethics" (which would classify his behavior as malfeasance), his defense council rejected the prosecution's central claim that the retired head of the Police Department should be declared and judged as a member of a criminal organization.[11]

After the hour-long speech of his lawyer, Lopukhin was invited to give his final testimony. He began by outlining the history of his appointment as the head of the Police Department. The chairman stopped Lopukhin, asking him to get to the point, but the defendant continued with his general statements, now aimed at demonstrating that his views on secret police prerogatives rested on directives from his superiors, former Interior Minister von Plehve and his deputy, State-Secretary Petr Durnovo, both of whom, according to Lopukhin, insisted that secret agents must never enter the center of a revolutionary party. When the chairman stopped him again, Lopukhin declared that he would limit his remarks to the following argument: after learning about Azef's role within the PSR, Lopukhin had decided that he would have every political murder and execution in the country on his conscience unless he exposed the provocateur. He felt that an appeal to the highest state authorities would have been to no avail, since ambitious police officers would have found a way to beguile him in order to embellish themselves in the eyes of their superiors.[12] For this reason, Lopukhin concluded his speech, he had collaborated with the radicals.

The testimony succeeded only in harming the defendant. The judges knew that Lopukhin had implanted Azef at the very center of the PSR in full accordance with Plehve's sanctions, and to deny his obvious awareness of the spy's active role within the party was a lost cause. One is left to wonder why Passover, as competent an attorney as he was, did so little to lead Lopukhin out of his predicament in some way that would have been a bit more discriminating than a vapid lie. In any case, on the final day of the proceedings, 30 April 1909, at 2:15 in the afternoon, the judges announced their decision. They issued a guilty verdict, convicting Lopukhin of taking part in an illegal association. In accordance with paragraphs 1 and 3, Article 102, as well as Articles 53 and 16 of the Criminal Code, he was sentenced to five years of hard labor. His appeal for a release on bail was denied once again.[13] Yet, considering certain "extenuating circumstances" and the harshness of the punishment—especially given Lopukhin's well-known name, former distinguished position, and deteriorating health—on 3 July 1909, Nicholas II commuted the sentence: Lopukhin was deprived of his property rights and exiled to Siberia for life.[14]

One of the most astonishing and baffling aspects of the trial was the fact that in her testimony, Varvara Lopukhina's governess, who was present as a witness, did not choose to report on the kidnapping. Nor did the judges question her about this incident,[15] which, to all logic, should have attracted their immediate attention especially because as early as 1907 police officials had come to speculate on Lopukhin's possible "desire to conceal the circumstances" of his daughter's abduction. These suspicions had been triggered by reports in the British newspapers about his dismissal of Varvara's governess. She had been loyal to the Lopukhin family for years, and was discharged solely because she had made the kidnapping public knowledge by appealing for help to Scotland Yard.[16] The judges, however, failed to relate Lopukhin's 1907 behavior to his role in the Azef affair. Lopukhin's wife, who appeared as another witness at the trial and seemed "completely enervated," exercised her privilege, guaranteed by Article 705 of the Criminal Code, not to give testimony.[17] This evasive behavior might be explained by obvious concern for the Lopukhin family safety; conceivably, the revolutionaries had threatened further coercion unless the defendant and the witnesses at the trial conformed to the line that the former police chief had exposed the crimes of his ex-employee—a version quite suitable for the radical cause. Thus, what should have been treated as the central episode in the "case of Lopukhin" was simply overlooked and cast aside.

Most government opponents saw Lopukhin as a repented sinner who had acted valiantly in accordance with his ethical convictions and had suffered in the hands of the unscrupulous tsarist administration. Impressed by what struck them as Lopukhin's undaunted and principled behavior during the Azef affair, people in the antigovernment circles were all too willing to absolve Lopukhin's former crimes as the director of the Police Department. In fact, they were eager to embrace him as one of the victims of the oppressive regime, so much so that after the verdict some members of the Duma's Left wrote to Mme Ekaterina Lopukhina to express their sympathy.[18]

In August 1909 Lopukhin arrived at his designated place of exile, Eniseisk province, where he settled in the town of Minusinsk with his family, who followed him to Siberia. From then on Lopukhin led a very quiet and completely secluded life, evading any contact with other exiled political criminals. With the governor's permission he occupied himself with arranging a small library at the Minusinsk museum. In 1910 he was allowed to take a job at the Minusinsk division of the Siberian Trade Bank; and in 1911 he received permission to settle in Krasnoiarsk, where he became deputy-director of the local branch of the same bank, receiving a substantial annual salary of 3,000 rubles. According to the local police authorities responsible for keeping an eye on him, Lopukhin's lifestyle was "irreproachable." His contacts were limited exclusively to his family and his associates in the business world, thus "giving no cause to suspect him of having links to antigovernment activity of any kind."[19] The central administration paid him back in kind: in February 1913, as a result of the general amnesty in connection with the three-hundred-year anniversary of the Romanov dynasty, Nicholas II approved a supplication from Colonel Dmitrii

Lopukhin, allowing his banished brother to return to St. Petersburg after only four years of exile.[20]

Among the mysteries surrounding Azef's exposure, one remains unsolved. Why did Lopukhin not disclose the truth at his 1909 trial, or years later, after the downfall of the Russian autocracy in 1917, in his testimonies before the Extraordinary Investigation Committee *(Chrezvy-chainaia sledstvennaia kommissiia)* of the Provisional Government? Indeed, he never mentioned his daughter's kidnapping as being the catalyst for his subsequent relations with the revolutionaries, and instead went along entirely with Burtsev's version of the story. Difficult as it is to hypothesize about his motives, it is arguable that when Lopukhin claimed he had only "fulfilled his moral patriotic duty" by disclosing Azef's "most villainous crimes," he assumed the posture of a selfless hero. Had he conceded that at least his initial cooperation with the revolutionaries, and probably his subsequent behavior to a certain extent, were the result of coercion, he would have implicitly admitted to malfeasance.[21] According to Nicolaevsky, "Lopukhin was so deeply involved in the Azef affair that he could simply lie because of his wish to purify his name in history."[22] This conjecture fits the image of Lopukhin held by a fellow statesman, a former governor and senator, A. V. Bel'gard: "A. A. Lopukhin was first of all a careerist, always ready to be more of a rightist or leftist, depending on his personal egotistic interests. . . . He did not have either his own convictions, or even his own thoughts."[23]

After the trial and banishment, Lopukhin's fate did not interest anyone outside his family. The real hero of the day was Burtsev. For months, he received loud applause from the numerous opponents of the Russian autocracy at home and abroad, hailing him for having rendered an invaluable service to the revolution.[24] For months Burtsev would provide newspapers all over Europe and the United States with the most incredible interviews and stories about how he exposed Azef. These stories combined factual information and retrospective—and largely frivolous—interpretation in a kaleidoscopic fashion, partly with the aim of enhancing Burtsev's own image as a winner, and partly to portray the Russian government in the worst possible light.

Burtsev made full use of the fact that the public craved sensational new information about the crimes of the tsarist regime. One of many examples of his catering to public opinion was the following assertion, unsupported by any evidence: "There was a consultation in St. Petersburg in which it was decided to kill me. I even know the names of those who accepted this commission, and I know that the Russian authorities in Finland have received orders not to arrest me, but to shoot me in case I happen to go there."[25] Burtsev also claimed that the tsarist authorities plotted to kill him in France.[26] He thus provided increasingly mysterious, stirring, and scandalous information, rather than a rational explanation of the facts, presenting Azef as a monstrous and almost superhuman villain and his government protectors as virulent hardened criminals.

Now that he was on the same side of the barricades with the SRs and no longer a pariah in revolutionary circles, Burtsev's cause célèbre was to rescue the prestige of the revolutionary movement and the terrorist idea by shifting attention away from the radicals' failures to the alleged crimes of the authorities. If the police spy in the center of the PSR had caused so much damage to the revolutionary movement, the SRs, Burtsev held, should at least try to pay the tsarist administration back in kind by demonstrating to the public that Azef had been an agent provocateur, armed with the support of important government functionaries who knew about his criminal exploits, yet closed their eyes to them as long as he served their interests. Convinced by Burtsev's arguments, the revolutionaries expected that the news about the government's employment of criminal methods would ruin its reputation and "create great trouble in the country"[27] by turning the party scandal into "the Dreyfus case of the Russian autocracy."[28]

The first reaction of the SR Central Committee to Azef's escape was a silence that betrayed the party leaders' confusion and indecision.[29] Two days had gone by, and on 8 January 1909, when it was no longer possible to avoid facing the inevitable, the SR leadership went public with the case, revealing Azef's police connections in an official party statement.[30] Seeking desperately to save the party's image, the Central Committee then made repeated announcements to the effect that even though Azef's treachery brought considerable harm to the PSR, and especially its terrorist policy, his role in the Combat Organization was not as crucial as it had appeared to be. SR terror, they argued, had not begun with Azef's entrance into the PSR, and would not end with his exposure; despite this major setback, political assassinations had not at all been discredited as a revolutionary tool and should not be renounced.

This initial interpretation of the significance of Azef's role did little to improve the party's prestige in the eyes of the public. Additionally, it drew strong criticism of the Central Committee from various SR circles, whose members accused the SR leaders of using contradictory and obviously infeasible evidence in a clumsy attempt to rescue the party's prestige by partially acquitting Azef and minimizing his role in the PSR.[31] The Central Committee was quickly forced to alter its

position and, together with Burtsev, to come up with a different interpretation of the Azef affair that would be more suitable for the SRs'
general aims.[32] Indeed, the SR public statements came to differ radically from their initial evaluations of Azef's role.

Even though the SR movement had been discredited, the top party
leaders sought at least to use the situation to bring maximum damage
to the government: on 20 January 1909 they issued another official
statement proclaiming Azef an agent provocateur, thus implicating
the tsarist authorities in the crime of provocation.[33] The SR leadership
had initially asserted that all the assassination attempts of which Azef
had any knowledge had been doomed to failure from the start and
that, conversely, many terrorist ventures in which he had not been
involved had succeeded.[34] The Central Committee now changed its
approach and publicly announced that Azef had been the organizer
and the leader of all major terrorist acts perpetrated by the PSR
between 1902 and 1908.

Without providing any evidence to substantiate their claims even
in part, the SRs proceeded to argue that Azef had frequently obtained
the secret approval and sanction of his protectors among the state's
highest officials before proceeding with these acts of revolutionary terror. Formulating their announcements in the tones of sensational jour-
nalism, the SRs asserted, for example, that Azef had arranged the 1903
assassination of the Ufa city governor, N. M. Bogdanovich, with the
explicit approval of Interior Minister Plehve, who had allegedly been
having an affair with Bogdanovich's wife and therefore wished to dis-
pose of her husband. Shortly after the fatal outcome of this romantic
drama, Plehve himself fell victim to an SR assassin, and in the new SR
version of the story, Azef bore primary responsibility for organizing
the attack. He was purported to have acted on the orders of Petr
Rachkovskii, who was hungry for revenge after having been forced
into temporary retirement in 1902 following his conflict with the minister of the interior.[35] Azef thus emerged from the SR stories as a pawn
in the blood-stained intrigues of the highest spheres.[36] The SRs issued
these statements under the (generally correct) assumption that society was susceptible to any negative rumor about the tsarist regime at
the time, and was all too willing to condemn the autocracy for all
imaginable offenses, thereby further undermining its reputation and
stability and contributing to its eventual downfall.

In the meantime, Burtsev did all he could to reinforce this antigovernment public opinion campaign. Once on the war path, he stopped
at nothing and was prepared even to suffer severe criticism from fellow radicals for breaking the revolutionary code of honor by sending

open appeals to various high-level government representatives, retired dignitaries, notable figures in the conservative circles, and even members of the imperial family, demanding that Azef and Stolypin be brought to trial.[37] To the public, Burtsev's efforts may have seemed idealistic and naive, and likely doomed to failure. The true purpose of his agitation campaign was much more pragmatic, however: he undoubtedly knew that he could not make the government of Nicholas II legally responsible for harboring a spy, but by pressing the charges, he could make sure that the public at home and abroad would look askance at the highest officials in the tsarist regime.[38]

The government chose not to complete its formal investigation of Azef's activity as a police agent before it issued the only official statement in connection with the entire affair—a speech that Stolypin made before the Third Duma on 11 February 1909. On that day, the Tauride Palace where the Duma deputies convened was packed with zesty journalists; ministerial seats were all occupied; in a crowd of excited visitors one could see many dignitaries from the State Council, members of the Russian imperial family, and foreign diplomats. Everyone wanted to hear Stolypin's reply to the January interpolation that the Kadet faction had issued with regard to Azef's role and the government's involvement in the practice of provocation.[39] Acknowledging Azef's employment in the secret police, Stolypin categorically denied all charges of the government's criminal misuse of its agent, arguing that the words "provocation" and "provocateur" were frequently abused in radical circles. Their meanings had been distorted, he said, to the point that, according to revolutionary terminology, a police agent either recruited from among the radicals or sent into the revolutionary ranks from the outside for the purpose of gathering information would, upon exposure, not be called a traitor or a spy, "but would be labelled a *provocateur*."[40] Thus, the SR party's very first public communiqué announcing Azef's exposure may be noted for its word choice:

> The Central Committee of the Socialist Revolutionary party wishes all comrades of the party to know that the engineer Yevno Filipovich Azef . . . a member of the Socialist Revolutionary party since its foundation . . . has been convicted of having entered into relations with the Russian political police and is hereby declared a provocateur.[41]

In contrast, although repeatedly declaring that means of provocation were "entirely unacceptable, criminal, and categorically proscribed" in the security organs,[42] the Russian government conformed to the standard definition of the term provocateur—the interpretation congruous with all Russian and Western legal usage of the term—that

first and foremost implied instigation to a certain act. In this definition an agent provocateur would be someone who "incited another
person to a criminal act with the exclusive goal of turning him over
into the hands of justice and punishing him."[43] As Stolypin put it, the
government "considered a provocateur only such an individual who
takes upon himself the initiative for a crime, involving in it other persons who choose this path at the instigation of an agent provocateur."[44]
Stolypin's speech was intended to demonstrate that Azef had done nothing of the sort, and therefore must be regarded as a police informer,
whose activity among the radicals was authorized and expressly permitted in Police Department regulations.[45] Since the use of secret agents
was common practice in political investigations, Azef's case was unusual only by virtue of the exceptionally long and accomplished career of
the master spy.

As a result of Stolypin's attempt to justify the methods of the Russian secret police, the majority of the Duma, including a number of the
prime minister's political opponents, acknowledged that his explanation logically and convincingly demonstrated the legitimacy of the
government's use of Azef. He had acted only as a secret informer and
not as a provocateur or double agent who, according to the Burtsev-
SR version of the story, had betrayed both the police and the revolutionaries. Excerpts from Stolypin's Duma speech were published in all the
major newspapers in Russia and abroad, and despite opposition from
the Kadet faction, the Duma rejected the interpolation. The Octobrist,
the moderate conservative, and the nationalist factions issued a joint
resolution that recognized the government's explanation as "satisfactory and exhaustive."[46] "The entire edifice of the grandiose and sensational allegations aimed at an all-European scandal was built on
sand," wrote the Octobrist newspaper *Golos Moskvy (The Voice of
Moscow)*.[47] Still more significantly, even many of the government's
most vehement opponents among the radicals accepted Stolypin's
interpretation of Azef's role as legitimate. Revolutionary S. M. Bleklov
(Senzharskii), a member of the SR committee of inquiry into the Azef
affair, asserted explicitly:

> As far as his [Azef's] participation in the revolutionary struggle, the
> government, represented by Stolypin, presents an evaluation of his
> activity which is much closer, it seems, to the reality. This may be seen
> in Stolypin's speech when he says that Azef participated only super-
> ficially, without taking close part in terrorist affairs. Now I am under
> the impression that this assessment of Stolypin's is much closer to the
> truth than all these stories about his [Azef's] illustrious revolution-
> ary work, about his very close involvement in terrorist acts.[48]

This resolution, of course, did not end the passionate public debate over the Azef affair, and particularly over the legitimacy of police methods employed against the revolutionaries. The word *provocation* was on everyone's lips and made its way into the everyday language of the beau monde and intelligentsia circles, with its meaning discussed in salons and the press. The general consensus among government critics in the opposition circles was that Azef's exploits served as a vivid confirmation of what they have always maintained: that the Russian autocracy was corrupted to its very core, and that it sustained itself against the forces of freedom solely by means of shameless provocation. At the same time, however, Vladimir Nabokov, an eminent liberal Russian jurist, summarized the independent legal interpretation of the controversy, underscoring the argument that "not any spy is a provocateur. The essential difference is that a spy does not incite to commit crimes: he observes and reports.... A spy may even participate in preparations for the crimes in order to deceive his comrades and betray them at an opportune moment." Nabokov compared a police spy to a scout who puts on the enemy's uniform and makes his way into the opposite camp: in so doing he runs the risk of being shot by the enemy, but he should not have to expect to be persecuted by those who had sent him there.[49] In essence, this illustration reinforced the official position of the Russian authorities, who continuously dismissed any demands to initiate an official investigation by declaring that the government had not found any new evidence to justify a reevaluation of its stand on the Azef affair.[50] Rumors, such as that Mikhail Trusevich, the director of the Police Department, would soon be fired for having compromised himself with illegal dealings along with Rachkovskii,[51] remained just that—empty rumors.

Contrary to the purpose of Burtsev's public statements, which, as he admitted, aimed to "give a deadly blow to the moral prestige" of the Russian government,[52] the scandal had an infinitely greater repercussion for the PSR than it did for the Russian imperial authorities.[53] Even when all the evidence had been against Azef, most rank-and-file radicals could not bring themselves to doubt his loyalty to the revolutionary cause; for them, a revelation about Azef's involvement with the police was analogous to finding out that Mikhail Gots or Grigorii Gershuni were secret agents.[54] Members of the Combat Organization, initially reluctant to give credence to Azef's involvement with the police, were especially determined to defend him. They perceived the campaign against him as a typical attempt by the civilian SRs to interfere with the affairs of the fighters. *Boevik* Petr Karpovich threatened to shoot the entire Central Committee if it dared to prosecute the terror-

ists' chief.[55] Other terrorists were no less adamant: the *boevik* Esfir'
Lapina (Bella) declared that comrades ought to put her under guard,
lest she kill the PSR leaders because they dared to suspect Azef.[56] The
combatants were all indignant about the surveillance of Azef's apartment; in fact, the Central Committee could count only on three or four
combatants who would not sabotage SR plans by divulging them to
Azef.[57] Even after his escape, some combatants were unprepared to
pronounce Azef a police agent.[58]

By mid-January 1909, however, with no one able to find excuses for
Azef's behavior any longer, there was a general atmosphere of profound
confusion, acrimony, and strife in the PSR circles. A police source delin-
eates the SRs' reaction to the devastating news: during a meeting of
PSR leaders devoted to the party's predicament Chernov made a
speech about Azef's treason, after which "chairman Il'ia Fundamin-
skii (Bunakov) and many among the present were crying; others sat
silently, their heads bent low."[59] "Everyone was dumbfounded, mortified by the shock of the enormous fact of provocation; people became
stupefied."[60]

In May 1909 the Fifth Council of the PSR convened and authorized
a special Investigatory-Judiciary Committee on the Azef affair *(Sudebno-sledstvennaia komissiia po delu Azefa)* to inquire into the details of the
spy's role in the party. The four-man Committee began its proceedings
in November 1909 under the chairmanship of Aleksei Bakh, and after
seventy-three meetings, having interrogated thirty-one persons, published in April 1911 the final product of its labors as a special volume
entitled *The Conclusions of the Investigatory-Judiciary Committee on the
Azef Affair (Zakliuchenie sudebno-sledstvennoi komissii po delu Azefa).*[61]
Besides presenting essential information about Azef's activities since the
beginning of his involvement with revolution, the report makes fascinating reading for its principal argument, which amounts to severe criticism of the SR Combat Organization and the party's Central Committee.

It follows from *The Conclusions* that the tactic of organized terror, elevated to the highest pedestal in the PSR, was to a large extent responsible for all the evil Azef brought onto the party. Excessive reliance on
terrorist methods—unavoidably clandestine by their very nature—
created a situation in which the Combat Organization was allowed to
turn into a semi-autonomous body within the PSR, practically independent from and indifferent to the party's leadership and its overall
objectives. The *boeviki* hardly concealed their scorn toward the "bab-
bling theoreticians and pen pushers."[62] At the same time, the practi-
tioners of terror and especially their leaders enjoyed a special position
of honor, prestige, and unbounded trust—something that allowed Azef

to continue his game without evoking suspicions. According to *The Conclusions*, absolute confidence was not something that Azef had earned; he had inherited it from Gershuni, who, as the first leader of the terrorists, was surrounded by an almost mystical aura of veneration that was automatically extended to Azef, his successor. Affirming the terrorists' resistance to any control from the SR civilian leadership and their sour relationship with the Central Committee,[63] *The Conclusions* assigned much of the responsibility for this situation to Azef, who had continuously incited the combatants against the Central Committee, instigating their desire for autonomy for his own purposes. The judges also blamed the Central Committee members, who for years were quite satisfied to exercise their authority over the *boeviki* exclusively via Azef, who was assumed to have been beyond suspicion. In the meantime, *The Conclusions* found, the sect-like Combat Organization had turned into a non-party assassination squad, largely extraneous to the movement's general interests and practices. It lived a life of its own—and was being manipulated by Azef. Indirectly, therefore, the blame for the Azef affair lay on the very nature of the SR practice of terrorism.

Among other findings of the Investigatory-Judiciary Committee was the startling revelation that Azef had enjoyed almost unlimited access to the SR funds. Considering that back in 1906, the Central Committee's expenditures were as high as one thousand rubles a day (allocations for the combat operations excluded),[64] the spy had the chance to avail himself of bulky resources. Since the terrorists were always given as much money from the party as they claimed they needed for the combat work, even at the expense of other PSR activity, Azef could use the immense sums allocated directly to the Combat Organization even more freely than he utilized the Central Committee funds. Owing to their unconditional trust, none of the SR leaders or terrorists ever bothered to inquire into the details of how thousands of rubles were spent,[65] even after Azef took twenty thousand rubles from the party's treasury after his retirement from the Combat Organization in late 1906— allegedly for the purpose of creating a "flying machine" to be used for assassinations.[66] During the period prior to his exposure, he stole a few thousand francs directly from the treasury of the Combat Organization and also from PSR funds that were to be used for a secret party venture abroad.[67] No wonder he was able to astonish a comrade by accidently pulling a five-hundred-ruble bill out of his pocket, justifying the casual handling of such a large sum by the requirements of his revolutionary work.[68]

Many SRs criticized the denigrating *Conclusions of the Investigatory-Judiciary Committee*, protesting that its findings were presented in the form of an act of indictment and simultaneously a verdict issued to the party's leadership.[69] The terrorists were particularly outraged by the judges' opinion on their activities: "What petty-vengeful rancor breathes through every line directed against the Combat Organization," wrote Petr Karpovich upon having read *The Conclusions;* "I feel sorry for the dead" fighters. Among other *boeviki*, Karpovich believed that the entire purpose of the Committee's effort was to shift the blame from the central PSR leadership to the combatants, who did not receive fair treatment by the judges.[70] "In all truth," he wrote, "I don't know who is better: such freedom fighters as Bakh and Co. or the Russian autocracy. Because at least the gendarmes interrogate, and these gentlemen ... spit at people in print, confident that they will remain tongue-tied."[71] Still, while cherishing little hope of gaining attention, the combatants, under Boris Savinkov's guidance, issued a collective protest against the direct accusations maligning their honor, as well as against various "insinuations, omissions, misinterpretations, discrepancies, and factual errors" found in *The Conclusions*.[72]

Members of the Investigatory-Judicial Committee defended their arguments and turned against those of their comrades who had had something to contribute to the investigation process but had failed to do so. The judges claimed that when the Committee had issued its appeal to the revolutionaries, asking their fellow SRs to volunteer with their testimonies about the Azef affair, there was only one volunteer—Mikhail Bakai.[73] The party members were either skeptical about the Committee's competence to "achieve positive results" through its investigation or simply did not want to think about Azef and disturb old wounds.[74] Thus, even though the Committee members were likely not entirely immune to preconception and intolerance with regard to the kind of terrorism perpetrated by the Combat Organization, Karpovich's complaints about having been unfairly judged seemed out of place, especially in light of his later statements about how glad he was not to have collaborated with the Committee's ignominious efforts to establish the truth about Azef's role in the party.[75]

The Conclusions suggests that the central SR leadership was but a bunch of impractical romantics duped by an unscrupulous scoundrel who on occasion did not even bother to make wholehearted efforts to fool them. In fact, Azef was almost frank with them at times. During a conversation with the gullible Savinkov on the eve of Azef's exposure, the spy, while feigning offended integrity, suddenly burst out with a laugh: "Of course you are not so bright as to make it impossible to deceive you" he said, referring to the entire SR leadership.[76] Many of the ordinary party members now began to view their hapless leaders exactly this way, accusing them of naïveté bordering on irresponsibility.

Overwhelmed by the desire to shift the blame from the movement as a whole to a few individuals in command, the rank-and-file SRs refused to consider that in their relationship with Azef, the party generals seemed to have been victims of an archetypal psychological pitfall. For years the SR leaders—idealistic and impractical as they were[77]—thankfully acknowledged a quality in Azef that they lacked—his unparalleled pragmatism. At the same time they projected certain traits onto him that many of them had in abundance—integrity, devotion to the cause, personal morality, and the like. Such behavior is typical of a romantic, who "creates for himself a situation of imaginary circumstances and imaginary people—in his own image."[78]

Be that as it may, the entire SR Central Committee submitted a collective resignation and demanded a trial by the revolutionary court, which was to determine the extent of their misconduct in neglecting to investigate earlier charges against Azef.[79] The party's leadership was replaced, but the Paris Group of Socialist Revolutionaries, whose members' antagonism to the Central Committee had become a tradition, now argued that a painful conclusion ought to be drawn from this devastating experience with treason: "The attempt to forge a large centralized party had failed." Its concentrated leadership "had been a plaything in the hands of the police," and lest a bitter lesson be lost, the PSR must undergo total reorganization and decentralization. Various party institutions would have to be rebuilt on a federative basis, but, most importantly, terrorism operations should be entrusted to autonomous squads, so that in case of police infiltration, the consequences "would be immeasurably less than if all terrorist activity were concentrated in the hands of one or several members of the Central Committee."[80] Some radicals "demanded that terrorism be abandoned until the time when it could be practiced in a way that would restore its former lustre"; others even went as far as to doubt the expediency of political assassination as an SR tactic.[81]

The oppositionists in Paris, as well as their like-minded comrades in other SR centers in Russia and abroad, were destined always to remain in the minority, and the party survived as a centralized political formation; nonetheless, the Azef affair had a calamitous effect on the numerous satellite PSR groups throughout the Russian Empire. It first caused shock and then profound pessimism among the provincial and regional cadres. According to Vladimir Zenzinov, who visited the peripheral party centers throughout Russia in the spring of 1909, the local SRs were in "utter disarray:" "What was most intolerable was the sense of psychological breakdown that one felt during the meetings with the comrades and that shaped the atmosphere in which they were compelled to work. One had the clear feeling that the Azef's treason had plowed a deep furrow in the psychology of the party workers. This was one of the most painful feelings that I have ever experienced during the course of my work for society."[82]

"The transition from 'Azef-comrade' to 'Azef-provocateur' took away all strength and will not only from members of the Central Committee [and from the rank-and-file SRs], but also from . . . the *boeviki*."[83] Now that they could no longer avoid dealing with their belated realization of Azef's perfidy, the terrorists not only blamed themselves for their former credulity but—going to the other extreme—also began distrusting one another, for the most part solely as a reaction to the painful lesson that no one was beyond suspicion.[84] For a while, rumors circulated in the émigré circles that party leader Viktor Chernov was a secret security employee; some even reported that he had been seen in a police uniform.[85] Relationships among "the chosen few" consequently quickly deteriorated, contributing to the increased demoralization in their ranks. Although several champions of immediate retribution in Burtsev's entourage offered their services for carrying out Azef's execution,[86] most of the disheartened terrorists did not even have the tenacity to start looking for the exposed spy in order to avenge themselves and the idea of terror.[87] Daunted and guilt-ridden, many of them went into deep depression; some even committed suicide, as did Lapina, who killed herself in the spring of 1909, feeling that everything that was important to her—the revolutionary struggle, the self-sacrifice of the terrorists, the honor of the party—"was defiled and turned into a sinister farce."[88]

Azef became an idée fixe; the leading SR Vladimir Zenzinov remembered, "In the course of a year there was not a day or night when I did not think about him.[89] A growing number of radicals, unable to overcome their despondency amidst the all-pervading "bacchanalia of helplessness" and dejection, began to resign from the PSR and desert the revolutionary movement altogether.[90] Thus Karpovich wrote to Savinkov, depicting himself as a "man with an ailing soul" and declaring, "I have left the revolution finally and irreversibly; now this is entirely clear to me."[91] Savinkov himself appeared mortified and depleted, giving the air of an enervated man disillusioned with everything. He no longer impressed his acquaintances with his vigor and spirit, admitting to "having been broken by the Azef affair."[92] Perhaps his greatest difficulty was to reconcile himself with the growing antiterrorist sentiments in wide party circles, rendering meaningless his career as a combatant and leaving him with no sense of the future.

Faced with general demoralization in the party and seeking to salvage the combatants' image (as well as their own) by assuring the rank-and-file comrades that Azef and terrorism were not synonymous, the SR leaders confirmed that "the heroes, who went for the acts, did so not for Azef but for the revolutionary cause," just as terror as a party policy "was not inspired by Azef."[93] Savinkov was particularly enthusiastic in embracing this line of thought. Justifying—as much to himself as to the other *boeviki*—the need to resist self-pity, misanthropy, and impotence by adopting a proper prospective on Azef's role, the terrorist leader contended that "2000 years ago Judas had turned Jesus over to the Romans, yet Christianity is still flourishing. Would anyone dare say that the sins of Judas had desecrated the doctrine of love? . . . Had Azef's sins desecrated the doctrine of socialism? . . . It was not Azef who had created terrorism, nor was it he who had breathed life into it. Therefore he could not destroy the temple which his hands had not erected." Savinkov's reasoning was hardly flawless, but it was permeated by genuine ardor. Azef, he concluded, "had sold his soul, yet terrorism remained as pure as it had always been."[94]

This method of intellectual exhilaration allowed Savinkov to develop relatively quickly a somewhat more optimistic outlook on the future. Consumed by the urge to prove that "the sacred terror" contained an inherent value and meaning, and that no government spy could make it inexpedient, Savinkov proceeded from words to deeds. In January 1909, almost immediately after Azef's escape, a meeting took place between members of the Central Committee and a group of *boeviki* under Savinkov's leadership. Their goal was to resurrect central terror. Despite Savinkov's reputation as a "revolutionary cavalier-guard," heretic, and troublemaker in the party, he was the natural nominee as the head of the new combat squad, given all his previous terrorist experience.[95] Fighting his gloom and apathy, he forced himself to make an attempt to "invigorate the purity of terrorism" and to prove that just as Azef had not created central terror, so was his unmasking ineffectual in abrogating the concept and its appropriateness as a revolutionary tactic.[96]

The attempt was a foreordained fiasco, however—and not only because the public was much less receptive to the idea of political violence in the aftermath of the flawed 1905–1907 revolutionary experience, particularly after the disgraceful Azef episode. Nor were Savinkov's efforts doomed only as a consequence of the terrorists' demoralization and spy mania. Equally critical was the SR Central Committee's refusal to provide the new combat union with regular funds now that they were under attack for having overemphasized terrorism earlier. Due to insufficient resources, Savinkov could not reactivate the "flying appa-ratus" project that the engineer S. I. Bukhalo had inaugurated on Azef's initiative. Savinkov also cherished plans to use a submarine boat for the purpose of regicide, but its estimated cost of eighty thousand rubles rendered the enterprise equally unfeasible.[97]

The terrorists' esprit de corps further suffered when two members of the Combat Organization fell under suspicion of collaboration with the Okhrana.[98] But the final stroke of misfortune for the terrorist cause came when *boevik* I. P. Kiriukhin, who had been admitted to the Com-bat Organization on Stepan Sletov's recommendation, was exposed as a police informer in September 1910. There seemed to be no retreat from treachery in the terrorist world, and in December, Savinkov con-fessed in a letter to his close friend Mariia Prokof'eva: "I have tried for two years, but nothing came out of my labors—worse, much worse, than nothing."[99] Savinkov was now "tormented by conscience for all misfortunes and failures," of which he felt he alone was guilty.[100] A few of his disillusioned comrades,[101] still technically under his command yet convinced that all of their efforts would be to no avail, were also ready to give up. Thus, in early 1911 they voted to formalize what was already a reality, acknowledging that the Combat Organization had fallen apart and no longer existed.[102]

The shock of Azef's exposure had been so tremendous that the PSR never fully recovered from the terrible moral wound that had been inflict-ed upon it; "ultimately, it was the entire party that paid the true price."[103] Still, perhaps it was an exaggeration when the newspaper *Revoliut-sionnaia mysl' (Revolutionary Thought)* pronounced its crestfallen con-clusion: "The PSR does not exist as an organization. . . . It has been defeated and [has] fallen apart."[104]

The widespread disintegration of the SR forces was not caused by the Azef affair alone. All revolutionary organizations within Russia sustained grave losses after the terrorist wave of 1905–1907 had ebbed, owing in part to the implacable measures of Prime Minister Stolypin. Although the party eventually re-emerged from the Azef crisis and remained a leading participant in Russian domestic politics, the wound of 1909 proved mortal for the PSR Combat Organization and drasti-cally reduced the terrorist activities of the radical camp as a whole. Even the most adamant supporters of radicalism admitted that when the slime of Azef's perfidy "stained the immaculate reputation of ter-ror, it died out."[105] Many revolutionaries regarded the Azef period ("Azefshchina") as a tragedy for their cause,[106] and some argued that the spy's exposure "was not only the Party's affair, but also the affair of Russian society and Russian history."[107] With terror discredited as a revolutionary tool and the *boeviki* demoralized, never again did the PSR or any other antigovernment organization in the Russian Empire possess adequate strength to mount an assassination campaign against the leading statesmen of autocratic Russia—politically motivated murders that might have had quite a profound impact on the course of Russian history.[108]

7

Fugitive Incognito

Shame and honor are like a dress: the more worn out they are, the more recklessly you treat them.
—Lucius Apuleius[1]

Until October 1908, Liubov' Menkina had no idea that her husband was under suspicion of being a traitor to the PSR. Over the years she had continued to be undiscerning and was obsequious to the point of being stifled and suppressed. She had long tried her hardest to win if not Azef's love, at least his favor and companionship by going along with his every wish. All of her efforts were in vain: just as earlier in their relationship, her goodwill was invariably crushed by her husband's callous rudeness. "I would wait for him for a whole year," she later griped. "He would return . . . and be bored. This irritated me so that in the last years I could not even talk to him. . . . I often came to the conclusion that I had to run away, simply escape at any cost, that, in any case, I could not live like this any longer; I suffocated." She also complained that people close to her had no idea about her true life. "Everyone thought I was a very happy person. . . . No one knew that I went through hell when we were together."[2]

Azef totally controlled the family finances by keeping his wife entirely uninformed about money matters.[3] Whereas his secret annual police salary had by the end of his service reached the prodigious figure of fourteen thousand rubles,[4] she operated on a more than limited budget, compatible with her husband's small party income of 125 rubles a month.[5] Menkina "was in debt and constantly borrowing money," and Azef "always reproved" her for spending too much, "rebuking for every penny used, while spending a great deal on himself."[6] He kept his personal expenditures secret, of course; in the eyes of most radicals Azef remained an ascetic who "lived on bread and herring" and, while traveling, declined the help of porters in order not to waste party funds.[7]

Menkina was perpetually preoccupied with household chores, struggling to take care of her two boys and barely making a living by keeping a small hat-manufacturing shop.[8] This down-to-earth routine, devoid of any revolutionary excitement, clearly plagued her. She even wrote to Savinkov, declaring her wish to be useful to the cause and not "to remain without anything to do."[9] However—and understandably so—Azef did not want his wife to be involved in the antigovernment struggle, justifying his attitude by pointing to the more immediate needs of the family. He preferred not even to discuss general party business with Menkina; "I never found out anything from him," she would later complain.[10]

Azef said nothing to Liubov' about Burtsev's accusations, and when she at last realized the extent of the problem, she was shocked and confused. Still, far from suspecting him of double dealing, she resolved to suffer side by side with her husband. Perhaps she was even a bit grateful for the situation, which she could use as an opportunity to prove her loyalty and empathy and thus win his appreciation and maybe even a little kindness from him. Menkina did not mince words when expressing her indignation with the SR leaders, who in her eyes turned out to be unfair and ungrateful to the man who had done so much for the party.[11]

Menkina's unfailing support notwithstanding, all through the fall of 1908 Azef was plagued by anxiety and tormented by doubts about his wife. What if, he thought, she in fact suspected him of collaboration with the secret police and for reasons yet unclear—perhaps to gather more evidence?—decided to feign devotion for the time being? What if the PSR leaders chose her as a striking hand of the revolutionary nemesis? What if she, convinced of his guilt, would take justice into her own hands? Even the undiscerning Liubov' could see that Azef did not trust her. He jumped up in terror when she approached him; he woke up in the middle of the night to question her as to why she was not sleeping; he constantly, though unsuccessfully, sought to cajole her into going to Switzerland to restore her health and nerves.[12] Her life turned into "real torment" not only as a result of the humiliating investigation by the Central Committee, but also because of her husband's way of handling the crisis. His slow agony caused him to forfeit all inner restraints, and he obviously used Liubov' as a target when expunging his anxiety with outbursts of flagrant rudeness—outbursts that she excused with the servility of a battered woman.[13]

Menkina was not present at the 5 January 1909 interrogation at the Azefs' apartment in Paris. She understood that she was to remain in another room for the entire interview, at the end of which her husband received a final warning from his three former comrades. Shortly before two o'clock in the morning, they were gone, and Liubov' came into Azef's study to find her flustered husband frantically destroying his papers, packing a small suitcase, and mumbling something about the need to go away at once—only for three days, he told his gullible wife—to gather additional "proof of his innocence before 'they' killed him."

At half past three, the couple left their apartment, the mise-en-scène of the spy's defeat. Azef was in such a great hurry that he neglected to cast a last look at his sleeping children, although he did remember to take three hundred francs from the total sum of five hundred found in the house.[14] Liubov'—despondent, confused, yet still trusting and obedient—took her husband to the railroad station to board the first train to Germany.[15] His behavior was "really detestable, terribly repulsive"; he seemed hysterical, "looking awfully pitiful." This was a rare moment when fear, Azef's fateful, yet ordinarily repressed companion, was allowed to reign supreme. Under the circumstances, fear seemed to be a legitimate response rather than a psychological anomaly; therefore, it required no displacement, inundating his personality and momentarily baring Azef's terror-stricken self.

As he stumbled heavily along snowy boulevards, where street lamps illuminated the murky silhouettes of occasional passers-by, Azef everywhere saw specters of SRs hungry for murder. He could only think of putting himself out of danger, repeating again and again that if he noticed revolutionaries trailing him on the train, he would call the police. At the North Station, he gruffly pushed his wife away when she tried to kiss him good-bye: "Now the situation is such that we may skip this part!"[16] Finally, by five o'clock in the morning he was gone, having left Menkina a forwarding address in Vienna. His actual point of destination, however, was the Saxon town of Friedrichsdorf; there, Azef joined a female friend who had been waiting for him in Germany since the beginning of November and who was to remain his devoted companion until the end of his life.[17]

The German-born Frau Hedwig Klöpfer, better known as "*la belle Hedy de Hero*," was a star singer at the St. Petersburg music hall Aquarium; she also performed in the famed Moscow nightclub Iar, as well as in Kharkov's Tivoli, Kiev's Chateau-de-fleurs, and other cabarets. "Oh, my name was widely known in Russia then" she would boast years later.[18] Azef had met Hedy in one of these "first-class" restaurants in late 1907. Her looks were very much to his taste: a "sumptuous woman,"[19] tall, with long white arms and a large sensuous mouth. She wore gaudy clothes, excessive makeup and, in all honesty, was rather tawdry, crass, and unmistakably provincial. In the same year, she followed

Azef abroad as his mistress, evidently quite content and comfortable with the role Azef designated for her. Most probably Hedy was genuinely attached to her lover, which hardly made her relationship with "her only bunny" and her dear "daddy" less corny.[20]

Even though Hedy had to know that Azef led a life of danger, he found it unsuitable to inform her about the technicalities of his secret occupation. Burtsev was correct in considering Azef to be "a man on his own" *(odinochka)*,[21] who always preferred to get by alone, without accomplices. He never trusted anyone, and perhaps the secret of his success was that he relied on no personal or emotional allegiances that could ruin his strictly calculated game. Be that as it may, to maintain a relationship with Azef, Hedy had to prove herself a patient and devoted concubine—something that she evidently managed to do prior to his exposure. On the ominous night of 5–6 January 1909, the haunted spy deemed it best to unite his fate with hers. Without yet knowing it, Liubov' Menkina had lost her husband to another woman; she was never to see him again.[22]

A day after his escape, Azef wrote a letter addressed to the three revolutionaries who had come to his apartment to demand his confession. The letter is exemplary in demonstrating profound indignation, anger, and resentment toward "the gentlemen" who dared to "stain his honor together with the police." Vowing never to forgive the insult and the moral wound caused by all the "dirt that was thrown" at him, Azef promised to take his own measures to clear his impeccable reputation as a revolutionary who had been a key figure in the party from the day of its formation. "This behavior of yours will, of course, be evaluated by history," he intimated in a half-concealed threat to his judges.[23]

The party leaders responded with the publication of an official SR statement about Azef's police connections. Menkina, suddenly finding herself at the center of an ugly scandal, was on the verge of suicide. She could no longer have any illusions about her husband's innocence. Moreover, she faced another personal predicament: numerous revolutionaries abroad simply refused to believe that she had nothing to do with Azef's exploits. How could she not know anything about the person she had lived with for so many years? Was it at all likely that she had never asked Azef about the source of his income, which was many times larger than what he received from the party? Many SRs thus came to a firm conclusion: "It was impossible, absolutely impossible for his wife not to suspect" anything.[24] Certain revolutionaries went as far as to accuse Menkina directly of collaborating with Azef in his treacherous activities and declared that they "could not stand her."[25] When they accidentally encountered her, some comrades simply ran away, "as if she were blighted by a contagious illness," causing her to sink into despair. "It is so sad when I have to defend myself and say that I am an honest person," she complained.[26]

Shaken as much by her comrades' suspicions as by the exposure of her husband's covert life, Menkina repeatedly appealed to the SR Investigatory-Judiciary Committee, demanding formal questioning and an unambiguous resolution concerning her own involvement in Azef's exploits.[27] Having subjected her to thorough interrogation, the SR leaders and Burtsev remained fully confident that this naive and imperceptive woman had been completely oblivious of her husband's police activities. Although Menkina had been guilty of having helped Azef in his escape,[28] which from the point of view of party discipline was an obnoxious impropriety, many of Azef's former comrades and their families supported her at this time of public humiliation and intense personal drama. Of all the SRs, Viktor Chernov was particularly congenial, always treating her with understanding and kindness,[29] though cherishing little hope of compensating for her tragedy. Chernov's stepdaughter Olga remembers that she, her twin-sister, and their older brother remained friends with Azef's children, Leonid and Valentin, amidst the general estrangement and rancor surrounding the boys' family following their father's disgrace.[30]

"Could it be true that fourteen years together did not reveal my soul to you?"[31] Azef wrote to his wife soon after his exposure when he had become a villain par excellence in the eyes of the public at large. "It is such an absurdity to think that everything on my part was a joker's performance.... Is it possible always to play" a role?[32] It was indeed possible for Azef to go on with his pretenses for so long, but while the revolutionaries belatedly blamed themselves for their naïveté in taking the government spy for a comrade, another facet of the Azef phenomenon always remained a riddle. No one was able to fathom how he could appear a perfect husband and father, a man of family values and puritanical principles for many years, during which he had multiple secret romantic liaisons and incidental affairs without eliciting the slightest doubt about his probity either from his wife or from his party colleagues.

Azef occasionally had revealed "incredible cynicism, at least as far as relations between the sexes were concerned. This question was apparently of special interest to him," some of his fellow radicals testified. They were appalled by the manifest vulgarity—quite uncommon in the revolutionary milieu—he exhibited when he raised "tacky and extremely boorish issues," notwithstanding the presence of "thoroughly proper and well-esteemed ladies"[33] Yet, knowing how to touch people with an impetuous show of emotions, Azef skillfully built the image of a man who had a secret sentimental side to his uncouth personality. Thus, Savinkov remembered Azef's "meticulously concealed tenderness toward his family,"[34] especially toward his two boys, whom he seemed to have relished. Many a time he would be seen happily playing on the floor with them, apparently enjoying the roughhousing as much as they did. "With a maudlin face," Azef would take out of his pocket a postcard with his little son's scribbles and, as if somehow relevant, show it to a female comrade who had treated him somewhat cautiously on their first encounter. Without overdoing his act, he managed to create a touching scene, especially effective because the female SR knew Azef as a hardened terrorist, involved in bloody combat work.[35]

According to Menkina, Azef "always harassed others by accusing them of lying,"[36] thus indirectly enhancing his own image as a meticulously honest and righteous person. His wife's behavior, too, contributed a great deal to Azef's success in building this reputation. Although she would subsequently claim to have reconciled herself to the fact she had virtually no private life,[37] for years she tried to conceal any marriage problems—be they conflicts, disappointments, or resentment—even from herself. She did this not only to preserve peace in the family, but to protect Azef's status as a virtuous man and an exemplary husband and father. Largely owing to Azef's wife, the SRs retained this image until his exposure.[38]

Several comrades had seen Azef in questionable places of entertainment and in the company of women of debatable reputation.[39] But they explained his behavior as having purely conspiratorial motives. The image that Azef projected with the help of his wife left the SRs with little choice but to accept his excuses at face value. For example, one comrade happened to run into Azef as the spy was leaving a boutique, having just purchased a pearl necklace worth several thousand rubles. Contrary to Azef's assurances, the gift was obviously not intended for his simple and undemanding wife, whom the acquaintance had trouble imagining ever wearing such exquisite jewelry. And yet, although greatly surprised, the revolutionary did not doubt Azef's words for a moment.[40] Similarly, the SRs believed him when, having been spotted in the front row of a theater, he justified this extravagance by the necessity to meet an actress who was allegedly in a position to provide him important information about a certain state dignitary.[41] The radicals immediately assumed that the dignitary was a potential target of the Combat Organization. The revolutionaries saw no need to inform Azef's trusting wife about these characteristic episodes. In situations that in anyone else's case might have been interpreted as incompatible with a revolutionary lifestyle and ethics, Azef was exempt from any judgment or criticism. By the end of his PSR career the austere "genius of terror" had even given up smoking and would not allow himself even a drop of alcohol.[42]

After his escape, while hiding from the radicals in the pleasant company of his mistress, Azef wrote to Menkina several times, pleading for understanding and claiming that he had only served the revolution. As he could not provide any proof of his innocence or a plausible explanation of his by now evident dealings with the secret police, Azef sought to impress his wife and elicit pity through melodramatic prattle and sheer demagoguery. He pledged his love for the "precious children," while also swearing "by their lives . . . by everything that is dear and sacred" to him, that, although he "had made an unforgivable mistake a long time ago," he always had behaved as a sincere revolutionary, was unconditionally devoted to the cause, and had never pursued his own interests.[43] With equal cynicism he complained of loneliness and insisted on his undying love for Liubov' herself: "Believe me, dear and precious one, that my letter contains only the truth. . . . Of course, it is only a dream that you can be mine. . . . What a tragedy!" Still, while feigning the greatest drama of his life, Azef could not help being quite down-to-earth and pragmatic as usual. Although he claimed that money had always interested him "less than anything else," and that he "never paid any attention to it," the overemotional tone of his letters to Menkina did not prevent him from discussing financial matters in substantial detail.[44]

In a letter of 13 April 1909, he complained that, except for a note written three months earlier, he had not received anything from her. He begged Liubov' to write for the sake of the children.[45] In May, he wrote to Menkina again, assuring his wife that he had the highest regard for her opinion about him.[46] Responding to his pleas, she finally decided to break the silence, but the tone of her brief message left no doubt that Azef was no longer in a position to manipulate her: she categorically refused to have any dealings with him and, without concealing her contempt, demanded an immediate divorce.

Realizing that their relationship had entered a new phase, Azef easily cast away most of his pretended feelings for Liubov'. He was far from heartbroken by her desire to break off their marriage, yet he insisted on his right to take part in their children's upbringing. Not that he had generous plans to support them financially, however: he offered Liubov' detailed monetary and other practical advice, but the lump sum he intended to give his wife to support their children was very modest—roughly the 1,500 rubles owed to him by his insurance company.[47] At the time his own fortune was substantial enough to allow him to travel extensively and to entertain himself and Hedy in lavish spas and casinos, where he could afford to lose up to seventy-five thousand francs a year without ruining his financial security.[48]

Voltaire once said that people never feel guilty as a result of those deeds that have become habit to them.[49] Without a doubt that was true of Azef, for whom lying was second nature, a routine occupation that invalidated the very awareness of his own untruthfulness. Perhaps, he even believed in his own sincerity while writing to his wife, and when, absorbed by self-pity, he lamented the crudeness of people's desires to intensify his sufferings after his exposure: "I am not a scoundrel," and "there was nothing low in my soul."[50] He certainly did not experience any qualms or pangs of guilt when he purposely lied, as he did when he wrote to his wife about his love, devotion, and respect for her—"the dearest person" in the world—at a time when he was living happily with his mistress.[51]

Throughout his life, ethical issues seemed to be largely irrelevant for Azef, who never had to work hard to avoid the discomfort and burden of conscience. The only values he took seriously were the practical—especially the material—costs and benefits of his behavior. Words, for instance, were immaterial and could be easily spared since they did not cost anything. When writing to his mistress a few years later, Azef did not hesitate to choose expressions almost identical to the ones he had used when writing to his wife: "You are the only person who is close to me, so close that I do not feel any difference between us; I do not know where you end and where I begin—and this is not a mere phrase."[52]

True to her resolution, Liubov' never answered Azef's letters again, even after he wrote to her in November 1910, two years after the outbreak of the scandal, promising to appear before a revolutionary tribunal. His only conditions were that his former party comrades be present at the trial and that they give their word not to use it as a chance to capture him. In exchange for an opportunity to "restore and purify his honor" from all defamation and falsifications associated with his name, Azef pledged to accept any decision of the judges, even if it was to be a death sentence.[53] It is entirely implausible that Azef had indeed planned to appear before the revolutionary court; it is equally unlikely that he missed his family and created an excuse to be in touch with his wife again. Most probably, he merely wanted to "test the ground," to find out how the SRs felt about him after all the passions associated with the affair had finally tapered off.

His circumspection was quite germane, since many of his former party comrades never gave up their intention to implement the death sentence the SRs had issued. As part of their efforts to establish his whereabouts, they even pored over Azef's letters to his wife and sought her assistance in setting up a trap for her ex-husband. Thus, in May 1909, after learning that she had received a letter from Azef, Chernov approached Menkina with a proposition. She ought to try to convince him to meet her in person—an opportunity the SRs would use to do away with him. Menkina complied; yet, for reasons still unclear, the SRs decided not to pursue this plan.[54] Most likely, yielding to practical considerations, they contained their emotions for the sake of averting a new wave of questionable publicity associated with what would be the final—and fatal—act of the Azef drama.

As it was, long after the SRs had publicly announced Azef's treason, an array of rumors, hearsay, and most incredible stories continued to circulate in Russia and abroad about both the tsarist government and the revolutionaries. The most popular accounts gave all sorts of thrilling details about the phenomenal exploits of the master spy. Azef quickly became a truly mythological figure, a villain par excellence, responsible for a motley of heinous crimes, which—many presumed—did not cease even after his exposure. In 1913, for example, two Russian newspapers reported a fantastic discovery: having won the trust of the Austrian government by providing it certain useful services, Azef was said to have been appointed as the head of a special section of secret military intelligence along the entire Russo-Austrian border.[55] Those who volunteered their contributions to the Azef saga fed the insatiable public demand for colorful and grandiose tales, "threatening to drown the reality in a sea of lies and fabrications."[56]

Every aspect of Azef's life suddenly turned into an unsolved controversy, including his physical appearance. Some described him as being above average in height and others remembered him to have been "surely no more than five feet six inches" and weighing at least a hundred and eighty pounds.[57] Azef's entire unsightly physical image—his markedly "stubby neck and broad, flabby face, greasy skin and heavy stare," exacerbated by a sulky expression and bourgeois air—was almost instantly transformed upon his exposure into a symbol of his moral wickedness.

In the past, when they first met Azef, some SRs were astonished by his unattractiveness and his unpleasant demeanor to the point of fear. Yet the general opinion prevailed: "Behind this coarse, unappealing appearance there hides the lofty, selfless soul of a revolutionary. Just look at his sad, pensive eyes."[58] Mikhail Gots, mild to a fault, sympathized with Azef's lifelong predicament: "What a pity God granted such an appearance to the man that at the first glance everyone thinks that he is straight from the police." Gots insisted, however, that in order to see Azef's true face, "one had to look closely at his eyes and especially at his child-like smile."[59] When Azef once broke down and cried inconsolably while listening to a revolutionary relate his brutal experiences as a hard-labor convict, Gots turned to the person sitting next to him and said: "Just look how kind and responsive he is at bottom."[60]

Tears always came easily to Azef, and so he had the good fortune to be able to leave the impression of a temperamental behemoth, outwardly coarse, yet deeply sensitive and gentle.[61] Azef's comrades occasionally heard him toss in bed, loudly moaning and sobbing in his sleep. Overwhelmed with pity, they liked to explain this by Azef's "acute conscience." "He is tortured not only by his thoughts about the dead comrades [and] about Jews murdered during pogroms, but also by compassion toward victims of terrorist assassinations. That is what does not let him sleep," whispered Azef's party colleagues to one another, giving themselves up to feelings of warmth toward the ugly giant who had inadvertently exposed his sensitivity.[62]

This tendency to absolve any and all of Azef's repulsive physical traits disappeared once he had been confirmed a police agent. Many revolutionaries suddenly remembered that Azef's hands were "feminine, flaccid, and mushy"; that to shake his hand was "like touching a cold frog or a slug"; that his eyes—"snake-like," according to one description—were always moving, as if looking for something; and that he had a caustic smile, his fat lips often showing "scornful displeasure and hostility."[63] People competed in their descriptions of the vividly repugnant details of his appearance and even invented much that they wished to add to the fast-growing list of Azef's negative physical traits. "He always chewed something. He had enormous jaws...."[64] A female radical, who had seen Azef once in 1898, subsequently affirmed that "she would have been afraid to meet him not only at night in the darkness of a forest, but also in broad daylight on the crowded Nevskii."[65] And many of his former comrades confirmed in unison that "the monster" had "an appearance of a professional killer."[66]

In their later commentaries on Azef's ethics, those who had met him before his rise in the PSR hierarchy often stressed that from his youth Azef's demeanor had betrayed a morally depraved and lascivious person. Yet, given Azef's quick admittance to the revolutionary milieu, it is difficult to believe that during his student years in Germany, his young friends had known enough about his sexual promiscuity and lewdness to have nicknamed him "a filthy beast."[67] Like so many of Azef's other acquaintances, these contemporaries simply could not disengage themselves from the shocking revelation of 1909 and substituted their thoroughly inimical subsequent judgment of the police spy for what must have been a milder initial impression.

Prior to Azef's exposure many people had commented on how gently and delicately he acted toward his comrades, exhibiting a sensitive and loving heart, how he was concerned with their private needs and problems, how he comforted them, how generously he gave his help. Sometimes, after a heated debate, Azef would abruptly get up and, as if seized by sudden emotion, approach one of his opponents, kiss him on the forehead, and leave the room at once. Many revolutionaries were quite impressed by such temperamental outbursts.[68] They also remembered how he suffered when his terrorist associates were leaving for Russia, perhaps to die there while preparing political assassinations.[69] According to many witnesses, he would treat such a comrade particularly warmly and even tenderly, hugging and kissing the departing friend and saying farewell "in a distinctive fatherly way."[70] Azef would greet a comrade who had just returned from a dangerous mission in much the same way; he "always liked to kiss," one SR recalled.[71]

Azef's exposure called for a new portrait of him, and after the announcement of his treason, revolutionaries rushed to recollect different impressions. "Azef was rude in his dealings with people; he liked to ridicule and belittle those who for some reason were not to his liking."[72] Azef was said to have had a particularly unpleasant propensity for discovering a ludicrous side to a person and would then "mock him endlessly."[73] Andrei Argunov claimed that various people disliked Azef for his characteristically impertinent manner.[74]

Boris Savinkov concurred. Azef was "sometimes quite stern and abrupt in his relations with the comrades," most of whom "did not love him—only respected and valued him extremely." Other radicals noted that Azef was incapable of keeping up a soulful conversation—a genuine emotional flaw, at least in the Russian culture, in which "spilling out one's soul" has always been held in high regard and considered part of the national tradition of unbreakable friendship. Savinkov claimed that he had had misgivings about Azef's character even prior to his exposure and admitted that he had always sought to justify to himself Azef's "great crudeness" and obvious deficiency in "emotional movement"; he simply "explained certain odd traits in Azef's personality by a lack of empathy in his heart and by harshness, which, within boundaries, was a duty" of the terrorist leader.[75]

Stepan Sletov, whose disagreements with Azef over tactical issues evolved into a bitter personal conflict, declared soon after the spy's exposure: "I must say that I have had doubts about Azef even before. Of course, I never thought that he was a police agent ... but I regarded him as a man who in certain circumstances may simply free himself from scruples."[76] Certainly a number of Azef's acquaintances instinctively felt that he was "an alien" among the intelligentsia in the revolutionary milieu.[77] In truth, however, most retrospective comments about him must be taken with a grain of salt, since they catered to the assumption that the historical image of the two-faced villain ought to remain utterly repulsive.

Many of those who published corny and sensational articles about the master spy resorted to baseless speculations or outright fabrications for lack of a true explanation for his motives. One such fabrication was "an open letter from Azef" that appeared on 21 July 1909, in the Polish journal *Volne slowo (Free Word)*. This fictitious letter aimed to reveal to the public the inner motives of the cryptic man about whom all Europe was talking:

> I laugh at you all. . . . I laugh loudly at both [sides]—your police order and your revolutionary disorder . . . I am filled with pride . . . since for many years I led all of you by the nose. . . . I am a greater artist and actor than Shakespeare. I wrote a play in life, not with a pen, but with bloody wounds, the bones of those blown to pieces, and with the mortal agony of the hanged. . . . I was the one who assigned the parts, who directed this infernal play, unprecedented in history. . . . In me, there were two souls, equally powerful, cunning, evil [and] bloodthirsty. . . . They fought one another on the surface, but inside me, they loved each other, inciting people to fraternal warfare, creating and killing executioners, while I always listened dispassionately to the surge of blood under my feet. . . . But why did I do all this? Because I hate all of you equally. . . . I hate and despise . . . both sides because they did not understand how I played with them and because they did their killing on my order. . . . So, the strength of Judas thrived in me. No, Judas is a child compared to me. . . . I reigned over *hundreds* of people, . . . I sent hundreds to the gallows. . . . And I received 100,000 rubles [for it]. . . . I know that satanical deeds such as mine ought to be done for the sake of the idea, for sheer pleasure. But I, in addition, received money for them. . . . I do not believe in God. . . . I do not believe in anything but Satan, who is incarnated in me. . . . And if I could be born into this world again, I would wish to be nobody else but Azef. . . . Beware: you will not hear me hissing like a snake, but my venom will poison your life for a long time yet.[78]

There is little doubt that Azef had nothing to do with this letter. His own style and manner of expression were entirely incompatible with these high-flown outpourings. Even chronologically, this letter could hardly be his. It was allegedly written by Azef right after the May 1909 note to his wife, in which he pleaded his innocence. More important, it came before his November 1910 letter to Menkina, in which he again expressed his desire to clear his name of all false charges.[79]

Many people treated such journalistic garbage seriously nonetheless, especially because it reflected the then fashionable propensity for playing with various forms of the supernatural, including worship of the devil—a tendency often cited as an inseparable part of Silver Age culture. Some of those who subsequently wrote about Azef borrowed much psychological nonsense from this letter attributed to him. Thus, a reporter of the British *Evening News* claimed to have interviewed the exposed spy in an obscure London hotel where he was hiding. According to this journalist, Azef quickly confessed his identity and proudly presented himself as a two-faced Janus and a criminal:

> [I] have not lost my principles . . . because I have never had any. As a revolutionary and as a spy I had magnificent accomplishment. Since 1897 I played a great role in the revolution and am responsible for all assassinations. Sipiagin, Plehve, the Grand Duke Sergei, Ignat'ev, Launnits, Gapon, and others died as a result of my efforts. As a police spy I . . . proved myself to be equally proficient. . . . If I killed many people, I also saved the lives of many others, the Tsar, for example.

Having unloaded his soul about his own accomplishments, Azef allegedly had a few things to reveal about his former police superiors, particularly Rachkovskii, a man "distinguished by a total lack of compassion." According to Azef's purported interviewer, Rachkovskii even used his own daughter in a assassination act provoked by the master spy. The innocent girl became a terrorist and ended up in Siberia, where, of course, she died of consumption—quite as dictated by the canon of post-Dostoyevskian popular literature.[80] There was hardly a word of truth in this or in similar tales about him, but the public, avid readers of the most improbable stories about his exploits, was willing to believe anything.

After Azef's exposure, various newspapers claimed—primarily as a result of Burtsev's incorrect insinuations—that the Russian secret police were on the lookout for their former agent. His photographs allegedly had been sent to every investigation office for the purpose of his immediate arrest.[81] "Where is Azeff?" the *New York Times* lead story of 7 February 1909 began under a large headline: "POLICE AND REDS BOTH HUNT AZEFF." "Who will get to him first? Who will be his executioner, the Russian police or the revolutionists[?]. These questions all Europe is asking."[82] Around the same time, newspapers reported that Azef had been arrested in Finland and transferred to St. Petersburg.[83] Reporters also periodically announced that the radicals had finally managed to get their hands on Azef, who was said to have been smuggled out of

Russia and kept in a secret revolutionary hideout in western Europe.[84] On numerous occasions newspapers around the world declared that Azef had been killed.[85]

Azef was said to have been seen almost simultaneously in St. Petersburg, Tsarskoe Selo, Simferopol, the French Riviera, Vienna, London, Finland, Switzerland, and Uruguay; he was allegedly "spotted" on the streets of New York; rumors had it that he had escaped to Japan.[86] At least twice the SRs initiated a hunt for Azef, based on new information about his whereabouts; both times their efforts led to no results. Several people nearly got into trouble with the revolutionaries due to their physical resemblance to the exposed spy.

As time went on, efforts to track Azef down became sluggish and gradually died out entirely.[87] Chernov later claimed—perhaps not entirely sincerely—that at one point the SRs spotted him in Berlin, but did nothing. "He had been rendered harmless, and we did not want to take revenge."[88] In any case, Azef never again confronted his adversaries from the revolutionary camp, except for one person—Vladimir Burtsev, the man who had caused his downfall, and with whom the former spy had a secret meeting in the Frankfurt café Bristol on 15 August 1912.

Burtsev, the sole beneficiary of the Azef affair, clearly enjoyed the fact that newspapers and magazines around the globe were publishing pictures of him next to multiple photographs and drawings of the "fallen angel of the revolution." Burtsev's unexpected popularity drove him to reinforce his prestige by making a career out of spy hunting. He worked himself up into "a mania of exposing provocateurs"[89] and turned into an object of mockery on the pages of popular satirical journals, which treated him as a frenzied psychopath.[90] Disregarding the ridicule, he worked to create a public image for himself as a revolutionary detective—a new Allen Pinkerton, entangled in a struggle against the crimes of the Okhrana.

At the peak of his triumph, he had acquired enormous funds from several radical organizations and also from numerous private admirers. Burtsev was said to have bragged about having received as much as one hundred thousand francs from various sponsors for the purpose of fighting provocation.[91] Equipped with financial and moral support, Burtsev organized a special "revolutionary detective bureau" in Paris that provided investigation services to all radical organizations seeking to ferret out government informers in their ranks. In 1912 one of Burtsev's clients was none other than Lenin, who feared there were a number of spies in the Social Democratic movement.[92] The revolutionary detective agency used information provided—usually for substantial pay—by renegade Okhrana officers such as Mikhail Bakai and Leonid

Men'shchikov. It succeeded in exposing a number of secret police agents in various antigovernment parties, including Zinaida Zhuchenko, Ia. Zhitomirskii, and I. Kaplinskii, but in the process ruined the reputations of several people whom Burtsev wrongly accused of spying or of otherwise collaborating with government authorities.[93]

Burtsev always remained "an independent warrior" *(vol'nyi strelok)*, or one who was said to belong to "the O. F. H.—'One-for-Himself' party,"[94] which soon led him into new altercations with the leaders of the PSR. For one thing, they objected to Burtsev's methods of obtaining compromising evidence against suspected government informers. Burtsev would enter into stealthy financial deals with most untrustworthy and shady characters who had records of previous association with the police world.[95] Even more objectionable from the viewpoint of revolutionary ethics was his reliance on information provided by secret employees who had infiltrated the Okhrana offices, in accordance with specific sanctions from their local radical cells, for the purpose of weeding out spies from their ranks.[96]

The SR leaders probably found even more intolerable Burtsev's attempt to monopolize all efforts to eliminate government spies from the radical milieu. He insisted on his exclusive rights to deal with former police officials and to use their information for spy-hunting purposes.[97] Outraged by Burtsev's behavior, leading SRs did not mince words in accusing him of "pursuing sensation and self-advertising *('samoreklama')*."[98] Whether or not this was the case—and here it appears that the SRs might have had a point[99]—Burtsev's popularity and prestige both in Russia and abroad remained for years nearly as high as they had been right after his disclosure of Azef's police ties. Thousands of people considered him a genius of detection, who provided invaluable services for the liberation movement, both by disabling police agents and by exposing the crimes of the tsarist regime.[100] In seeking to set up a rendezvous with Azef in 1912, Burtsev claimed to be pursuing one goal: to obtain supplementary compromising information about secret police operations—information that he would then employ as "additional ammunition for the political war he was then waging against the Tsarist government," and particularly against the Okhrana, which, in his view, was "the pillar of Russian reaction."[101]

Burtsev had expressed his opinion on the matter a year earlier on the pages of *Budushchee:*

> Azef has something to tell about the Stolypins, the Gerasimovs, the Truseviches, and right now he has no need to cover for them. He has no interest ... in preserving their secrets. ... Like any paid agent,

deep down he was always contemptuous of those he served. . . . Now, when the Okhrana no longer has any need for Azef, after all the revelations, and he is out of the Police Department, there is nothing more natural for him than to expose the Gerasimovs whom he has always despised. . . . The Azef period, the Azef affair are gone for good. Now begins the exposure of the Azefs, and in this period Azef's revelations . . . could play an important role.[102]

Burtsev's conjectures proved to be flawed. Whatever took place between him and Azef in Frankfurt—and we only have Burtsev's vague and uninformative statements[103]—Azef obviously did not despise his official superiors enough to provide the revolutionary detective with any sensational evidence about their crimes. The exposed spy agreed to an appointment with Burtsev only in the hope of convincing the radicals that although he had indeed provided the Okhrana with information, his services to the revolution exculpated him fully. Since he no longer had any connection with the Russian police,[104] the comrades should suspend their hunt for him and, in essence, cast him to the four winds.

Burtsev's secret rendezvous with Azef ruined his own relations with the SRs beyond any chance of reconciliation. The SRs had long been annoyed by Burtsev's continued public references to Azef as "a revolutionary resorting to ignoble means" to achieve his goals. Such behavior prompted them to curtail their collaboration with Burtsev.[105] His secret meeting with Azef was the last straw.

Burtsev had shared information on Azef's whereabouts with the revolutionaries, but when they sought to locate the spy, the address turned out to be incorrect. Assuming logically that Azef would never have consented to meet Burtsev unless he was certain the encounter would be confidential, the SRs felt duped and furious. They refused to listen to Burtsev's explanations about some sort of misunderstanding and believed that he had purposely kept Azef's hiding place a secret from them, despite their previous agreement to share information. "When they hear Burtsev's name," the revolutionary Evgenii Kolosov wrote to his wife, "they tremble with rage. They threaten—God knows what. They accuse him of having deliberately given them an incorrect address. . . ." This was "a shameless fraud," the SRs declared; Burtsev has "led us astray. . . . We will never forgive him."[106]

What probably vexed the SRs the most was not Burtsev's deception—they could have given him the benefit of the doubt and refused to blame him absolutely for their failure to track down Azef. Rather, they were more upset that Burtsev was stirring a new wave of discussions about Azef. By this time most PSR leaders wished only to proceed with party life and to relegate the Azef affair to oblivion. There was no chance that they would use the knowledge of his whereabouts to initiate judicial procedures or sanction his killing without a trial. Either choice would mean a new wave of unfavorable publicity for the PSR—exactly what its leaders wished to avoid.[107] In fact, it is unclear what they would have done if they had tracked Azef down using Burtsev's information.[108] Now, even more zealously than before, the SRs accused Burtsev of resorting to unethical means solely in order to resurrect his prestige as a spy hunter and fighter against provocation. His apologies notwithstanding, the SRs never accepted the legitimacy of what Burtsev imagined would be the long-term political consequences of his efforts to implant "the issue of provocation in the public consciousness." They perceived his campaign—merely a tactical tool he employed for the wider purpose of combating the tsarist regime—to be contrary to the interests of their party.[109] The SRs could not admit even to themselves that the immediate corporate interests of their movement were more dear to them than intangible revolutionary principles. And those of them who did acknowledge that Burtsev's motives might be a bit more upstanding than the banal desire to make the headlines still rejected his investigation activities, believing that they would inflict spiritual damage upon the revolution. Vera Figner was particularly outspoken in a letter to Burtsev:

> What a dark figure you represent, Vladimir Lvovich! You stride about like the angel of death bearing the scythe, even worse than the angel of death . . . like a black phantom with long, twisted fingers . . . and your dark shadow falls everywhere that you turn. From your black bag you pull out broadsheets on informers, on betrayal, on the selling of one's soul, on crimes against comradeship, against friendship, against everything that man holds precious and sacred. You sow suspicion, you sow loathing and contempt for people, for mankind in general. . . . You are a terrible person, you are dark-souled. . . . You want endless exposures, condemnations, proofs, judgements. Is that creative work? Is it for that that we must call on those who still remain in the ranks? . . . No, it is better that you remain alone. Go by yourself and complain about the cool indifference [accompanying you] in this murderous campaign.[110]

As for Azef, having finally escaped both the revolutionaries and the Okhrana, he lived with Hedy in accordance with his perfectly philistine perception of deluxe life. He continued to gamble and now invested in stocks, bought diamonds and silver table sets for his mistress, travelled with her to Italy, Greece, Egypt, and various seashore spas—in other words, he lived in accordance with his idea of what it meant to "live happily."[111] He presented himself everywhere as a businessman, and since "he always had the ability to comport himself with a certain aplomb, with self-assurance," flaunting confidence, and even subduing others by his poised demeanor,[112] people took him for a straitlaced entrepreneur.

Amazingly, it appears that Azef—quite out of character—was not overly concerned that the radicals might track him down. For example, he never chose to disguise himself with makeup or even to wear dark glasses. "He had always utterly despised the revolutionaries' abilities as technicians of combat," and soon after his exposure wrote to Gerasimov, "If they have the wits to employ the assistance of private detectives, then perhaps they would have a chance of trailing me."[113] Just in case, however, Azef had several Russian passports for foreign travel that he used at different times. In 1910 he lived in Berlin, in Dessau, and in Vienna under the name Lipchenko.[114] Most frequently, however, Azef presented himself as the merchant Alexander Neumayer, using identity papers he had received from the Russian authorities in St. Petersburg in 1909.[115]

Eventually, he and Hedy settled permanently in Berlin, renting an apartment at 21 Luitpoldstrasse. They decorated it with expensive furniture, silverware, and various other luxury items that Hedy loved so much—all costing Azef a small fortune of one hundred thousand German marks.[116] According to one estimate, his wealth at the time was about a million French francs, although he might in fact have been wealthier, largely due to the funds he had expropriated from the SR treasury.[117] At this stage of his life the exposed spy might have decided that it was time to count returns and reimburse himself for many years of turmoil and apprehension. He was no longer of use to the police, hardly a threat to the revolutionaries, and consequently of only a limited interest to either side, though clearly more prosperous than anyone might have imagined him to be. Why not finally enjoy the tranquil retirement of a respectable bourgeois?

This thought certainly does not imply that after his retirement from secret police service Azef suddenly found relief from his lifelong struggle with fear, which appears to be the determinant of his troubled personality. His chronic anxiety seems to have been free-floating and could not fade away as a result of an altered situation, since the dread was unconditional, rather than contingent on external circumstances. During the last and strictly private period of his life Azef must have experienced the recurrent attacks of panic that were always a characteristic of his psychic state. Azef regularly failed to recognize fear as a thing in itself, not necessarily rooted in external causes: during the years he was hiding from the revolutionaries these sudden paroxysms of horror were entirely justifiable and subject to facile rationalization. In fact, after his exposure, the spy's psychological situation was more favorable than it had ever been before: subconsciously he no longer needed to seek out and plunge himself in an objectively menacing situation for the sake of validating his fears as well-founded and reasonable. Paradoxically, by reminding himself occasionally that he had been sentenced to death, Azef from then on could live in peace with his frightened self without being actively compelled to forge truly threatening circumstances, as he had done in the past. In other words, as part of his perpetual struggle for inner balance and stability, he no longer had to damage himself.[118]

The outbreak of the First World War abruptly ruined the paradise on earth, bringing new hard times for Azef and his mistress. Azef's entire savings were invested in Russian bonds; in August 1914 they lost all value in Germany.[119] Financial bankruptcy and the prospects of a return to poverty must have initially plunged Azef into despair, but, in his typical manner, he resurfaced quickly and set out to exploit the new economic situation that was developing in Germany as a result of the war. The brainchild of his efforts was a small corset-manufacturing boutique. Unlike most of his contemporaries, who engaged in wishful thinking about the brevity of the hostilities, he, perspicacious as usual, understood that the Great European War would be a prolonged conflict that would cause increasing hardship for the civilian population. Consequently, he calculated that "ladies, subjected to a deficient diet, would continue to lose weight." He, therefore, proceeded to manufacture corsets of smaller sizes,[120] wrecking the competition and quickly improving his shattered financial resources.

Then came a new blow from where it could hardly have been expected. On 12 June 1915, Azef was arrested by the imperial police in Berlin and thrown into the Moabit prison as a dangerous subversive, anarchist, and terrorist. The former police agent was hardly in a position to appreciate the irony of this incident. Rather, he strove to use his notoriety as an exposed spy to regain his freedom by convincing the German authorities that his association with the revolutionaries was but a mandatory requirement of his previous secret employment. Yet, the Germans did not yield: instead of making an effort to investigate the unusual case, they evidently deemed it simpler to keep the suspicious citizen of a belligerent country in prison at least for the duration of the military hostilities. Thus, Azef found himself in confinement for the second time in his life, but under the onerous conditions of the war he could be certain that his predicament was bound to be far worse than his incidental imprisonment in April 1906.

Indeed, "from June until Christmas 1915, he was kept in solitary confinement in a cold, damp cell, without the right to receive visitors, to converse with other prisoners, or to read the daily newspapers." He would have had trouble reading anyway since his cell was dark until October, when he was finally provided with a gas lamp. Fighting the debilitating monotony of the prison routine in order "to maintain his mental balance, Azef kept his mind and spirit alive by refreshing his knowledge of electronics, by studying Italian and translating from the French, by corresponding with Hedy and by scanning books received from her."[121] His readings were a potpourri of fashionable titles and authors, ranging from Cesare Lombroso to M. P. Artsybashev. Azef particularly enjoyed the latter's *Sanin,* a novel of woeful quality that had made the best-seller list in 1907 amd was an early example of quasi-pornographic Russian literature. Azef was unaccustomed to systematic reading of any sort, however, and he spent much of his time in prison studying the intricacies of the stock exchange.[122]

In his letters to Hedy, written in flawed German, verbose, and whiny, he pursued several dominant themes, focusing particularly on his personal afflictions: "I was struck by misfortune, the greatest misfortune which can befall an innocent person, and which can only be compared with Dreyfus's adversity."[123] Evidently, Azef's prison experience did not cause him to reevaluate his past; he never exhibited signs of grief or remorse for anything he had done during his life—or with his life, filled with betrayals of those who had trusted him. The catch here was that he did not consider himself a traitor or a criminal. He had been a police agent, serving the government; why should he have worried about people who happened to consider him a comrade?

Azef's letters to his mistress were also permeated with complaints about loneliness. "All around me is a desert," he wrote to Hedy, professing his great love for her, "the only one interested" in him. In return, Azef manifested his empathy with Hedy's gloom and offered advice on how to conduct their business, which suffered major setbacks in his absence.[124] Yet, while attempting to solve the strictly practical problems his mistress was experiencing, in his intentionally poignant letters to Hedy, Azef persistently returned to an entirely new and unexpected theme in his correspondence—the question of faith, and particularly Christian ethics and values.

In the manner of an accomplished missionary, Azef instructed Hedy: "Do not despise people; do not hate them; do not ridicule them too much—have compassion for them." He also reported: "After a prayer I am usually cheerful and feel good and strong in my soul. Even suffering sometimes strengthens me. Yes, even in suffering there is happiness, closeness to God. In our troubled and hasty times, a person usually forgets the best part in him, and only suffering gives him bliss, forces him to view himself from a better side, and to approach God submissively."[125]

His newly acquired religious conviction was vague, superficial, and highly questionable; it was an amalgam of poorly assimilated Russian Orthodox concepts (possibly snatched randomly from Dostoyevsky) and fickle philosophical truisms, reiterated thoughtlessly and barely intelligibly. His was the religion of a philistine, who happened to find himself in an insurmountable situation with no functional resolution and little choice but to appeal to the supernatural in the hope of magic. Azef always remained a pragmatist, however, immune to the slightest appreciation for spirituality or mysticism; to the end he was a down-to-earth man, a perfect utilitarian, deaf to the slightest vibration on the metaphysical plane of existence. Indeed, there could not have been anything less likely than communion between Azef and the transcendental.[126]

Azef was not altogether sincere in complaining about being neglected by everyone but Hedy, for she was not his only correspondent at the time. While in prison, he received letters from another female acquaintance, a mysterious lady from Moscow, who sometimes called herself Mariia, but preferred to go by Magdalene. Apparently she took the name seriously, for her numerous love letters and postcards reveal not only her boundless and all-consuming infatuation with Azef, but also the fact that in her eyes he was a being equal in magnitude to Christ himself: "My love for You is a religious ecstasy, a sacred paroxysm," she confessed. Imploring Azef to come to Moscow, she promised to welcome him "as Maria Magdalene welcomed Christ." "I will wash Your feet and dry them with my hair. . . ."[127]

"I am thinking of you," Mariia kept writing to Azef in a frenzy. "Where are you? Do you remember me? You are so tender, so wonderful, so lovable, so mysterious, so kind, so cruel; are you so mean to forget? I weep because of love for you. . . . How I want to kiss your dear hands, my darling, my love!"[128] She called him "a genius, a great person;" she praised his "wonderfully beautiful face. . . . "[129] There is hardly a doubt that this woman—no longer young and apparently afflicted by her fading health and looks—was a psychopath. Her correspondence reveals unmistakable signs of emotional instability and hysteria when judged by handwriting alone—not to mention the style and content.

She would begin her letters (she sometimes wrote several a day) in a calm tone, and her handwriting would be rather small, accurate, discernible, reflecting a relatively collected state. As she proceeded, however, Mariia would gradually lose control of herself and of what she was trying to express, and her handwriting would deteriorate visibly: the letters would become larger, sloppier, more tilted and distorted; spaces between characters and lines would also increase and become lopsided, contributing to the increasingly hysterical tone of the composition, which by the end would be almost maniacal. Suddenly she would begin an overwrought digression about seeing "angels" or being followed by some shady characters and "the Masons."[130] Then she would turn on Azef and accuse him of such things as ruining her financially, subjecting her to extreme poverty and hunger, and humiliating her morally. She even went as far as to accuse him of being the cause of her son's death: "You destroyed my life; you slaughtered my poor baby; and you led his tormented, suffering mother to sin. His blood is on you and your children." She threatened to leave him and to betray him as he had betrayed his comrades; she also repeatedly warned him that she was very close to suicide.[131] "I am not some cheap blackmailer . . . I never demanded anything from you, not . . . even what *belonged to me*." But "you don't let me live." "I am not a thing," and "I cry, I weep," but "if you loved me a little, you would not wish me to cry. . . ."[132] Mariia would write to Azef this way and then in her next day's letter contradict her lamentations with long and teary apologies for "the slander" against him, admitting that she alone was to blame for everything and calling herself "his slave" who adored him no end.[133]

We will probably never know how Azef responded to these hysterical appeals, although Mariia did refer to his letters, showing "traces of his precious tears," in which Azef allegedly pledged his devotion to her and claimed that he wished no other reward for years of suffering than her love.[134] Indeed, we will most likely never be sure whether Azef in fact had an affair with Magdalene, although their correspondence did exist, and hence their relationship was not merely a product of her troubled consciousness. Otherwise, it would have been impossible to explain how Mariia could come to know about Azef's illness, of which she claimed to have learned from his letter to her.[135] Nor would it be clear how she managed to find out Azef's address not only in the Moabit prison, but—more precisely—at the prison hospital. It is certain, in any case, that the former spy admitted to Hedy that in prison he received packages containing dried flowers, tea, delicacies, and books from an obscure female sympathizer in Moscow, whose motives for turning Azef into the target of her charity were allegedly a mystery to him.[136] He never said a word to his mistress about his sizable collection of love letters from Mariia.

In the meantime, Hedy was despondent about the strictly practical realities of wartime survival. Her financial situation was exigent. The corset shop went out of business, and she was forced to sell her jewelry and other valuables—vestiges of the luxuriant past—and support herself with the little money that remained from the proceeds.

Things soon went from bad to worse. Hedy had no choice but to resort to food rations at the communal dining room, selflessly sacrificing her weekly share of butter and cheese for her "unfortunate beloved," who in April 1916 had been taken to the prison hospital, Lazarett des Zellengefängnisses, on account of his rapidly deteriorating health.[137]

Suffering from fatigue and agonizing back pain, Azef spent twenty months in the clinic's solitary confinement. Having customarily pampered himself, he did not have the willpower to engage in physical exercise, for which he always had distaste; instead, he grew increasingly lethargic, slept most of the time, and got up from his bed only to write a whiny letter to his sympathetic and indulgent mistress. As could be expected, his health problems intensified. His heart gave him trouble, and by October 1916 he "had lost more than thirty pounds and could not walk without losing his breath. He had struck bottom." Azef was now apathetic to everything except the one thought that kept him going: "the expectation of peace, and with it, of release."[138]

In February 1917 mass disturbances in St. Petersburg swiftly evolved into a full-fledged revolution, eventually overthrowing the government of Nicholas II and terminating the country's imperial order. Azef was not swept off his feet by the momentous political developments in Russia; he was still preoccupied exclusively with his personal ordeal, which was not resolved by the immediate cessation of hostilities on the eastern front, since the newly formed Provisional Government had declared its loyalty to the Allied cause and insisted on fighting for total victory. On the other hand, "when Lenin's Bolsheviks took power in November under the banner of 'Peace, Land, and Bread', Azef knew that his own liberation was near." Indeed, having begun the Brest-Litovsk peace negotiations, the Soviets and the Germans signed a temporary armistice, which, among other things, included a clause about the release of civilian prisoners. Azef was one of the earliest beneficiaries; just before Christmas, he regained his freedom after two and a half years in confinement.[139]

All he wanted now was to leave Germany, which had turned out to be so inhospitable, and move to the neutral Switzerland, but at the time of his release, his health was still poor. The most troubling ailment was acute kidney inflammation; during the next three months the pain intensified, and in April 1918, Azef was placed in the Westend Hospital. His case was hopeless, and the doctors predicted a fatal outcome within a month. Indeed, his condition deteriorated quickly, and on 24 April 1918, Azef died at the age of forty-nine.[140] Two days later, the grief-stricken Hedy buried him at their neighborhood cemetery in Wilmersdorf. His gravestone had no inscription, only the cemetery number 446.

"There are so many Russians here now," Hedy explained. "Somebody could read [the inscription], remember the old days, cause troubles. It is better this way."[141]

At Azef's funeral the devoted Hedy was the only mourner, but in Moscow Magdalene kept writing frantic love letters addressed to him at the Moabit prison hospital; she did not find out about his death for several more months.[142] Nor did the radicals learn of the fate of the man who had been responsible for so much damage to their cause. For all practical purposes, they had given up their attempts to establish his whereabouts even before the outbreak of the First World War; the 1917 revolution and the catastrophic civil war in Russia relegated the Azef affair to the annals of the past. Not until 1925 did the participants of the 1909 drama—scattered all over the world by the tumultuous political events in their home country—find out about the master spy's death in Berlin seven years earlier.[143]

Epilogue

Among the numerous human vices . . . cowardice, no doubt, is one of the most terrible. . . . No, philosopher, I object: it is the most terrible vice.
—Mikhail Bulgakov, *The Master and Margarita*[1]

The Azef affair remained in history as a classic case study of the criminal nature of the tsarist regime, which hinged on villainy for its very existence.[2] Petr Stolypin's Duma speech was drowned in an avalanche of antigovernment rhetoric, and, very much in accordance with the radicals' intentions, in the eyes of posterity the scandal served only as "the definitive exposé of the 'Russian system of provocation,' which was roundly condemned by writers and political figures throughout the West. It served to reinforce the image of the tsar's government as a barbaric, police-ridden autocracy, and gave even the Kaiser's regime cause to congratulate itself on its relative liberalism."[3]

A reevaluation of the practical aspects of Azef's career, however, suggests that much of the inaccuracy in the traditional conception of his role is largely a result of misleading terminology, particularly the term "provocation." As first noted by Stolypin in 1909, the words "provocation" and "provocateur" were frequently misemployed in revolutionary rhetoric, and in dealing with questions of police infiltration of the radical camp, subsequent scholarship tended to adopt the language of the radicals without modification. Thus, Boris Nicolaevsky, among many others, used the words "agent" and "provocateur" interchangeably in referring to a police spy, just as Vladimir Burtsev and the SRs had previously done.[4]

The employment of secret informers was a regular police procedure in many European countries, such as France, Germany and Austria, long before it became a standard political safety measure in tsarist Russia. There, according to a rough estimate, in the period from the end of the 1870s to the collapse of the tsarist regime in 1917, at least ten thousand spies provided services to security organs throughout the empire.[5] Given the dubious nature of their occupation, it is little wonder that some of these characters were less than saintly in their ethical standards and could not flaunt virtuous private lives.[6] A number of high-ranking government officials acknowledged that from the point of view of strict juridical formality, police spies in underground organizations might technically be considered criminals due to the very fact of their belonging to illegal societies. At the same time, no one involved in political investigation ever doubted the absolute expediency of sending a spy into the heart of a revolutionary organization for the purpose of thwarting its subversive plans.[7]

Indeed, years of experience in the struggle against the insurgents had convinced the Okhrana personnel that "the only truly reliable means of procuring information" about the radical camp was "internal surveillance."[8] According to Aleksandr Gerasimov, "in order to throw some light upon a certain [secret] society, it is essential that an agent be quite at home there, otherwise it is impossible to find out anything";[9] to direct the political police without such agents is "like doing without eyes."[10] And Mikhail Trusevich, a one-time director of the Police Department, declared even more categorically that "it is either one or the other: either the regime has to renounce its existence, or it must accept the only measures available" to defend itself by using secret informers among the terrorists.[11]

Still, the authorities were equally conscious of the fact that police informants among the radicals inevitably faced the risk of turning into criminal provocateurs. The two categories of government-paid agents in the revolutionary camp were separated "by quite a narrow line," which was "very easy to cross." The security personnel therefore were explicitly warned that "the ability not to cross this line is the key to the art of successful political investigation."[12] Police spies within revolutionary organizations were expressly forbidden "under any circumstances to engage in so-called 'provocation,' i.e., to initiate criminal acts and to prompt others— those who play secondary roles in this activity—to become responsible for the deeds." Although required to remain thoroughly embroiled in the radical affairs in order to maintain their positions in the underground world, the agents were advised to shun participation in the most perilous extremist ventures.[13] Given this official attitude, to pronounce Azef a criminal, guilty of illegal machinations, the government had first to determine whether he had indeed incited acts of political violence.

Evidence suggests that Azef was not engaged in provoking or inciting of any kind. Following the orders of his police superiors, he did present himself as a partisan of terrorist methods as early as his affiliation with emigré radicals and his period of service as an agent in the Northern Union of the Socialist Revolutionaries. Yet, the spy never instigated its members to combat practices; according to the Union's leader Andrei Argunov, Azef knew that terrorism was already "becoming central to the movement"—something that was naturally a primary concern of the authorities. In conjunction with his police duties, he therefore professed bogus enthusiasm for political violence, doing so not to provoke it, however, but merely to create a suitable image for himself and to demonstrate to the radicals that his place was indeed among them.[14]

Similarly, the SR Judicial-Investigatory Committee on the Azef affair declared erroneous any source stating that Azef had introduced terror as the SR party's tactic.[15] He held no responsibility for establishing the Combat Organization; nor did he demonstrate any desire to enter it,[16] much less an ambition to become its leader. When, following the 1903 arrest of Grigorii Gershuni, Azef nevertheless found himself increasingly immersed in the central terrorist operations of the PSR—coincidentally at the insistence of both the revolutionaries and his police superiors—he never attempted to draw anyone into the Combat Organization.[17] On the contrary, according to his former comrades, he exhibited a definite proclivity to discourage applicants. Most Combat Organization members, including its major figures—Boris Savinkov, Egor Sazonov, Ivan Kaliaev, Aleksei Pokotilov, Maximilian Shveitser, and Dora Brilliant—joined the terrorist group without any inducement from Azef, who played no role in their decision to engage themselves in combat work.[18]

Nor did the master spy initiate any specific terrorist attacks, and although eager to demonstrate his role as a provocateur, the SR leaders admitted that the PSR Central Committee, not Azef, had always selected the targets of the terrorist campaign, guided—as its members declared with revolutionary fervor—by "the voice of the people."[19] General policy with regard to the Combat Organization's terrorist ventures was thus beyond Azef's personal prerogative. Among the rest of the PSR leadership, Mikhail Gots in particular made it his business to monitor the party's central terror; in essence, "not one enterprise was undertaken without Gots' approval, sanction, or knowledge."[20]

Even so, while pretending to operate in accordance with the main party line—something that any secret informer would do if he wished to remain useful to his employers—on every convenient occasion Azef sought to persuade the Central Committee to curtail or to end its terrorist policy. He pursued this course following the promulgation of constitutional rule in Russia in October 1905. Moreover, when the SRs resolved to revive terrorist activity in the summer of 1906, after the dissolution of the First Duma, they acted against Azef's recommendations.[21] Having been offered the leadership of the Combat Organization, he did his best to convince the party leaders of the necessity "to discontinue terror entirely."[22] Only after his efforts failed, did Azef accept—on explicit orders from his police superiors—his new position, intending to fight the Combat Organization from within.[23]

By seeking pretexts that would enable him to leave the Combat Organization, Azef aspired to sabotage the SR central terror still further, and at least once, in late fall of 1906, this tactic proved successful. Finally, pursuing the same objective of moderating the PSR's radical course, Azef "drew the party toward agreement with the moderately liberal groups,"[24] lending additional weight to the argument that he received the label of *agent provocateur* quite inappropriately. This book has sought to modify this inaccurate label, which is still prevalent and has at its core the PSR leaders' desire to discredit the tsarist regime.

The study has also contended that it would be improper to accept the revolutionaries' initial explanations for the tsarist authorities' alleged support of political violence. The government, according to the radicals, sponsored terrorist acts as a means of "resolving" internal personal intrigues. Azef was said to have been employed by his police chiefs in order to stage assassinations of their political rivals. There is no basis whatsoever to consider as anything but pure fiction the story that the jealous interior minister, Plehve, initiated the murder of Governor Bogdanovich. Equally unconvincing is the trendy argument that Aleksei Lopukhin deliberately tolerated Plehve's assassination because Count Witte, chairman of the Council of Ministers, had "asked him to do so."[25] Nor is there any validity in the persistent charges—taken at face value by some historians[26]—that Azef conspired with Petr Rachkovskii, who allegedly directed his agent's murderous game that resulted in the 1904 murder of Plehve—Rachkovskii's mortal enemy.[27] "I know beyond all doubt," Azef's police superior Leonid Rataev certified, that Rachkovskii "never had either direct or indirect contact with Azef and did not lay eyes on him until 8 August 1905 when, having applied for retirement, I introduced Azef to him and transferred him to . . . [Rachkovskii's] disposal."[28] Later, the PSR leaders acknowledged that the political assassinations were "not dictated by Azef's concerns or the concerns of those who stood behind him."[29] They based this assertion on the findings of the Judiciary Investigatory Committee, which concluded that it found no evidence to support "Burtsev's initial suggestion that Azef's participation in the party's terrorist activity, particularly the assassinations of Plehve and the Grand Duke Sergei . . . took place with the awareness and consent of the highest police officials. Presently Comrade Burtsev himself has renounced his claim."[30]

Indeed, soon after the initial wave of passion associated with the Azef affair had subsided, Burtsev denied that he had ever claimed that Azef had killed Plehve in collaboration with the Police Department, or that Gerasimov had plotted with his secret agent to assassinate the tsar and to stage other terrorist acts. Burtsev obviously contradicted his previous statements, including the charge that the head of the St. Petersburg Okhrana was a provocateur and a criminal.[31] Eventually, Burtsev summarized his opinion as follows: the tsarist authorities, although not compensating Azef directly for helping them to square accounts among themselves, knew and tolerated the fact that Azef carried out terrorist acts. According to him, it was as if the government was saying: "He is a useful person for us, we will utilize him. . . . And if he kills certain people, what is there to be done? It does not matter."[32] This study has demonstrated, however, that there is no validity even in the modified version of Burtsev's argument, just as there is no evidence to support another generally accepted charge against Azef—that the master spy was also a double agent.

Azef was not a terrorist or even a revolutionary when he offered his services to the Police Department,[33] and he began his career in the PSR when he was already a secret employee of the tsarist police. That Azef was not a double agent is equally evident from the fact that it was the Police Department which insisted on his closer ties with the newly formed PSR Combat Organization and its leader Gershuni after the assassination of Interior Minister Sipiagin in April 1902. After reviewing all the incriminating evidence against Azef following his escape, Savinkov repudiated any claims that his former terrorist colleague had ever in good faith championed the radicals' cause.[34] Burtsev also rejected categorically the possibility of Azef's "reincarnation" from a bona fide revolutionary into a government spy.[35] Thus, after 1909 when the radicals referred to Azef as Judas, emphasizing what they thought was his symbolic penchant for kissing, the analogy was as flippant as it was tempting, for Azef had never been a friend, a disciple, or a believer.

Certain contemporaries and later historians of the Azef affair insisted that he not only had instigated political assassination attempts, but was also responsible for their realization on those numerous occasions when he allegedly failed to notify his police superiors of the terrorists' plans. While being paid for his services in fighting state enemies, Azef was said to have been actively working for their success in combat undertakings when it suited his personal aims. According to this view, such behavior was primarily motivated by Azef's desire to enhance his reputation in revolutionary circles as an organizer of triumphal terrorist attacks, thus obstructing any suspicion of his double role. He also allegedly wanted to convince the Central Committee that the enormous funds transferred into the hands of the terrorists were not wasted—a strategy that gave him significant control over the finances of the Combat Organization and a great opportunity to make a personal profit.[36]

It is true that as a member of the Central Committee Azef was actively involved in laying out general guidelines for the terrorists and that later he outlined the details of the Combat Organization operations. It would be erroneous, however, to label him a double agent in the true sense of the term on this basis alone. Even some of the most ardent opponents of the government's position in the Azef affair acknowledged that it would be impossible "systematically to reveal political assassinations without taking part in them, *de facto* and *de jure*." No police agent who wished to penetrate a terrorist organization could reasonably avoid engaging himself personally in preparations for political assassinations if he hoped to present himself as a useful and trustworthy member of the conspiracy and yet retain his value for the government.[37] To be effective, any informer would be required to build his revolutionary reputation and credibility through active duty, and to hold that against him would be to pronounce espionage tantamount to political villainy. Logically, every successful spy could then be labeled a criminal, which would, of course, be a manifestly inaccurate designation.

Azef's role as a secret agent would not have been feasible unless he had acted precisely as he did on the police directive to establish himself at the center of the SR movement. But such an active participation in terrorist undertakings does warrant suspicions that the police spy could also have been a traitor to the government's cause and a state criminal. However, Azef could legitimately be considered a double agent only if there were evidence to support the fact that he had organized political assassinations without informing the police or without making serious efforts to prevent them by other means at his disposal. In attempting an objective evaluation of Azef's true role, this book has sought to assess the degree of his association with PSR terrorist activity during various periods. His reports to the police must be compared with his actual knowledge of the terrorists' affairs.

Rataev did not doubt that Azef was an unconditionally honest servant of the government in the initial decade of his police employment, from 1893 to the summer of 1902.[38] Having failed to find any evidence confirming his participation in the assassination attempts against Dmitrii Sipiagin, Konstantin Pobedonostsev, Prince Obolenskii, and others, even Burtsev and the SRs were never able to build a strong case for Azef's alleged double game in this early period of his police service. Similarly, every attempt by the revolutionaries to convince the public that Azef purposely allowed the 1903 attempt on N. M. Bogdanovich to take place appears to be unjustified, since all evidence suggests that he was not aware of the preparations, sanctioned by Grigorii Gershuni and planned in strict secrecy by local revolutionaries in Ufa.[39]

The next period of Azef's police career, from Gershuni's arrest in May 1903, to October 1905, when the party temporarily ceased its centrally organized terror, is much more difficult to reconstruct, primarily because there is little evidence to compare with the party-sanctioned testimonies of the SRs. While it cannot be denied that Azef's connections with the terrorists became significantly closer after Gershuni's imprisonment, it would be misleading to accept statements found in the SR sources at face value, since they deliberately exaggerated Azef's role among the *boeviki*. Savinkov was the true practical organizer of all the party's central terrorist operations from 1903 to 1905, while Azef functioned more as the Central Committee overseer in the Combat Organization. Despite his detached role, however, Azef demonstrated his extreme usefulness to the authorities following the arrest of Gershuni by thwarting several terrorist plots in the capitals and in such outlying areas as Irkutsk and Baku. According to official evidence, "All information from him, with rare exceptions, was outstanding in its precision, and the great significance of Azef's services . . . was beyond any doubt."[40]

At the same time, as early as 1903, Azef began to conceal some relatively important information about the radicals from his police superiors. As this study has sought to demonstrate, however, Azef's behavior from this point on ought to be explained by his growing fear of being compromised and exposed. He was forced to become increasingly cautious in dealing with the Russian authorities. Consequently, Azef does not emerge as a selfless enthusiast for the government's cause or as a courageous man, but it is not appropriate to convict him of serving two masters simply because he desired to prevent terrorist acts with minimal risk to himself. "A certain self-protective concealment was to be expected of such spies," and even Burtsev acknowledged that "as a general rule, no *provocateur* [read "police agent"] ever reports everything that he knows."[41] Azef's behavior thus does not immediately qualify him as a traitor, criminal, or a double agent, especially because his carefully selected information proved extremely valuable for the initial phases of police investigation.[42]

Sergei Zubatov accurately described Azef as "in the highest degree a prudent, almost cowardly, agent,"[43] who was often inclined to protect himself by not disclosing all the information at his disposal. According to this police official, Azef "passed over serious [information] in silence not out of sympathy toward the revolutionaries, but due to fear" of police actions that might have been harmful to him personally. "His position became increasingly dangerous as he moved up in the revolutionary hierarchy, and he kept silent more and more, limiting [his reports] to hints," which still, Zubatov admitted, could be understood, if only "after serious thinking and comparing."[44]

Azef invariably provided his superiors with enough clues to prevent terrorist acts, and he can hardly be blamed for every occasion in which the Police Department proved incapable of carrying out surveillance thoroughly enough to uncover political assassinations. It is useful to remember that the police force was undergoing reorganization in the years 1903–05, and was in a state of disarray. In the words of Rataev, it was "reminiscent of an army which has rearmed itself and trained its recruits under enemy fire."[45] The imperial security forces were "underarmed, poorly trained, and rent by internal squabbling. . . . [They] were in no position to control the mounting terrorist campaign."[46] The fact that the SRs succeeded in staging several central assassinations in this period of Azef's service can thus be largely attributed to the incompetence, inefficiency, and negligence of police investigation procedures, perhaps most clearly exemplified by the compelling fact that Gershuni, who was wanted throughout the empire, managed to stay in the capital for three days under his own name and passport prior to his accidental detention in Kiev.[47] Under such circumstances, if the secret agent is to be blamed at all, it could be only for overestimating the capabilities of the police, as well as his own ability to jeopardize the terrorists' plans. But the results of Azef's behavior speak for themselves. Despite their wish to portray Azef as a double agent, the revolutionaries admitted that whereas "many successful acts were unknown to Azef, . . . the grandiose plans under his leadership and participation fell through."[48]

The scarcity of sources does not allow for the clarification of all questions and doubts about Azef's activities during the five-month hiatus in his police employment. However, his two final years as an agent, from April 1906, when he again placed himself at the disposal of the St. Petersburg Okhrana, to May 1908, when he finally secured his long-desired retirement from police service, are adequately accounted for, and thus are the least problematic for evaluation. This was also the period when Azef, acting on Stolypin's explicit orders, became most actively involved in the terrorist affairs of the PSR, and, according to Gerasimov, turned out to be the government's "best agent," providing extremely valuable and detailed reports and rendering the Combat Organization powerless in every single one of its undertakings.[49] The information Azef supplied the police was truly essential, especially considering the fact that after he left the Combat Organization, "the rate of success in militant activity immediately improved."[50] That fact also clearly speaks against all claims that Azef was implicated in a double game during the final period of his police service.

The accusations against Azef often refer to the large number of terrorist attacks committed throughout the empire for which the Party of Socialist Revolutionaries claimed responsibility in the years 1906–07. His accusers attributed the primary role in all SR-perpetrated violence to him and sought to demonstrate that the party's terrorist success owed much to the fact that Azef concealed information from the police. According to Burtsev's public statements and the recollections of many other revolutionaries, Azef was almost omnipresent, and the authorities were unable to prevent political assassinations throughout Russia solely because he chose not to help them—for reasons of his own. After Azef's exposure, there was also a tendency to attribute every failure of the terrorists or every successful police action in the country to the presence of the master spy. For many he had acquired the reputation of a truly mythological being.[51]

Azef's role was far more modest, however. As he had warned Gerasimov, "he could be responsible only for the activities of the central Combat Organization, but not for all the smaller terrorist groups" of the PSR.[52] Indeed, it was dangerous for Azef to reveal excessive interest in the affairs of independent or local terrorist units, since such indiscreet inquisitiveness would surely have aroused suspicions against him. Therefore, Azef knew little about the smaller terrorist detachments, whether in St. Petersburg and Moscow or in the provinces. Only occasionally did he come across very general information pertaining to certain peripheral combat ventures because, according to the local radicals, "he gave no advice or directions; nor did he express any desire to find out the details about [their] organization."[53] Thus, when the SRs succeeded in killing Governor Shuvalov of Moscow, General Min, and Chief Military Prosecutor Pavlov, along with a number of other leading military and state figures, the high police officials held no grudge against Azef for not having notified them about these operations ahead of time. They obviously realized that it would be not only impossible but frankly imprudent for him to attempt to collect information on every terrorist plot. In fact, Gerasimov was explicit in permitting Azef not to endanger himself by getting entangled in the affairs of less important terrorist groups. Instead he urged him to concentrate his attention exclusively on the Combat Organization.[54]

Still, when he acquired information on independent combat groups, Azef readily reported their activities to his police superiors, provided these revelations would not lead to his exposure. For instance, he did inform Gerasimov of the whereabouts of a small, yet dangerous terrorist band, the Central Combat Detachment, led by Lev Zil'berberg, which was established after the Combat Organization broke up following Azef's and Savinkov's retirement in 1906. According to one *boevik,* "Ivan Nikolaevich [Azef] demonstrated special attention, was extremely concerned," and took very close to heart all the affairs of this new combat group; he involved himself in literally every detail of their operations, and the terrorists "approached him whenever they needed advice."[55] The consequences of Azef's particular commitment to this terrorist unit were predictable: Zil'berberg and several of his associates were captured, tried, and executed.[56]

According to Gerasimov, Azef's role in combating terrorism was truly historic:

> I categorically assert: if I had not had for an employee a man like Azef, who occupied a central position in the [SR] party, the political police, despite all their efforts, almost certainly would not have been able so successfully and so systematically to disrupt all of the terrorist undertakings. And it is difficult to imagine what would have happened with Russia if the terrorists in 1906–07 had accomplished two or three "central" terrorist acts.[57]

A number of police officials, including Azef's former chief, Rataev, who initially recognized the SRs' intent to ruin the government's reputation by proclaiming Azef an agent provocateur,[58] were subsequently overwhelmed by the avalanche of literature portraying Azef as a self-seeking traitor. Some of them eventually accepted the prevalent image of the spy as a double agent and even did their share in promoting it.[59] Thus, partly to justify his own behavior, Aleksei Lopukhin declared that in 1904 he had intended to bring Azef to trial for deceiving the police by denying his membership in the PSR. Lopukhin's assertion had nothing to do with reality, if only because Plehve had sanctioned Azef to penetrate the party's center and the Combat Organization as early as 1902, and any denial of his affiliation with the PSR was unthinkable.[60] In fact, in the summer of that year Azef complained to Zubatov that his position had "become somewhat dangerous" because he was "now playing a very active part among the revolutionaries."[61] There is no indication that prior to his train conversation with Burtsev, Lopukhin possessed any information about Azef as a traitor, a sinister criminal, or indeed anything other than a police informer. In his dealings with the revolutionaries the retired statesman contributed no evidence to support their claims that Azef was involved in a double game or other illicit activity; he merely confirmed that Azef had worked for the Police

Department.[62] Grateful for his past services, the highest officials in the empire continued to assist Azef after his exposure by providing him with fresh passports and defending him publicly—even at the cost of being themselves accused of covering up provocation and double dealing. They did not sever contact with the alleged criminal until approximately 1910, despite the fact that Azef was already absolutely useless as an agent.[63] In the following years, although the Police Department did issue orders to its agents abroad to establish Azef's whereabouts, there is no evidence to justify the myth that the government had placed Azef on a "wanted list" in order to put him on trial upon his arrest.[64]

This book has evaluated the evidence produced by Azef's contemporaries in both the radical and the government camps and argued that just as it is inappropriate to consider Azef an agent provocateur, so too are there no valid reasons to hold him accountable for playing a double game. At the same time, it has sought to enhance our understanding of Azef's unprecedented success. The study has also aspired to discredit the persistent tale of a "demonic Azef."[65]

To a degree, Nicolaevsky is correct in judging him to be "a typical petty bourgeois and a business man . . . adroit, sharp, very prudent and self-restrained, who knew how to risk a great deal when it was necessary, in life as in a game of cards, but who was never prepared to stake everything, who knew people and possessed a certain initiative and even the talent of an organizer—everything that was required of a good business man."[66] Aware that the figure of the police spy had been inflated into that of a "melodramatic villain,"[67] Nicolaevsky rejected all insinuations of Azef's "super-human" qualities, which had allegedly allowed him to lead a life of danger and vice: "There was not a grain of the 'heroic' or 'demonic' in his personality."[68] The writer Maksim Gor'kii advanced a similar interpretation of Azef's character, outlining a portrait of "a monstrously 'simple man' . . . intellectually dumb, semi-literate," and limited in every way, plus a typical "streamline philistine," who played with people's lives for the sake of personal comfort.[69] Several other contemporaries, including Leon Trotsky, were also indignant to witness "the cult of Azef's demonism," regarding him rather as "a complete knucklehead":

> To carry on for seventeen years the devil's game, to be fraudulent without appearing so, to lie without ever getting caught, one either has to be a genius, or, conversely, a man with an extremely simplified mechanism of the brain and the heart, simply a dimwit, who proceeded with his play crudely, in a straightforward way, audaciously, without adapting to the psychology of others, not bothering about

details—and precisely because of this emerging on top. But . . . it is far more natural to assume that Azef was a dimwit rather than a genius, firstly, because dimwits are encountered much more frequently. . . and secondly—and most importantly—because geniuses tend to apply their abilities outside the walls of the Okhrana.[70]

Trotsky offers what seems to be the most plausible explanation of Azef's success: had he attempted to play an intricate psychological game with the refined intellectuals among whom he found himself, he would certainly have botched it and made his fraud obvious every step of the way. The spy's ugly visage would have stuck out from under the mask of a man driven by ideas. Perhaps the perspicacious Azef followed his keen intuition in not attempting to play such a game at all, and

instead openly exposed his mug, physical, as well as spiritual. He forced people to get used to him not by thought-out behavior, developed in accordance with a plan, but solely by instinctive force of his dull inability to change himself. His comrades . . . must have said to themselves: 'What a character! A perfect boor, but his deeds speak for him.' Of course, not everyone dared to call him a boor . . . but everyone must have felt roughly so. And this saved him.[71]

Trotsky's judgment is convincing: Azef must have been instinctively aware of his image as a stranger, the odd man out in revolutionary circles. He made a halfhearted attempt not to veer too much from the accepted SR lifestyle; for instance, he provided himself with "a rather sizable library" and in his letters and conversation with his comrades made casual references to artistic masterpieces. He projected the image of a man not entirely devoid of intellectual interests[72]—only perhaps too busy with matters of grave revolutionary importance to allow himself a chance to enjoy culture. Occasionally he would engage in a philosophical argument with party theoretician Chernov, taking care to limit the discussion to matters related to the field of mathematics—the one area where he knew he had a chance to assert himself at the expense of the uninitiated.[73] Yet, typically, he did not attempt to replace his image of a "well-to-do entrepreneur"[74] with that of a freedom fighter, which the radicals would have preferred; instead, he forced his comrades to reconcile themselves to every side of his personality, including those they found strange or unpleasant.[75] Azef sought to compensate for his shortcomings with something that the SRs were sure to be impressed by: his thorough pragmatism.

For the most part, the SR's leaders were highly impractical people; they were intellectuals, and some of them were not only idealists, but also utopian dreamers. They must have been aware of their shortcomings, however, and of their need for a down-to-earth realist with a superbly efficient mind, phenomenal utilitarian abilities, and unmatched functional qualities.[76] Thus, Rubanovich, while considering Azef a rather "limited person," respected him as a "brilliant technician of combat," much as did Gots, who liked to compare Azef to Gershuni, emphasizing that whereas the latter had been a "romantic" of terror, the former "was its splendid practitioner."[77] Natanson expressed a similar view as to why the SRs appreciated Azef so much: "I rarely met a man who, given a certain problem, would proceed with such mathematical consistency toward its resolution.... To use a comparison with a game of chess: ... usually a player thinks three or four or five, or at most eight or nine moves ahead, but he can analyze fifteen or more moves."[78] Natanson was not alone in invoking the image of a chess master when talking about the master spy: Chernov also liked the analogy, referring to Azef as someone whose way of thinking was very much akin to that of "an experienced chess player" who reviews all possible variants at every step of the way. Gots and Gershuni, while praising Azef's "mathematical intellect," even reproved him for what in their minds was his only strategical shortcoming—a tendency "to regard people as if they were not human material, but simply chess pieces" who would always behave as ordered.[79]

Finally, we come to the issue that ran as a red thread through the entire story of Azef's life—his motives for having taken up the career of a police agent among terrorists and leading a life permeated with danger and bloodshed. Clearly, it would be an oversimplification to accept Nicolaevsky's explanation of Azef as a self-seeking man who "never identified himself wholly with either" camp and, acting "in two worlds, . . . now betrayed the revolutionaries, now the police," playing a fantastic game in which he sent the revolutionaries to the scaffold while simultaneously inciting them to blow up the carriages of the highest officials of the Russian state, all for the sake of the one goal that dominated his entire life—personal enrichment.[80]

The SRs who were close to Azef for many years believed that Nicolaevsky was wrong to explain the spy's "bizarre activities only by cupidity"; obviously, his "motives were more complicated."[81] The standard alternative hypothesis also inaccurately explains Azef's "treachery," primarily by the argument that "by nature he was a gambler; he wagered with his own and other people's heads, and this game, in which he must have felt himself a master, gave him power that intoxicated him—power over the government and over the revolution."[82] This seemingly misconstrued view turns Azef's figure into a true Goliath of conceit with an uncontrollable urge to dominate by way of "his titanic game, where the bets were gold and the heads of ministers and revolutionaries. Azef kept making bets . . . and paid with heads."[83]

German Lopatin is observant in suggesting that Azef had chosen "the profession of a police agent, exactly the way people chose the occupation of a doctor, a lawyer, and so forth."[84] Soon, he must have realized that his initial decision to provide the tsarist secret service with information about the radicals might keep him entangled in what could be a long-term game of political espionage. Under the circumstances, Azef continuously expanded his experience and occupational expertise, demonstrating not only competence but indeed genuine mastery of his trade. Still, as it is essential for any biographical probe to inquire into the person's rational and perhaps also subconscious motivations for choosing a particular career path, so it must be in the case of the professional—and virtuoso—spy.

Azef was not an idealist risking his life for the sake of fighting "the revolutionary menace"; of this, incidentally, the authorities were fully aware. Although he was a man for whom money was always "a very important consideration,"[85] for all his avidity and deep necessity for self-indulgence, Azef was probably not driven predominantly by a perpetual desire for enrichment or by a penchant for every material pleasure that money could buy. Nor is there a very convincing argument for presenting Azef primarily as a victim of socio-pathology, although it might have been an element of his troubled personality.[86] Amidst the intricate interplay of various behavior stimuli, the dominant force that seems to have led Azef to take up—and stay with—the dangerous job of a police agent among the radicals was relentless fear, an indigenous trait of his rueful self and "the greatest devil" in his anxious soul.[87] This anxiety appears to have led a life of its own, regardless of external circumstances, for "to him who is afraid everything rustles."[88]

Ironically, the constant hazard associated with Azef's involvement in political conspiracy might even have been psychologically advantageous for him in at least one respect: it relieved the fainthearted man of the necessity to deal with the very cause of his predicament—his immanent anxiety. Having plunged himself in an objectively dangerous situation, Azef no longer had to look for a rational explanation or a remedy for his inner tensions; the external conditions of his life provided plenty of reasons for experiencing chronic fear. As the practical aspects of his menacing existence gradually concealed Azef's rudimentary psychological condition, they also served to provide him with soothing, if beguiled, complacency by intimating that there was nothing wrong with him emotionally, and his incalculable fear was in fact the perfectly natural reaction of a man walking on a tightrope between life and death. Based on what we know about Azef, would it be imprudent to infer that he—perhaps typically for individuals in a similar mental state—was prepared and indeed required psychologically to force himself into a situation of extreme peril, stress and "justified anxiety" in order to escape the relentless fear existing in the realm of the inexplicable or the irrational?

Azef "was pathologically craven,"[89] "a coward at heart."[90] "His vile faintheartedness" led to all other vices, one of the greatest of which was his falseness—"for no other passion leads to such great measure of baseness as cowardice."[91] A brutal and compelling fear dominated and shaped not only the career, but also the entire mesmerizing, if piteous, life of Azef, the Russian master spy.

Abbreviations Used in Notes

Archives

Arkhiv Men'shchikova: Arkhiv L. P. Men'shchikova, International Institute of Social History, Amsterdam

Burtsev: Vladimir L. Burtsev Collection, Hoover Institution Archives, Stanford, California

GARF: Gosudarstvennyi Arkhiv Rossiiskoi Federatsii, Moscow, Russia

Nic.: Boris I. Nicolaevsky Collection, Hoover Institution Archives, Stanford, California

Okhrana: Arkhiv Zagranichnoi Agentury Departamenta Politsii (Okhrana Collection), Hoover Institution Archives, Stanford, California

PSR: Arkhiv Partii Sotsialistov-Revoliutsionerov, International Institute of Social History, Amsterdam

RGIA: Rossiiskii Gosudarstvennyi Istoricheskii Arkhiv, St. Petersburg, Russia

Other Abbreviations

DPD: Director of the Police Department

Delo Lopukhina: Delo A. A. Lopukhina v osobom prisutstvii pravitel'stvuiushchego Senata. Stenograficheskii otchet (St. Petersburg, 1910).

References to Western archival materials use short forms for box and folder numbers. Okhrana XVIc-2 thus refers to the Okhrana Collection, box XVIc, folder 2.

The Russian GARF and RGIA citations use other abbreviations: f. for *fond* refers to the document's collection; op. for *opis'* refers to the inventory list; d. for *delo* refers to the case file.

Notes

Introduction, 1–10

1. Quoted in *The Merriam-Webster Dictionary of Quotations* (Springfield, MA: Merriam-Webster, 1992), 142.

2. For a recent literary reference see Mikhail Bezrodnyi, *Konets tsitaty* (St. Petersburg: Izdatel'stvo Ivana Limbakha, 1996), 36.

3. Aleksandr Blok, "The Intelligentsia and the Revolution," in Marc Raeff, ed., *Russian Intellectual History: An Anthology* (New Jersey: Humanities Press, 1978), 364.

4. Aleksei Tolstoi, "Azef, kak teatral'naia maska," in A. Tolstoi and P. Shchegolev, eds., *Azef* (Leningrad: Academia, 1926), 15. Tolstoi and Shchegolev also wrote a play *Azef,* published in the first issue of *Krasnaia nov'* in 1926 Istorik, "Azef v izobrazhenii P. E. Shchegoleva," *Katorga i ssylka* 26 (1926): 241. Unless indicated otherwise all Russian-language sources are translated into English by this author.

5. L. Trotskii, "Evno Azef," in A. Lunacharskii, K. Radek, L. Trotskii, eds., *Siluety: Politicheskie portrety* (Moscow: Izdatel'stvo politicheskoi literatury, 1991), 227–28.

6. Boris I. Nicolaevsky Collection, Hoover Institution Archives, Stanford, California, box 615, folder 11 (hereafter cited as Nic., with box and folder numbers).

7. Report to the Director of the Police Department (hereafter cited as DPD), 22 October [4 November] 1912, Arkhiv Zagranichnoi Agentury Departamenta Politsii (Okhrana Collection), Hoover Institution Archives, Stanford, California, box XVIc, folder 2 (hereafter cited as Okhrana, with box and folder numbers); and N. Irten'ev, "Sotrudnichestvo," excerpt from the newspaper *Priamur'e* (11 April 1909), Gosudarstvennyi arkhiv Rossiiskoi Federatsii (hereafter cited as "GARF"), *fond* (hereafter cited as f.) 102, 7 *deloproizvodstvo*, 1909, *delo* (hereafter cited as d.) 891.

8. Boris I. Nikolajewsky, *Aseff the Spy: Russian Terrorist and Police Stool* (New York: Doubleday, Doran and Company, 1934), vi. Incidentally, the correct spelling of Azef's name is Azev, and the generally accepted way of writing it—adopted in this book—derived from the French version of his surname—"Azeff"—which carried over into the Russian (see B. Nikolaevskii, *Konets Azefa* [Leningrad: Gosudarstvennoe izdatel'stvo, 1926], 7n).

9. On the less than congenial relationship between the central PSR leadership and the terrorists see Anna Geifman, *Thou Shalt Kill: Revolutionary Terrorism in Russia, 1894–1917* (Princeton: Princeton University Press, 1993), 48–58.

10. One ruble at the turn of the twentieth century was worth roughly nine U.S. dollars in the 1990s (Richard E. Rubenstein, *Comrade Valentine* [New York: Harcourt Brace and Company, 1994], xviii).

11. P. A. Stolypin, *Polnoe sobranie rechei predsedatelia Soveta ministrov P. A. Stolypina v Gosudarstvennoi dume i Gosudarstvennom sovete (1907–1911 gg.)* (New York: Teleks, 1990), 160. See also idem, *Nam nuzhna velikaia Rossiia* (Moscow: Molodaia gvardiia, 1991).

12. D. B. Pavlov, Preface to "Pis'ma Azefa," *Voprosy istorii* 4 (1993): 100.

13. V. A. Gerasimov, *Na lezvii s terroristami* (Paris: YMCA-Press, 1985), 131; and Feliks Lur'e, *Politseiskie i provokatory* (St. Petersburg: Chas pik, 1992), 369. See also report to DPD, 22 October (4 November) 1912, Okhrana XVIc-2.

14. Viktor Chernov as A. V. (V. Tuchkin), *Za kulisami okhrannogo otdeleniia* (Berlin: Heinrich Gaspari Verlagsbuchhandlung, 1910), 27.

15. Romain Gary, *White Dog* (New York: World Publishing Company, 1970), 97.

16. Sheldon Kopp, *Raise Your Right Hand against Fear* (Minneapolis: Comp Care Publishers, 1988), 27.

17. Bonaro W. Overstreet, *Understanding Fear* (New York: Harper, 1951), 16.

18. Ibid., 6.

19. Ibid., 3.

20. Ibid., 3–4, 15.

21. Roman Gul', *Azef* (New York: Most, 1974), 301.

22. L. Bernstein, *L'Affaire Azeff: Histoire et documents* (Paris: Société des amis du peuple russe, 1909), 3.

23. See, for example, "Izveshchenie Tsentral'nogo Komiteta o provokatsii E. F. Azefa" (7 [20] January 1909), 1, Arkhiv Partii Sotsialistov-Revoliutsionerov, International Institute of Social History, Amsterdam, box 3, no. 168 (hereafter cited as PSR, with box and document numbers); Gerasimov, *Na lezvii*, 136 *Otchet o sostoiavshemsia 1/14 ianvaria 1909 g. v Parizhe sekretnom zasedanii*, Okhrana XVIc-9. See also copy of a letter from E. E. Lazarev to M. A. Natanson in Paris, 20 January 1909, Okhrana XIIIb (1)–1A, Outgoing Dispatches, document no. 28.

24. Pavlov, Preface to "Pis'ma Azefa," 100.

25. V. Burtsev, "Azef i ego uchastie v terroristicheskikh aktakh," *Budushchee* (10 December 1911), Nic. 205–21.

26. Azef himself subsequently insisted that the chief motive behind much of what the SRs stated publicly about him was to compromise the government (see "Opravdatel'naia zapiska Azefa," in Nikolaevskii, *Konets Azefa*, 64–65).

27. About Lopukhin's appointment as the director of the Police Department, see Rossiiskii Gosudarstvennyi Istoricheskii Arkhiv (hereafter cited as RGIA), f. 1284, op. 52, d. 91a, pp. 5, 15, 20, 22; and RGIA, f. 1284, opis' (hereafter cited as op.) 52, d. 91b, pp. 7–8.

28. "Azeff's Career, Told by Vladimir Bourtzeff," *New York Tribune* (31 August 1912); and "Russian Spy Admits Guilt," *The Sun* (15 September 1912), PSR 1–19.

29. See, for example, [V. Burtsev], "Gerasimov i Azef," *Budushchee* 45 (n.d.), Okhrana XXIVa-1B; and [V. Burtsev], "Stolypin i Azef," *Budushchee* (31 March 1912), PSR 3–279.

30. Gerasimov, *Na lezvii*, 136.

31. V. M. Chernov, *Pered burei* (New York: Izdatel'stvo imeni Chekhova, 1953), 272.

32. Nikolajewsky, *Aseff the Spy*, vi.

33. Azef's letters and reports have not been preserved in their entirety. In accordance with his request, two of his high-posted employers, A. V. Gerasimov and P. I. Rachkovskii, at different times removed many of them from the

police archives and destroyed them, lest their agent be compromised if the documents happened to fall into the hands of the revolutionaries (Pavlov, Preface to "Pis'ma Azefa," 102). Equally unfortunate is that none of Azef's police superiors left extensive memoirs, with the sole exception of General Gerasimov, whose reminiscences first appeared after the publication of Nicolaevsky's study in 1934, and portrayed Azef in an entirely new light. Similarly, the voluminous files of the Foreign Agency of the Okhrana, indispensable for any serious scrutiny of the Azef affair, have become available only since the late 1950s. Unfortunately, Nicolaevsky did not footnote his evidence, and readers are often left to make educated guesses about his sources of information.

34. The SR leaders admitted that even after the investigation the party knew little about Azef's operations (Chernov, *Pered burei*, 272).

35. Report to DPD, 28 March 1912, Okhrana XVIb (3)–4. On numerous cases of misinformation in Savinkov's memoirs, see N. S. Tiutchev, "Zametki o vospominaniiakh B. V. Savinkova," *Katorga i ssylka* 5 (12), (1924): 49–72. Tiutchev also notes Savinkov's tendency to embellish his narrative with psychological and stylistic ornamentations, turning his memoirs into an inferior sample of belles lettres (ibid., 71). Not suspecting either the severe censorship to which the SR leaders subjected Savinkov's memoirs or the apparent factual errors that they contain, subsequent commentators have treated this volume as one of the main sources supporting the official SR version of the Azef affair. The memoirs even exerted a considerable influence on Azef's police superiors, one of whom wrote: "On the basis of my official experience, I am not of a very high opinion of Savinkov's moral qualities. But this story of his breathes such truthfulness . . . that somehow one is tempted to believe everything he says" (L. A. Rataev, "Evno Azef," *Byloe* 2 [24] [August 1917]: 187, 193). For his part, however, Savinkov protested against the use of his memoirs as part of the process of investigating the Azef affair partly because all chapters of his reminiscences were "subject to revision" (undated letter from B. V. Savinkov to "Sudebno-sledstvennaia komissiia," GARF, f. 1699, op. 1, d. 89). In frequent references to Savinkov's memoirs (Boris Savinkov, *Vospominaniia terrorista* [Kharkov: Proletarii, 1926]), this study uses information selectively, only if it is corroborated by other evidence.

36. In another instance in 1912, an SR, B. V. Bartold, occupied himself with "fabricating" the second edition of the memoirs of party comrade A. A. Petrov, a police informer who tried to avenge his ruined reputation by murdering his police superior, Colonel Karpov, in December 1909. See a copy of a note from the head of the St. Petersburg Okhrana to the director of the Police Department, 24 June 1912, Okhrana XVIb [3]-1B. Portions of Petrov's manuscript are held in PSR 3-219. On censorship within the PSR, see R. A. Gorodnitskii, "B. V. Savinkov i sudebno-sledstvennaia komissiia po delu Azefa," *Minuvshee* 18 (Moscow-St. Petersburg: Atheneum-Feniks, 1995), 231.

37. See, for example, a letter from B. I. Nicolaevsky to V. K. Agafonov, 30 October 1932, Nic. 471-9.

38. Several months before completing his study, Nicolaevsky confessed: "I have now collected all the literature on the subject and feel more acutely than ever that this is not enough. A whole range of questions of primary significance will not be possible to resolve" (letter from B. I. Nicolaevsky to V. K. Agafonov, 11 April 1931, Nic. 471-79; see also letter from Nicolaevsky to Andreev, 17 October 1961).

39. Manfred Hildermeier, for instance, takes it for granted that "this agent provocateur . . . had cheated his paymasters and had committed double treachery" (Manfred Hildermeier, "The Terrorist Strategies of the Socialist Revolutionary

Party in Russia, 1900–1914," in Wolfgang J. Mommsen and Gerhard Hirschfeld, eds., *Social Protest, Violence and Terror in Nineteenth- and Twentieth-Century Europe* [New York: St. Martin's Press, 1982], 83). Similarly, Maureen Perrie labels Azef "an agent provocateur in the employ of the tsarist security police" (Maureen Perrie, "Political and Economic Terror in the Tactics of the Russian Socialist Revolutionary Party before 1914," in Mommsen and Hirschfeld, eds., *Social Protest*, 65; see also Edward H. Judge, *Plehve: Repression and Reform in Imperial Russia, 1902–1904* [Syracuse, NY: Syracuse University Press, 1983], 225–34). Nurit Schleifman's study, *Undercover Agents in the Russian Revolutionary Movement: The SR Party, 1902–1914* [New York: St. Martin's Press, 1988] and the important recent work by Jonathan W. Daly, *Autocracy under Seige: Security Police and Opposition in Russia, 1866–1905* [DeKalb, IL: Northern Illinois University Press, 1998], the only substantial treatments of the Okhrana's secret informers, concur almost entirely with Nicolaevsky's hypothesis in its fundamental argument concerning Azef. Soviet and post-Soviet scholars have also followed the traditional interpretation of the Azef affair, insisting that "regardless of the fact that Azef was an agent in the Police Department, we will consider him to be undoubtedly an active participant in the struggle against representatives of the tsarist bureaucracy" (P. A. Gorodnitskii, "Tri stilia rukovodstva boevoi organizatsiei partii sotsialistov-revoliutsionerov: Gershuni, Azef, Savinkov," *Individual'nyi politicheskii terror v Rossii XIX-nachalo XX v.* [Moscow: Memorial, 1996], 52). The most recent monograph on Azef, Rubenstein's *Comrade Valentine*, while challenging Nicolaevsky's psychological evaluation of the master spy, agrees with his historical interpretation in the most important points of his argument. And several works of historical fiction depicting Azef's exploits, of which Roman Gul's *Azef* is most notable, also generally adopt the SR-Burtsev-Nicolaevsky version of the events.

40. It would hardly be appropriate to rely on Azef's letters to his former comrades and to his wife, in which, immediately prior to and following his exposure, he tried to save his reputation and ultimately his life by posing as a man who had "served the revolution and the revolution only" ("Priznanie Azefa," *Budushchee* 3 [5 November 1911], PSR 3-279; see also Savinkov, *Vospominaniia*, 369).

Chapter 1, A Frightened Child, 11–29

1. As a psychiatrist perceptively notes, in reading the biographies of famous people, "one gains the impression that their lives began at puberty. Before that, we are told, they had a 'happy,' 'contented,' or 'untroubled' childhood, or one that was 'full of deprivation' or 'very stimulating.' But what a particular childhood really was like does not seem to interest these biographers—as if the roots of a whole life were not hidden and entwined in its childhood" (Alice Miller, *Prisoners of Childhood* [New York: Basic Books, 1981], 4).

2. This town was sometimes referred to as Liskowo (*Pistsovaia kniga grodnenskoi ekonomii s pribavleniiami, izdannaia vilenskoiu komissieiu dlia razbora drevnikh aktov*, Part 1 [Vilna, 1881], 408).

3. Mark Zborowski and Elizabeth Herzog, *Life Is with People: The Culture of the Shtetl* (New York: Schocken Books, 1952), 61–62.

4. Ibid., 63, 66, 62.

5. Nikolajewsky, *Aseff the Spy*, 22.

6. Overstreet, *Understanding Fear*, 36.

7. "Iz istorii Partii S.-R.," *Novyi zhurnal* 100 (1970): 281n.

8. Rostov grew rapidly indeed: whereas in 1860 its population was approximately 18,000, by 1897, according to the census conducted that year, its inhabitants had increased to almost 120,000 (S. Shvetsov, *V starom Rostove* [Rostov: Rostovskoe knizhnoe izdatel'stvo, 1971], 7–8, 12; *Rostov-na-Donu: Ocherki o gorode* [Rostov: Rostovskoe knizhnoe izdatel'stvo, 1973], 26).

9. Oleg V. Budnitskii, "Political Leaders among Jews in Rostov-on-Don, 1900–1920," in *Proceedings of the Eleventh World Congress of Jewish Studies*, Division B (The History of the Jewish People), vol. 3 (Jerusalem, 1994), 37.

10. Shvetsov, *V starom Rostove*, 12, 23; Nikolajewsky, *Aseff the Spy*, 22–23.

11. Shvetsov, *V starom Rostove*, 56.

12. Ibid., 57, 60.

13. Nikolajewsky, *Aseff the Spy*, 24, 28.

14. As a child, Evno must have been exposed to horror stories people recounted to one another about Russia's "first modern massacre of Jews: the Odessa pogrom of 1871." He was not even twelve years old when "a wave of pogroms swept southern and western Russia" as an aftermath of the 1 March 1881 terrorist assassination of Alexander II; "160 communities were attacked, with hundreds of lives lost and countless homes and shops destroyed" (Rubenstein, *Comrade Valentine*, 6, 12).

15. Overstreet, *Understanding Fear*, 35.

16. Ibid., 36–37.

17. Victimized by fearful parents, the child frequently carries their anxiety into his own adulthood. See, for example, Diane F. Hailparn, *Fear No More* (New York: St. Martin's Press, 1988), 108.

18. "Pokazaniia L. G. Azef," GARF, f. 1699, op. 1, d. 126, p. 2.

19. Ibid., 3–4.

20. Zh. Longe and G. Zil'ber, *Terroristy i okhranka* (Moscow, 1991), 47.

21. The Gemara is the part of the Talmud that interprets Jewish law. See Zborowski and Herzog, *Life Is with People*, 85, 438. For similar illustrations of the importance of education for the Jewish tradition see S. A. An-skii, "Evreiskoe narodnoe tvorchestvo," in A. Lokshin, ed., *Evrei v Rossiiskoi imperii 18–19 vekov: sbornik trudov evreiskikh istorikov* (Moscow-Jerusalem: Gesharim, 1995), 662.

22. P. Berlin, "Ob odnom poveshennom," *Katorga i ssylka* 59 (1929): 94–95. See also Oleg V. Budnitskii, "The Jews in Rostov-on-Don in 1918–1919," *Jews and Jewish Topics in the Soviet Union and Eastern Europe* (Jerusalem: The Hebrew University of Jerusalem, Winter, 1993), 17, n. 7. Nicolaevsky incorrectly assumed that Azef had studied in a classical gymnasium in Rostov, although at the time the young man received his secondary education there was no such school in the city. Shvetsov, *V starom Rostove*, 109. Other biographers simply repeated Nicolaevsky's premise. See, for example, Rubenstein, *Comrade Valentine*, 9. Azef's wife claimed not to have had Azef's gymnasium diploma "but some other document *(bumazhka)*" ("Pokazaniia L. G. Azef," GARF, f. 1699, op. 1, d. 126, p. 3).

23. Among numerous examples, see Azef's letter to L. G. Menkina, 13 April 1909, GARF, f. 1699, op. 1, d. 20; and Azef's letter to L. G. Menkina, postmarked 14 May 1909, GARF, f. 1699, op. 1, d. 21.

24. Nikolajewsky, *Aseff the Spy*, 28.

25. A useful analysis of innate fear stimuli may be found in Jeffrey A. Gray, *The Neuropsychology of Anxiety: An Enquiry into the Functions of the Septo-Hippocampal System* (New York: Oxford University Press, 1982).

26. Nikolajewsky, *Aseff the Spy*, 23; Rubenstein, *Comrade Valentine*, 9–10. According to one source, Azef barely made it to the sixth grade and then was expelled as a result of some scandalous episode. For the next three years he studied in absentia for his diploma, while struggling to support himself with private lessons (Longe and Zil'ber, *Terroristy i okhranka*, 48).

27. Overstreet, *Understanding Fear*, 25.

28. On Azef's misgivings about his Jewish identity and the lack of attachment to his heritage see "Pokazaniia L. G. Azef," GARF, f. 1699, op. 1, d. 126, p. 9; letter from N. A. Rubakin to B. I. Nicolaevsky, 8 March 1935, Nic. 206-8; and Leonid Praisman, "Fenomen Azefa," *Individual'nyi politicheskii terror v Rossii XIX-nachalo XX v.* (Moscow: Memorial, 1996), 68.

29. Zborowski and Herzog, *Life Is with People*, 67.

30. For a radically different reaction to the secular school experience, from the perspective of a Jew who later became Azef's colleague in the PSR, see Mark Vishniak, *Dan' proshlomu* (New York: Izdatel'stvo imeni Chekhova, 1954), 22–23, 26–27. To a great extent, Vishniak's inner security may be explained by a healthier climate in his household, as well as by the fact that his family, although a traditional Jewish one, resided in Moscow and was thus spared the harsher reality of the Pale (ibid., 13–14, 33–34).

31. Berlin, "Ob odnom poveshennom," 95.

32. Ibid.

33. Longe and Zil'ber, *Terroristy i okhranka*, 47. See also Bernstein, *L'Affaire Azeff*, 35–36.

34. "Zapiska o predpolozheniiakh i slukhakh kasatel'no sushchestvovaniia ser'eznoi provokatsii vnutri P.S.R.," GARF, f. 1699, op. 1, d. 44; Nikolajewsky, *Aseff the Spy*, 28.

35. Vishniak, *Dan' proshlomu*, 37.

36. Nikolajewsky, *Aseff the Spy*, 24, 28.

37. Nikolajewsky, *Aseff the Spy*, 28; Longe and Zil'ber, *Terroristy i okhranka*, 45; Rubenstein, *Comrade Valentine*, 2; and P. S. Ivanovskaia, "Delo Pleve," *Byloe* 23 (1924): 190.

38. Maksim Gor'kii, "O predateliakh," *Sobranie sochinenii*, vol. 25 (Moscow: Gosudarstvennoe izdatel'stvo khudozhestvennoi literatury, 1953), 195.

39. Leaflet "Provokator Evgenii Filippovich Azev," GARF, f. 1699, op. 1, d. 146.

40. Longe and Zil'ber, *Terroristy i okhranka*, 48.

41. Zborowski and Herzog, *Life Is with People*, 135.

42. In the Jewish fairy tales, "a man of disguised virtue" takes the place of the simpleton, who by the end of the story attains prosperity and happiness—largely by going along with his characteristically naive and innocuous instincts. In his appearance the virtuous Jew is as pathetic as Ivan the Fool, but when his hidden goodness is finally revealed, in the Jewish tradition it takes the form of a superior intellect. The wretched-looking sage (who was thought to be dumb and illiterate) knows not only "the entire Torah" but also all the "secret wisdom" (An-skii, "Evreiskoe narodnoe tvorchestvo," 676).

43. Zborowski and Herzog, *Life Is with People*, 102.

44. In pursuing the comparison with the Russian Orthodox tradition, one would be wise to remember that "Christianity turned this criterion inside out. . . . The criterion of good and evil was placed in the individual's soul and became subjective. If the soul is filled with love, everything is in order: that

man is good and everything he does is good" (Milan Kundera, *Immortality* [London-Boston: Faber and Faber, 1991], 216).

45. An-skii, "Evreiskoe narodnoe tvorchestvo," 650.

46. Zborowski and Herzog, *Life Is with People*, 85. For a variant of this lullaby see An-skii, "Evreiskoe narodnoe tvorchestvo," 661.

47. Vishniak, *Dan' proshlomu*, 37.

48. Geifman, *Thou Shalt Kill*, 175–76.

49. P. Berlin, "Stranitsa proshlogo. O dvukh poveshennykh," *Novoe russkoe slovo*, 7 September 1952, in Nic. 438–28; Berlin, "Ob odnom poveshennom," 95, 97; A. V. Gerasimov, *Na lezvii s terroristami* (Paris: YMCA-Press, 1985), 88, 91–93; D. B. Pavlov, *Esery-maksimalisty v pervoi Rossiiskoi revoliutsii* (Moscow, 1989), 14n, 169–72, 179–180, 183; A. I. Spiridovich, *Partiia Sotsialistov-revoliutsionerov i ee predshestvenniki (1886–1916)* (Petrograd, 1918), 310.

50. In general, as one author put it, "The development of a group is the experience of victory over seemingly insoluble human dilemmas" (Charles Hampden-Turner, *Radical Man* [New York: Anchor Books, 1971], 187).

51. As modern psychology has it, "By definition, an immature adult is one who still feels threatened by problems that should long ago have been brought to some solution" (Overstreet, *Understanding Fear*, 69).

52. Walter Reich, ed., *Origins of Terrorism* (Cambridge, U.K.: Cambridge University Press, 1990), 33.

53. Longe and Zil'ber, *Terroristy i okhranka*, 44.

54. Ibid., 45n.

55. See, for example, Stenograficheskii otchet 26 zasedaniia sudebno-sledstvennoi komissii, 2 maia 1910 g., p. 27, GARF, f. 1699, op. 1, d. 136; "Pokazaniia M. A. Natansona," GARF, f. 1699, op. 1, d. 123, p. 76; "Pokazaniia Iriny, Ritinoi (Rakitnikovoi), Rubanovicha, Burtseva, dannye sudebno-sledstvennoi komissii po delu Azefa," GARF, f. 1699, op. 1, d. 129, pp. 8–9; and Longe and Zil'ber, *Terroristy i okhranka*, 45, 47.

56. Nikolajewsky, *Aseff the Spy*, 23; Longe and Zil'ber, *Terroristy i okhranka*, 48; Shvetsov, *V starom Rostove*, 174, 179.

57. Nikolajewsky, *Aseff the Spy*, 23–24.

58. Years later, one of Azef's comrades was astonished to realize that the terrorist veteran was unable to conceal his dread of even the hypothetical idea of imprisonment (unsigned manuscript [probably written by Andrei Argunov], entitled "Pervaia vstrecha s Azefom," GARF, f. 1699, op. 1, d. 78, p. 26).

59. Nikolajewsky, *Aseff the Spy*, 24.

60. Ibid. Azef's brother Vladimir confirmed the fact of Evno's thievery ("Pokazaniia L. G. Azef," GARF, f. 1699, op. 1, d. 126, p. 3). According to an alternative, yet unconfirmed version, Azef's comrades in Rostov extorted from him the money that belonged to another person, forcing him to escape abroad (Mark Aldanov, "Azef," *Istoki* [Moscow: Izvestiia, 1991], 402).

61. Overstreet, *Understanding Fear*, 37.

Chapter 2, Yet Another Way to Sell Your Soul, 31–49

1. According to Azef's wife, he first went to Vienna, then moved to Munich, and only afterwards arrived in Karlsruhe ("Pokazaniia L. G. Azef," GARF, f. 1699, op. 1, d. 126, pp. 4–5).

2. Nikolajewsky, *Aseff the Spy*, 24, 27; Longe and Zil'ber, *Terroristy i okhranka*, 48.

3. Nikolajewsky, *Aseff the Spy*, 24; see also "Pokazaniia L. G. Azef," GARF, f. 1699, op. 1, d. 126, p. 2). Living under these onerous conditions, Azef is said to have also developed "a chronic throat infection" (Rubenstein, *Comrade Valentine*, 21).

4. According to one of Azef's acquaintances in Karlsruhe, the young people's situation was difficult but hardly life-threatening, since émigré students helped one another (see Aldanov, "Azef," *Istoki*, 433n).

5. See, for example, "Pokazaniia L. G. Azef," GARF, f. 1699, op. 1, d. 126, pp. 26–27; and P. Shchegolev, "Istoricheskii Azef," in Tolstoi and Shchegolev, eds., *Azef*, 9.

6. GARF, f. 1699, op. 2, d. 142.

7. In his State Duma speech concerning the Azef affair, Stolypin asserted that Azef had become a police agent as early as 1892 (Stolypin, *Polnoe sobranie rechei*, 160; see also *Gosudarstvennaia Duma. III sozyv. Stenograficheskie otchety,* Session II, zasedanie 50 [11 February 1909], 1422). Based on Stolypin's speech, Bernstein, the first historian of Azef's career, asserted that Azef's initial contact with the security police took place in 1892 in Ekaterinoslav (Bernstein, *L'Affaire Azeff*, 36–37). For corroboration of this date, see *Obvinitel'nyi akt ob otstavnom deistvitel'nom statskom sovetnike Aleksee Aleksandroviche Lopukhine, obviniaemom v gosudarstvennom prestuplenii,* GARF, f. 102, 7 deloproizvodstvo, 1909, d. 891 and *Delo A. A. Lopukhina v osobom prisutstvii pravitel'stvuiushchego Senata. Stenograficheskii otchet* (St. Petersburg, 1910), 9 (cited hereafter as *Delo Lopukhina*). However, the earliest available letter from Azef to the police authorities is dated 6 April 1893. D. B. Pavlov and Z. I. Peregudova, eds., *Pis'ma Azefa (1893–1917)* (Moscow: Terra, 1994), 14. All previous studies of Azef's collaboration with the secret police mistakenly assumed that his first letter to the Russian authorities was written on 4 April 1893 and addressed to the Police Department in St. Petersburg. See, for example, Nikolajewsky, *Aseff the Spy*, 25; Rubenstein, *Comrade Valentine*, 21; Praisman, "Fenomen Azefa," 66. In fact, this was his second letter, written on 10 April 1893 (Pavlov and Peregudova, eds., *Pis'ma Azefa*, 14–15).

8. The letter was signed "W. Sch." Pavlov and Peregudova, *Pis'ma Azefa*, 14.

9. Letter from V. M. Zenzinov to B. I. Nicolaevsky, 19 July 1931, Nic. 206–10.

10. Aldanov, "Azef," *Istoki*, 402.

11. Cited in Nikolajewsky, *Aseff the Spy*, 26.

12. Ibid., 27.

13. "Pokazaniia V. L. Burtseva, dannye sudebno-sledstvennoi komissii po delu Azefa," GARF, f. 1699, op. 1, d. 129, p. 151.

14. "Iz istorii Partii S.-R.," *Novyi zhurnal* 100 (1970): 293.

15. "Pokazaniia V. L. Burtseva, dannye sudebno-sledstvennoi komissii po delu Azefa," GARF, f. 1699, op. 1, d. 129, p. 72.

16. "Pokazaniia L. G. Azef," GARF, f. 1699, op. 1, d. 126, p. 11.

17. Aldanov, "Azef," *Istoki*, 406.

18. Ibid., 402–3.

19. "Pokazaniia V. L. Burtseva, dannye sudebno-sledstvennoi komissii po delu Azefa," GARF, f. 1699, op. 1, d. 129, p. 73.

20. Praisman, "Fenomen Azefa," 66.

21. A copy of Azef's diploma is held at the Hoover Institution Archives, Nic. 205-5.

22. Azef had no reason to complain about his salary, since around the turn of the century "informants generally received an average of 30 to 40 rubles per month" (Daly, *Autocracy under Seige*, 91).

23. Nikolajewsky, *Aseff the Spy,* 29.
24. Kopp, *Raise Your Right Hand Against Fear,* 26.
25. Nikolajewsky, *Aseff the Spy,* 30.
26. For a detailed description of the revolutionaries' efforts to unify their forces, see Norman M. Naimark, *Terrorists and Social Democrats: The Russian Revolutionary Movement under Alexander III* (Cambridge, MA: Harvard University Press, 1983).
27. See, for example, "Pis'ma Azefa," *Voprosy istorii* 4 (1993), 106–7; and Pavlov and Peregudova, eds., *Pis'ma Azefa,* 103, 105, 117, 125.
28. "Pokazaniia L. G. Azef," p. 9, GARF, f. 1699, op. 1, d. 126; "Dopros Azefa," 14 June 1915, GARF, f. 1699, op. 2, d. 142.
29. It is more than unlikely that "the poor tailor's son imagined himself arriving in Moscow and St. Petersburg like a Jewish Monte Cristo, his diploma in hand and righteous anger in his heart" (Rubenstein, *Comrade Valentine,* 25).
30. Longe and Zil'ber, *Terroristy i okhranka,* 50; and untitled manuscript by Olga Chernov Andreyev, p. 41, Olga Andreyev Carlisle private archive, San Francisco, CA. Azef's family joined him in Russia a year later ("Pokazaniia L. G. Azef," GARF, f. 1699, op. 1, d. 126, pp. 10–11).
31. "Pokazaniia L. G. Azef," GARF, f. 1699, op. 1, d. 126, pp. 1–2.
32. See, for example, Stenograficheskii otchet 26 zasedaniia sudebno-sledstvennoi komissii, 2 maia 1910 g., GARF, f. 1699, op. 1, d. 136, p. 9; "Pokazaniia V. L. Burtseva, dannye sudebno-sledstvennoi komissii po delu Azefa," GARF, f. 1699, op. 1, d. 129, p. 146; and "Vyderzhka iz pokazanii Lapina (Iudelevskogo)," GARF, f. 1699, op. 1, d. 134, pp. 1, 5.
33. Nikolajewsky, *Aseff the Spy,* 30.
34. "Pokazaniia L. G. Azef," GARF, f. 1699, op. 1, d. 126, p. 2.
35. Rubenstein, *Comrade Valentine,* 25.
36. "Pokazaniia L. G. Azef," GARF, f. 1699, op. 1, d. 126, p. 26. Azef's police superiors also remembered him as a "very avaricious" man (Longe and Zil'ber, *Terroristy i okhranka,* 52).
37. "Pokazaniia L. G. Azef," GARF, f. 1699, op. 1, d. 126, p. 2.
38. Ibid., 2–3, 5.
39. To the end Liubov' could never reconcile Azef's professed love for her and the fact that "he had very little interest" in her life. She claimed that Azef "could not live without her" and that he threatened to shoot himself if he lost her, if she ever decided to leave him. Yet she also admitted that even one week of living together invariably led to conflicts (ibid., pp. 5–6, 24).
40. Ibid., 3.
41. Ibid., 17–18.
42. Ibid., 12.
43. Niccolo Machiavelli in *The Merriam-Webster Dictionary of Quotations,* 142.
44. This argument contradicts the assumption that "Azef was smitten" by love for Liubov' (Rubenstein, *Comrade Valentine,* 25).
45. "Pokazaniia L. G. Azef," GARF, f. 1699, op. 1, d. 126, p. 4. Azef's relations with his second brother were "very rancorous" ("Pokazaniia Iriny, Ritinoi (Rakitnikovoi), Rubanovicha, Burtseva, dannye sudebno-sledstvennoi komissii po delu Azefa," GARF, f. 1699, op. 1, d. 129, p. 150).
46. "Pokazaniia L. G. Azef," GARF, f. 1699, op. 1, d. 126, p. 14.
47. Ibid., 14.
48. When Azef felt that it was time to justify his improved financial status, he simply told Liubov' that some friend of his, being an ill man, decided

to put a few thousand marks in Azef's account, allowing him to use the funds occasionally. Liubov' accepted the story without any questions (ibid., 6–7).

49. See a letter from Nicolaevsky to Agafonov dated 30 October 1932, Nic. 471–9. See also notes on Azef by Men'shchikov, in Arkhiv L. P. Men'shchikova (cited hereafter as Arkhiv Men'shchikova), box 10, folder EE, p. 5, International Institute of Social History, Amsterdam.

50. At the time, such tenuous assertions "astonished" even Azef's credulous comrades (Boris Savinkov's testimony in "Stenograficheskii otchet zasedaniia C. C. K. [Sudepans-sledstvennoi komissii] 9 noiabria 1910 goda," GARF, f. 1699, op. 1, d. 133, p. 35).

51. Gorodnitskii, "Tri stilia rukovodstva boevoi organizatsiei," 57.

52. Cited in Gor'kii, "O predateliakh," 193. See also Nikolaevskii, *Konets Azefa*, 36.

53. Gor'kii, "O predateliakh," 192.

54. Aldanov, "Azef," *Istoki*, 437.

55. "Pokazaniia L. G. Azef," GARF, f. 1699, op. 1, d. 126, p. 16; and Longe and Zil'ber, *Terroristy i okhranka*, 52–53.

56. Shchegolev, "Istoricheskii Azef," 8.

57. Publius Ovidius Naso, *Tristia* (Moscow: Nauka, 1978), 6 (author's translation).

58. Gary, *White Dog*, 58.

59. Shchegolev, "Istoricheskii Azef," 8.

60. This is why Dostoyevsky vouched that "beauty would save the world," Joseph Brodsky argued in his Nobel Prize Lecture (1987), which was partly devoted to the idea that "aesthetics is the mother of ethics."

61. "Pokazaniia L. G. Azef," GARF, f. 1699, op. 1, d. 126, p. 27.

62. "Pokazaniia V. L. Burtseva, dannye sudebno-sledstvennoi komissii po delu Azefa," GARF, f. 1699, op. 1, d. 129, p. 163.

63. Longe and Zil'ber, *Terroristy i okhranka*, 50, 52.

64. Shchegolev, "Istoricheskii Azef," 8. See also Longe and Zil'ber, *Terroristy i okhranka*, 52.

65. Biographical sketch of Azef, Arkhiv Men'shchikova, box 10, folder EE, p. 5; Aldanov, "Azef," *Istoki*, 405.

66. For a discussion of gambling as a means to escape deep anxiety, see Kopp, *Raise Your Right Hand against Fear*, 25–26.

67. Pavlov and Peregudova, eds., *Pis'ma Azefa*, 50, 241 n. 110; and Longe and Zil'ber, *Terroristy i okhranka*, 49. Azef's salary was 225 rubles a month, according to other sources (Charles Ruud and Sergei Stepanov, *Fontanka, 16. Politicheskii sysk pri tsariakh* [Moscow: Mysl', 1993], 176).

68. "Pokazaniia L. G. Azef," GARF, f. 1699, o. 1, d. 126, p. 12. See also P. E. Shchegolev, ed., *Provokator* (Leningrad: Priboi, 1929), 5.

69. Longe and Zil'ber, *Terroristy i okhranka*, 49. See also Ruud and Stepanov, *Fontanka*, 16, 176.

70. Azef's police salary at the time was already close to what he was making as an engineer—150 rubles per month (Ruud and Stepanov, *Fontanka*, 16, 180).

71. Nikolajewsky, *Aseff the Spy*, 32–33, 37–38.

72. Ibid., 39.

73. Ibid., 39–40.

74. Cited in ibid., 41.

75. "Pokazaniia M. F. S. [Seliuk]," GARF, f. 1699, op. 1, d. 132, p. 2.

76. Cited in Nikolajewsky, *Aseff the Spy*, 41–42.

77. A famous case demonstrating this tendency was that of Pavel Miliukov, future leader of the Constitutional Democratic Party, whose one-year prison sentence was, on his wife's request, substituted with an official permission to leave Russia for Bulgaria in 1896 (Thomas Riha, *A Russian European: Paul Miliukov in Russian Politics* [Notre Dame-London: University of Notre Dame Press, 1969], 33).

78. A. I. Spiridovich, *Zapiski zhandarma* (Moscow: Proletarii, 1991), 80–81.

79. Nikolajewsky, *Aseff the Spy*, 41–42. See also Rataev, "Evno Azef," 195.

80. Only rarely did the Russian authorities succeed in securing the cooperation of other governments in their struggle against the radicals, and for the most part, foreign administrations limited their collaboration to joint efforts against the anarchists (see 17 March 1904 police report, Okhrana XIIId [1], 9; and "Protokol," Okhrana Va, 3).

81. F. M. Lur'e and Z. I. Peregudova, "Tsarskaia Okhranka i provokatsiia," *Iz glubiny vremen*, I (St. Petersburg: Elektrotekhnicheskii institut sviazi imeni M. A. Bonch-Bruevicha, 1992), 56–57.

82. Geifman, *Thou Shalt Kill*, 50. The next day the enigmatic signature "Organization" was disclosed in hundreds of leaflets which appeared in the capital under the heading "the Combat Organization of the Socialist Revolutionary Party" and which threatened the ministers with further violence "so long as they refuse to understand human language and to listen to the voice of the nation" (cited in Rubenstein, *Comrade Valentine*, 46–47).

83. Cited in Iurii Davydov, *Tainaia liga* (Moscow: Pravda, 1990), 18.

84. Nikolajewsky, *Aseff the Spy*, 56.

Chapter 3, Terrorist-Neophyte, 1902–1905, 51–73

1. Author's translation from *Izrecheniia kitaiskogo mudretsa Lao-Tze* (Moscow: Izdatel'stvo MGIK, 1992).

2. Gorodnitskii, "Tri stilia rukovodstva boevoi organizatsiei," 54; "Pis'mo S. V. Zubatova A. I. Spiridovichu," *Krasnyi arkhiv* 2 (1922): 281.

3. Rubenstein, *Comrade Valentine*, 38; cited in Geifman, *Thou Shalt Kill*, 45–46.

4. "Iz istorii Partii S.-R.," *Novyi zhurnal* 100 (1970): 284. See also Trotskii, "Evno Azef," 233.

5. Gerasimov, *Na lezvii s terroristami*, 195.

6. Gorodnitskii, "Tri stilia rukovodstva boevoi organizatsiei," 53.

7. Ibid., 54.

8. Ibid., 53. For an analogous description of Gershuni by a contemporary, see excerpt from an intercepted letter to Emiliia Kaufman in Geneva, 26 February 1904, Okhrana XVIIn-2A.

9. Another high-posted police officer was also of the opinion that Gershuni "possessed the power of influencing people almost to the point of hypnotism" (sources for all citations can be found in Geifman, *Thou Shalt Kill*, 51).

10. Gorodnitskii, "Tri stilia rukovodstva boevoi organizatsiei," 53. When Gershuni could not be present at the site of a terrorist operation, Kraft or Mel'nikov would take over for a while, as occurred during the terrorists' preparation of the attack against Prince Obolenskii ("Iz istorii Partii S.-R.," *Novyi zhurnal* 100 [1970]: 284–85).

11. Geifman, *Thou Shalt Kill*, 51.

12. Ibid., 50; "K delu Fomy Kochury," *Byloe*, 6 (June 1906): 102–4.

13. In making this assertion, Nicolaevsky contradicts the evidence provided by Rataev, Zubatov, and Bakai. Nikolajewsky, *Aseff the Spy*, 52–53.

14. "Pokazaniia L. G. Azef," GARF, f. 1699, op. 1, d. 126, p. 16.

15. Boris Savinkov's testimony in "Stenograficheskii otchet zasedaniia C. C. K. 6 noiabria 1910 goda," GARF, f. 1699, op. 1, d. 133, p. 6. According to official sources, "information provided by Azef in this time period, until 1904 . . . although it was very valuable in precluding revolutionary activity and preventing political assassinations inside Russia, in essence was of incidental, cursory character, depending on . . . accidental sources (*Obvinitel'nyi akt ob . . . Lopukhine*, GARF, f. 102, 7 *deloproizvodstvo*, 1909, d. 891; see also the testimony of Zubatov at Lopukhin's trial, in "Protses Lopukhina," *Delo Lopukhina*, 42 and "Gershuni i Azef po ofitsial'nym dokumentam," Byloe 15 [1913]: 36–37).

16. Rubenstein is incorrect in thinking that Evno and Liubov' Azef had a son and a daughter (Rubenstein, *Comrade Valentine*, xiv, 120).

17. See, for example, E. E. Lazarev, "Zhiznennyi podvig G. A. Gershuni" (unpublished manuscript), p. 11, Nic. 12-2; miscellaneous notes by V. L. Burtsev, p. 5, Nic. 150-1; decoded telegram from L. A. Rataev in St. Petersburg to the Moscow Okhrana director S. V. Zubatov, 13 January 1902, Nic. 150-1. In an ensuing dispatch Rataev wrote: "Gershuni will never be able to evade us now because he is operating quite close to our source of information. His immediate arrest, while leaving us in the dark, will be of little purpose and may compromise the agent" (confidential letter from L. A. Rataev to S. V. Zubatov, 30 January 1902, Nic. 150-1; see also "Gershuni i Azef po ofitsial'nym dokumentam," 36–40). Zubatov confirms that the police acquired all the information about Gershuni and the people close to him from Azef, *Delo Lopukhina*, 41.

18. Aldanov, "Azef," *Istoki*, 403.

19. Savinkov, *Vospominaniia*, 327; letter from Kolosov to Kolari, Okhrana XVIb (3)-10; and Aldanov, "Azef," *Istoki*, 403.

20. Detailed description of Gershuni dated February 1903, and decoded telegram from the director of the Police Department, A. A. Lopukhin, in St. Petersburg to the Moscow Okhrana director, 12 February 1903, Nic. 150-1. The police were able to arrest Mel'nikov only due to Azef's information (*Obvinitel'nyi akt ob . . . Lopukhine*, GARF, f. 102, 7 *deloproizvodstvo*, 1909, d. 891; *Delo Lopukhina*, 10; see also Rataev, "Evno Azef," 196).

21. *Obvinitel'nyi akt ob . . . Lopukhine*, GARF, f. 102, 7 *deloproizvodstvo*, 1909, d. 891; *Delo Lopukhina*, p. 10.

22. *Delo Lopukhina*, 10, 55; *Obvinitel'nyi akt ob . . . Lopukhine*, GARF, f. 102, 7 *deloproizvodstvo*, 1909, d. 891. See also Nikolajewsky, *Aseff the Spy*, 58, and Aldanov, "Azef," *Istoki*, 403.

23. The only indication that Azef had anything to do with the events in Ufa comes from his own letter to Savinkov, 10 October 1908, in which, already facing Burtsev's charges and obviously trying to exaggerate his role in SR terrorist activity at the time, he could only claim to have "sent people to Ufa," which did not at all mean that he knew about the local preparations for the act against Bogdanovich (Savinkov, *Vospominaniia*, 369). Indeed, in his later statement, Azef categorically denied any involvement in the Ufa affair ("Opravdatel'naia zapiska Azefa," 54–55). In his testimony, Zubatov also argued that Azef may not have known about this act (*Delo Lopukhina*, 42).

24. "Obvinitel'nyi akt ob otstavnom deistvitel'nom statskom sovetnike Aleksee Aleksandroviche Lopukhine, obvinennom v gosudarstvennom prestu-

plenii," *Byloe* 9–10 (1909): 234; "Iz zapisok M. E. Bakaia," *Byloe*, 9–10 (1909), 197.

25. Aldanov, "Azef," Istoki, 404. The fact that Azef did not know about all of Gershuni's operations is confirmed by Gorodnitskii, "Tri stilia rukovodstva boevoi organizatsiei," 53.

26. See, for example, Gorbunov, "Savinkov, kak memuarist," *Katorga i ssylka* 3 (40): 181.

27. See, for example, a note to L. A. Rataev from A. Harting, 19 November [2 December] 1902, Okhrana XIIc [1]–1A.

28. "Iz istorii Partii S.-R.," *Novyi zhurnal* 100 (1970): 296.

29. Grigorii Gershuni, *Iz nedavnego proshlogo* (Paris: Tribune Russe, 1908), 17.

30. There is evidence that in 1904 the authorities spared Gershuni's life in order to demonstrate to the public that he was a figure of exaggerated stature and reputation (report to DPD, 2 [15] March 1904, Okhrana XVIb[3]–4). Gershuni initially served time in Schlusselburg fortress, from where in January 1906 he was transferred to the Akatui hard-labor prison in Siberia.

31. "Izveshchenie Tsentral'nogo Komiteta," 1; *Otchet o sostoiavshemsia 1/14 ianvaria 1909 g. v Parizhe secretnom zasedanii*," Okhrana XVIc-9. Nicolaevsky also supports this precis of Azef's activity (Nikolajewsky, *Aseff the Spy*, 67–68).

32. "Izveshchenie Tsentral'nogo Komiteta," 1; see also Chernov in A. B. (V. Tuchkin), *Za kulisami okhrannogo otdeleniia*.

33. Along with his published works, see manuscripts held in Savinkov's literary archive in Arkhiv-Biblioteka Rossiiskogo Fonda Kul'tury, f. B. V. Savinkova, op. 1. For an analysis of Savinkov's two highly controversial novels, both published under the pseudonym "V. Ropshin," that throws some light on his intricate personality, see Geifman, *Thou Shalt Kill*, 53–54.

34. Dmitrii Filosofov cited in Dmitrii Zubarev, ed., "Boris Savinkov: chelovek, kotoryi khotel rasshirit' chelovecheskuiu svobodu," *Nezavisimaia gazeta* (23 May 1995), 3.

35. Letter from B. V. Savinkov to V. N. Figner, 3 July 1907, *Minuvshee* 18, 196.

36. Richard B. Spence, *Boris Savinkov: Renegade on the Left* (Boulder, CO: East European Monographs, 1991), 47, 53.

37. "Pokazaniia tt. Bobrova, Bol'shova, Kubova, Chernova, Bunakova i Moiseenko, dannye sudebno-sledstvennoi komissii," GARF, f. 1699, op. 1, d. 130, p. 189.

38. Spence, *Boris Savinkov*, 28.

39. Cited in Geifman, *Thou Shalt Kill*, 53.

40. Aleksandr Kuprin cited in Zubarev, ed., "Boris Savinkov: chelovek, kotoryi khotel rasshirit' chelovecheskuiu svobodu," 3.

41. Vladimir Zenzinov cited in ibid.

42. R. A. Gorodnitskii and G. S. Kan, preface to letter from Savinkov to Figner, *Minuvshee* 18, 195.

43. Gorodnitskii, "Tri stilia rukovodstva boevoi organizatsiei," 59–61; Gul', *Azef*, 37; Spence, *Boris Savinkov*, 29.

44. Marina Mogil'ner, "Boris Savinkov: 'podpol'naia' i 'legal'naia' Rossiia v peripetiiakh odnoi sud'by," *Obshchestvennye nauki i sovremennost' (ONS)* (New York, 1995), 88.

45. Filosofov cited in Zubarev, ed., "Boris Savinkov: chelovek, kotoryi khotel rasshirit' chelovecheskuiu svobodu," 3.

46. Cited in Gorodnitskii, "Tri stilia rukovodstva boevoi organizatsiei," 60.

47. "Iz istorii Partii S.-R.," *Novyi zhurnal* 100 (1970): 288–91; "Pokazaniia tt. Bobrova, Bol'shova, Kubova, Chernova, Bunakova i Moiseenko, dannye sudebno-sledstvennoi komissii," GARF, f. 1699, op. 1, d. 130, p. 80.

48. Amy Knight, "Female Terrorists in the Russian Socialist Revolutionary Party," *Russian Review* 38, no. 2 (April 1979): 147.

49. "Iz istorii Partii S.-R.," *Novyi zhurnal* 101 (1970): 180.

50. Boris Savinkov's testimony in "Stenograficheskii otchet zasedaniia C. C. K. 6 noiabria 1910 goda," GARF, f. 1699, op. 1, d. 133, pp. 2–3, 6.

51. Boris Savinkov's testimony in "Stenograficheskii otchet zasedaniia C. C. K. 9 noiabria 1910 goda," GARF, f. 1699, op. 1, d. 133, p. 20. In August 1904, the Combat Organization adopted its bylaws. They stated that the highest organ within the organization was the Central Committee, to which Azef was selected as chairman (*chlen-rasporiaditel'*) with Savinkov as his deputy. According to Savinkov, however, the bylaws were never complied with in practice: this document "always remained but a piece of paper," rather than serving as the "constitution" of the terrorist unit (Boris Savinkov's testimony in "Stenograficheskii otchet zasedaniia C. C. K. 6 noiabria 1910 goda," GARF, f. 1699, op. 1, d. 133, p. 4).

52. *Delo Lopukhina*, 60.

53. Boris Savinkov's testimony in "Stenograficheskii otchet zasedaniia C. C. K. 6 noiabria 1910 goda," GARF, f. 1699, op. 1, d. 133, pp. 2, 6; "Pokazaniia Iriny, Ritinoi (Rakitnikovoi), Rubanovicha, Burtseva, dannye sudebno-sledstvennoi komissii," GARF, f. 1699, op. 1, d. 129, p. 3.

54. Spiridovich, *Zapiski zhandarma*, 180; "Pokazaniia tt. Bobrova, Bol'shova, Kubova, Chernova, Bunakova i Moiseenko, dannye sudebno-sledstvennoi komissii," GARF, f. 1699, op. 1, d. 130, p. 189; Rubenstein, *Comrade Valentine*, 78; Mogil'ner, "Boris Savinkov," 87; Gorodnitskii, "B. V. Savinkov i sudebno-sledstvennaia komissiia po delu Azefa," 237.

55. Spence, *Boris Savinkov*, 20–21; Geifman, *Thou Shalt Kill*, 164; V. O. Levitskii, "A. D. Pokotilov," *Katorga i ssylka* 3 (1922): 159, 171.

56. O. V. Budnitskii, ed., *Zhenshchiny-terroristki v Rossii* (Rostov-on-Don: Feniks, 1996): 76–78.

57. "Iz istorii Partii S.-R.," *Novyi zhurnal* 101 (1970): 195.

58. Gorodnitskii, "Tri stilia rukovodstva boevoi organizatsiei," 54–55.

59. For a discussion of various dogmatic principles—ranging from neo-Kantian philosophy to Orthodox Christianity—that led the Combat Organization members to embrace terror, see Anna Geifman, *Thou Shalt Kill*, 49.

60. Gorodnitskii, "Tri stilia rukovodstva boevoi organizatsiei," 55.

61. N. Tiutchev, "Zametki o vospominaniiakh B. V. Savinkova," *Katorga i ssylka* 5 (12) (1924): 68–69.

62. See, for example, Rataev, "Evno Azef," 196–97. This information is confirmed by all available left-wing sources without exception.

63. Gerasimov, "E. Azef i A. A. Lopukhin" (undated manuscript), p. 9, Nicolaevsky, 206–14; and Rataev, "Evno Azef," 204.

64. "Pis'mo S. V. Zubatova A. I. Spiridovichu po povodu vykhoda v svet ego knigi 'Partiia s.-r. i ee predshestvenniki'," *Krasnyi Arkhiv* 2 (1922): 282.

65. Rataev, "Evno Azef," 204; report to DPD, 25 May (7 June) 1911, Okhrana XXIVb–6; and letter from N. A. Rubakin to B. I. Nicolaevsky, 8 March 1935, Nic. 206-8.

66. Rataev, "Evno Azef," 204, 209.

67. For instance, it was Azef who in early 1904 warned the police about the details of Savinkov's preparations to stage a terrorist act against Count Kutaisov, the governor-general of Irkutsk. In March of the same year Azef provided Lopukhin with enough evidence to arrest prominent PSR activist Khaim Levit, who had come to Russia from abroad in order to set up dynamite laboratories, organize various new "flying combat detachments," and prepare an attempt against the life of Nicholas II (*Obvinitel'nyi akt ob ... Lopukhine,* GARF, f. 102, 7 *deloproizvodstvo,* 1909, d. 891; *Delo Lopukhina,* 56, 58).

68. Iurii Davydov, *Tainaia liga* (Moscow: Izdatel'stvo Pravda, 1990), 18. "My security is totally dependable," Plehve would say, "I think that an assassination attempt may succeed only by chance" (Gul', *Azef,* 45). Nonetheless, at times the dignitary "gave vent to a kind of gallows humor. He refused to have the black bunting, which had been used for Sipiagin's funeral, removed from the staircase of his Fontanka home. When it was suggested that the cloth be taken down, the minister replied: 'No, you'd better save it; you can still use it for me'" (Judge, *Plehve,* 234).

69. Sazonov remained unconscious for several days. After he recovered, he was tried and sentenced to hard labor. He was spending his term at the Zerentui hard-labor prison, when on 27 November 1910 he committed suicide in protest against the harsh treatment of political convicts by the prison commandant Vysotsky (Spiridovich, *Zapiski zhandarma,* 156, 252).

70. Count M. V. Golitsyn cited in Davydov, *Tainaia liga,* 18.

71. "25 let nazad. Iz dnevnika L. Tikhomirova," *KA* 1 (38) (1930): 59–60; Sukhotina-Tolstaia cited in Davydov, *Tainaia liga,* 18.

72. See, for example, Tiutchev, "Zametki o vospominaniiakh B. V. Savinkova," *Katorga i ssylka* 5 (12) (1924): 63.

73. Cited in Rubenstein, *Comrade Valentine,* 109.

74. William Shakespeare, *Macbeth.*

75. Gray, *The Neuropsychology of Anxiety,* 461.

76. Savinkov, *Vospominaniia,* 66; Longe and Zil'ber, *Terroristy i okhranka,* 113.

77. Pokazaniia t. Bobrova (Natansona), typescript, p. 5, GARF, f. 1699, op. 1, d. 123; A. B., *Za kulisami okhrannogo otdeleniia,* 20.

78. "Pokazaniia Iriny, Ritinoi (Rakitnikovoi), Rubanovicha, Burtseva, dannye sudebno-sledstvennoi komissii," GARF, f. 1699, op. 1, d. 129, pp. 29–30.

79. See, for example, report to DPD, 18 April [1 May] 1908, Okhrana XIIc [1]–1a.

80. Gorodnitskii, "Tri stilia rukovodstva boevoi organizatsiei," 55.

81. Zenzinov, "Razoblachenie provokatsii Azeva," 1.

82. "Opravdatel'naia zapiska Azefa," in Nikolaevskii, *Konets Azefa,* 57.

83. Boris Savinkov's testimony in "Stenograficheskii otchet zasedaniia C. C. K. 12 noiabria 1910 goda," GARF, f. 1699, op. 1, d. 133, p. 18. Azef's association with Savinkov was hardly anything close to friendship; even during and after the hunt for Plehve, Savinkov deliberately accentuated his strictly "business relations" with Azef (Gorodnitskii, "B. V. Savinkov i sudebno-sledstvennaia komissiia po delu Azefa," *Minuvshee* 18, 209).

84. Stenograficheskii otchet 26 zasedaniia sudebno-sledstvennoi komissii, 2 maia 1910 g., p. 24, GARF, f. 1699, op. 1, d. 136.

85. "Pokazaniia V. L. Burtseva, dannye sudebno-sledstvennoi komissii po delu Azefa," GARF, f. 1699, op. 1, d. 129, p. 153.

86. "Doneseniia Evno Azefa (Perepiska Azefa s Rataevym v 1903-1905 gg.)," *Byloe* 1 (23) (July 1917): 227.

87. Stolypin, *Polnoe sobranie rechei*, 163.

88. Decoded telegram from St. Petersburg, 17 [30] December 1903, Okhrana XIIIc [3]–13, incoming telegram no. 1085.

89. Aldanov, "Azef," *Istoki*, 403.

90. Rataev, "Evno Azef," 206.

91. Spiridovich, *Zapiski zhandarma*, 154–55. According to both Spiridovich and Rataev, Azef, while giving correct information about the disposition of the combatants, protected his position by reporting that the terrorists were planning an attack not against Plehve, but against Lopukhin himself (Rataev, "Evno Azef," 207).

92. Rataev, "Evno Azef," 207–8.

93. Savinkov, *Vospominaniia*, 28.

94. Gerasimov remembered having personally burned this letter—at Azef's insistence (Gerasimov, *Na lezvii*, 137–38; Gerasimov, "E. Azef i A. A. Lopukhin, 9; see also Schleifman, *Undercover Agents*, 27).

95. Pavlov and Peregudova, *Pis'ma Azefa*, 100–101. Pokotilov's constantly trembling hands, a sign of alcoholism, may have caused the accidental bomb explosion that killed him (Geifman, *Thou Shalt Kill*, 164).

96. "Doneseniia Evno Azefa," *Byloe* (23) (July 1917): 206; Pavlov and Peregudova, *Pis'ma Azefa*, 101. See also Stolypin, *Polnoe sobranie rechei*, 163.

97. See Pavlov and Peregudova, *Pis'ma Azefa*, 100–109.

98. Gerasimov, *Na lezvii*, 138; Gerasimov, "E. Azef i A. A. Lopukhin," 9.

99. Rubenstein, *Comrade Valentine*, 111.

100. Lur'e, *Politseiskie i provokatory*, 310. Years later, Rataev suggested that Azef had began to conspire against government dignitaries under Gershuni's influence (Praisman, "Fenomen Azefa," 68). Some have accepted this hypothesis, which in fact was based on "neither direct not indirect evidence; Azef certainly was not one of the exalted youths, whose minds and hearts Gershuni usually captivated." Conversely, it was Azef who "deceived and used the renowned terrorist" (Ruud and Stepanov, *Fontanka*, 16, 197).

101. See, for example, F. Vinogradov-Iagodin and K. Protopopov, "Provokator-terrorist Evno Azef," p. 10, GARF, f. 533, op. 1, d. 1445, and Praisman, "Fenomen Azefa," 68. Nicolaevsky supports this generally accepted opinion (Nikolajewsky, *Aseff the Spy*, 68–69; see also a letter from Rubakin to Nicolaevsky, 8 March 1935; and a letter from B. I. Nicolaevsky to N. A. Rubakin, 20 March 1935, Nic. 206-8). Some even argue that Azef's alleged cooperation with the revolutionaries was due to his desire to take revenge on "generals and ministers" for the Jewish Pale and the pogroms (Tolstoi, "Azef, kak teatral'naia maska," 15–16).

102. For a police description of the surveillance and arrest of Klitchoglu's group, see the intelligence summary, 5 February 1904, pp. 4–7, Okhrana XIIIc (2)-4A. See also *Obvinitel'nyi akt ob . . . Lopukhine*, GARF, f. 102, 7 deloproizvodstvo, 1909, d. 891.

103. Rataev, "Evno Azef," 198. Director of the Police Department Lopukhin denied Plehve's responsibility for staging or instigating the Kishinev pogrom (L. Aizenberg, "Na slovakh i na dele [Po povodu memuarov S. Iu. Vitte i A. A. Lopukhina]," *Evreiskaia letopis'*, 3 [Leningrad-Moscow, 1924]: 37). For additional information see Judge, *Plehve*, 98–100.

104. Letter from N. A. Rubakin to B. I. Nicolaevsky, 8 March 1935, Nic. 206-8.

105. Azef might have felt slightly sentimental at the sight of raggedly clothed Jewish peddler boys—vestiges of his own wretched childhood—on the

streets of Vil'no and Warsaw, from whom his comrades often saw him buying pins, matches, and other trifles (P. S. Ivanovskaia in Budnitskii, ed., *Zhenshchiny-terroristki v Rossii*, 69–70). Perhaps—this cannot be entirely excluded—by showing outward signs of concern to the plight of the poor, Azef was simply adding another subtle touch to the compassionate and sensitive image he projected onto his comrades. Another possibility—perhaps not too far-fetched—is that by showing charity to Jewish children Azef subconsciously was underscoring the distance between his past and his present.

106. Cited in Praisman, "Fenomen Azefa," 68.

107. "Pokazaniia L. G. Azef," GARF, f. 1699, op. 1, d. 126, p. 9. There is reason to believe that Azef converted either to Russian Orthodoxy or Lutheranism on Zubatov's suggestion (Rubenstein, *Comrade Valentine*, 33; see also Nikolaevskii, *Konets Azefa*, 37). Years later, when interrogated by German police authorities, Azef left the question about his religious affiliation blank ("Dopros Azefa," 14 June 1915, GARF, f. 1699, op. 2, d. 142).

108. For a discussion of the controversy over agrarian and factory terror, see Geifman, *Thou Shalt Kill*, 72–73.

109. "Iz istorii Partii S.-R.," *Novyi zhurnal* 101 (1970): 177.

110. *Obvinitel'nyi akt ob . . . Lopukhine*, GARF, f. 102, 7 *deloproizvodstvo*, 1909, d. 891; "Pokazaniia V. L. Burtseva . . . po delu Azefa," GARF, f. 1699, op. 1, d. 129, p. 122.

111. Rataev, "Evno Azef," 191. For information on Zhuchenko see Anna Geifman, "Zinaida F. Zhuchenko," *Modern Encyclopedia of Russian and Soviet History*, vol. 55 (Gulf Breeze, Florida: Academic International Press), 1993, 230–31.

112. *Delo Lopukhina*, 57–58. The combatants were arrested on 16–17 March (Gorodnitskii, "B. V. Savinkov i sudebno-sledstvennaia komissiia po delu Azefa," 217).

113. Boris Savinkov's testimony in "Stenograficheskii otchet zasedaniia C. C. K. 12 noiabria 1910 goda," GARF, f. 1699, op. 1, d. 133, p. 7. Savinkov's contentious, almost aggressive, attitude toward Azef serves as an additional argument against the latter's close involvement in Combat Organization affairs in the earlier period: it seems inconceivable that a person who allegedly led the terrorists against Plehve suddenly became an alien in their eyes.

114. For instance, in January 1905, Azef provided the police with information about SR activity in the Caucasus, and owing to him the authorities were able to prevent the first assassination attempt against Count Nakashidze, the Governor of Baku. Around the same time, Azef informed the imperial police of the revolutionaries' plans to import into Russia shipments of explosives necessary for manufacturing the notoriously effective Macedonian bombs, and he provided the authorities with names of those who were selected to bring the explosives to Samara and Saratov from Bulgaria. Finally, in early August 1905, Azef's information allowed the police to prevent an attempt against General Unterberger, governor of Nizhnii Novgorod (*Obvinitel'nyi akt ob . . . Lopukhine*, GARF, f. 102, 7 *deloproizvodstvo*, 1909, d. 891; *Delo Lopukhina*, 56, 58).

115. Nicolaevsky claims that Azef's reports at the time sought primarily to turn over to the police his opponents within the PSR, such as Mariia Seliuk and Stepan Sletov, who were arrested in September 1904, and that he "deliberately intended to put the police on a false trail and divert suspicion from the real work" of the Combat Organization (Nikolajewsky, *Aseff the Spy*, 103–4). Azef's limited involvement in the affairs of the organization after July 1904

hardly justifies this assertion. For an evaluation of Azef's activities in the PSR, as established by various police sources, see Stolypin, *Polnoe sobranie rechei*, 160, 164; see also Pavlov and Peregudova, eds., *Pis'ma Azefa*, 105–6

116. "Izveshchenie Tsentra'nogo Komiteta," 2.

117. As in Plehve's case, some have sought to explain Azef's involvement in the attempt against the Grand Duke by the latter's reputation as an anti-Semite. Rabbi Maze, for instance, was convinced that both attempts were acts of "vengeance of a Jew against the great adversaries of the Jewish people" (cited in Praisman, "Fenomen Azefa," 69).

118. Gorodnitskii, "B. V. Savinkov i sudebno-sledstvennaia komissiia po delu Azefa," 217.

119. See, for example, "Pokazaniia V. L. Burtseva . . . po delu Azefa," GARF, f. 1699, op. 1, d. 129, p. 153; and "Pokazaniia tt. Bobrova, Bol'shova, Kubova, Chernova, Bunakova i Moiseenko, dannye sudebno-sledstvennoi komissii," GARF, f. 1699, op. 1, d. 130, p. 191. In fact, not until the SRs came up with their interpretation of Azef as a government agent mercilessly killing his own employers to build his revolutionary prestige did any sources—whether official investigation records or underground publications—accuse him of being implicated in this terrorist act in any direct way (Stolypin, *Polnoe sobranie rechei*, 164). All contrary evidence notwithstanding, scholars continue to hold Azef responsible for this terrorist act (see, for example, Gorodnitskii, "B. V. Savinkov i sudebno-sledstvennaia komissiia po delu Azefa," 209).

120. *Delo Lopukhina*, 57; Rataev, "Evno Azef," 210; see also Bernstein, *L'Affaire Azeff*, 56.

121. Boris Savinkov's testimony in "Stenograficheskii otchet zasedaniia C. C. K. 12 noiabria 1910 goda," GARF, f. 1699, op. 1, d. 133, p. 6.

122. "Pokazaniia tt. Bobrova, Bol'shova, Kubova, Chernova, Bunakova i Moiseenko, dannye sudebno-sledstvennoi komissii," GARF, f. 1699, op. 1, d. 130, p. 191.

123. Boris Savinkov's testimony in "Stenograficheskii otchet zasedaniia C. C. K. 12 noiabria 1910 goda," GARF, f. 1699, op. 1, d. 133, pp. 6–7.

124. *Obvinitel'nyi akt ob . . . Lopukhine*, GARF, f. 102, 7 *deloproizvodstvo*, 1909, d. 891. While supplying the police with facts of varying importance, Azef made a point of assuring his superiors that he did not take part in the activities of the Combat Organization (see his letter of 23 September 1904 in Pavlov and Peregudova, *Pis'ma Azefa*, 107–9).

125. "Iz zapisok M. E. Bakaia," 197; Savinkov, *Vospominaniia*, 327–28; Boris Savinkov's testimony in "Stenograficheskii otchet zasedaniia C. C. K. 12 noiabria 1910 goda," GARF, f. 1699, op. 1, d. 133, p. 6. See also miscellaneous notes by V. L. Burtsev, pp. 6–7, Nic. 150-1.

126. "Pokazaniia V. L. Burtseva, dannye sudebno-sledstvennoi komissii po delu Azefa," GARF, f. 1699, op. 1, d. 129, p. 125.

127. Savinkov, *Vospominaniia terrorista*, 102; and A. I. Spiridovich, *Partiia sotsialistov-revoliutsionerov i ee predshestvenniki (1886–1916)* (Petrograd, 1918), 188–89.

128. In contrast to the relatively lenient punishment of hard labor tsarist authorities had deemed appropriate for Sazonov following Plehve's assassination, Kaliaev was sentenced to death and hanged (Geifman, *Thou Shalt Kill*, 55).

129. Spiridovich, *Zapiski zhandarma*, 180–81.

130. Davydov, *Tainaia liga*, 24–25, 19. Interestingly, black humor associated with the Moscow assassination extended far beyond the Russian borders.

Thus, President Theodore Roosevelt wrote to a close friend on 17 February 1905: "I am having my own troubles here, and there are several eminent statesmen at the other end of Pennsylvania Avenue whom I would gladly lend to the Russian Government, if they cared to expend them as bodyguards for grand dukes whenever there was a likelihood of dynamite bombs being exploded!" (Elting E. Morison, ed., *The Letters of Theodore Roosevelt* [Cambridge, MA: Harvard University Press, 1951], 1129).

131. Pokazaniia t. Bobrova (Natansona), typescript, p. 5, GARF, f. 1699, op. 1, d. 123.

Chapter 4, Terrorist-Virtuoso, 1905–1908, 85–103

1. "Pokazaniia Iriny, Ritinoi (Rakitnikovoi), Rubanovicha, Burtseva, dannye sudebno-sledstvennoi komissii po delu Azefa," GARF, f. 1699, op. 1, d. 129, p. 9.

2. Pokazaniia t. Bobrova (Natansona), typescript, pp. 6, 11, GARF, f. 1699, op. 1, d. 123, and "Iz istorii Partii S.-R.," *Novyi zhurnal* 100 (1970): 305.

3. "Iz istorii Partii S.-R.," *Novyi zhurnal* 101 (1970): 173.

4. Gerasimov cited in Praisman, "Fenomen Azefa," 69.

5. "Pokazaniia Iriny, Ritinoi (Rakitnikovoi), Rubanovicha, Burtseva, dannye sudebno-sledstvennoi komissii," GARF, f. 1699, op. 1, d. 129, pp. 5–6.

6. "Iz istorii Partii S.-R.," *Novyi zhurnal* 100 (1970): 305.

7. Cited in Praisman, "Fenomen Azefa," 70.

8. Savinkov, *Vospominaniia*, 173–75.

9. Azef had nothing to do with a previous attempt on Trepov's life that had taken place in Moscow in accordance with a secret sanction of the local SR committee. The assassination attempt, carried out by a young man named Poltoratskii, took place on 2 January 1905 at Kurskii railway station, but turned out to be a failure (Tiutchev, "Zametki o vospominaniiakh B. V. Savinkova," 62). In the summer of 1905 Azef reported to the Police Department that terrorist Ivan Kazantsev had come to St. Petersburg in order to organize an attempt against Trepov (*Obvinitel'nyi akt ob ... Lopukhine*, GARF, f. 102, 7 *deloproizvodstvo*, 1909, d. 891).

10. "Pokazaniia Iriny, Ritinoi (Rakitnikovoi), Rubanovicha, Burtseva, dannye sudebno-sledstvennoi komissii po delu Azefa," GARF, f. 1699, op. 1, d. 129, pp. 23, 33.

11. "Iz istorii Partii S.-R.," *Novyi zhurnal* 100 (1970): 300; "Pokazaniia tt. Bobrova, Bol'shova, Kubova, Chernova, Bunakova i Moiseenko, dannye sudebno-sledstvennoi komissii," GARF, f. 1699, op. 1, d. 130, p. 85. There is no evidence to support the assertion that Chernov "learned a great deal from" Azef, whom the party ideologist believed to have "possessed fine knowledge of theoretical questions" (Gorodnitskii, "Tri stilia rukovodstva boevoi organizatsiei," 57).

12. Boris Savinkov's testimony in "Stenograficheskii otchet zasedaniia S. S. K. 9 noiabria 1910 goda," GARF, f. 1699, op. 1, d. 133, pp. 19, 21.

13. Gorodnitskii, "Tri stilia rukovodstva boevoi organizatsiei," 57; and Gorodnitskii, "B. V. Savinkov i Sudebno-Sledstvennaia komissiia po delu Azefa," 215. Gorodnitskii produces no evidence to substantiate his claims. Conversely, Azef's wife affirms that her husband "was a person poorly educated in theory, and when he had to say something, he could never put two words together" ("Pokazaniia L. G. Azef," GARF, f. 1699, op. 1, d. 126, p. 11).

Other SRs shared this opinion. See, for example, "Pokazaniia Iriny, Ritinoi (Rakitnikovoi), Rubanovicha, Burtseva, dannye sudebno-sledstvennoi komissii po delu Azefa," GARF, f. 1699, op. 1, d. 129, p. 32.

14. "Pokazaniia Iriny, Ritinoi (Rakitnikovoi), Rubanovicha, Burtseva, dannye sudebno-sledstvennoi komissii po delu Azefa," GARF, f. 1699, op. 1, d. 129, p. 8.

15. "Pokazaniia M. F. S. [Seliuk], GARF, f. 1699, op. 1, d. 132, p. 1.

16. See, for example, "Pokazaniia L. G. Azef," GARF, f. 1699, op. 1, d. 126, p. 14.

17. Trotskii, "Evno Azef," 230.

18. "Pokazaniia Iriny, Ritinoi (Rakitnikovoi), Rubanovicha, Burtseva, dannye sudebno-sledstvennoi komissii po delu Azefa," GARF, f. 1699, op. 1, d. 129, p. 31.

19. "Pokazaniia Iriny, Ritinoi (Rakitnikovoi), Rubanovicha, Burtseva, dannye sudebno-sledstvennoi komissii po delu Azefa," GARF, f. 1699, op. 1, d. 129, pp. 46, 67–68.

20. Gerasimov, *Na lezvii*, 72; Vinogradov-Iagodin and Protopopov, "Provokator-terrorist Evno Azef," GARF, f. 533, op. 1, d. 1445; letter from B. I. Nicolaevsky to V. M. Zenzinov, 21 July 1931, Nic. 206-10.

21. "Pokazaniia Iriny, Ritinoi (Rakitnikovoi), Rubanovicha, Burtseva, dannye sudebno-sledstvennoi komissii," GARF, f. 1699, op. 1, d. 129, p. 6.

22. Mikhail Gots was the one Central Committee member whom the terrorists knew personally, and therefore he was the only PSR leader about whom Azef always talked with reverence (*Zakliuchenie sudebno-sledstvennoi komissii po delu Azefa* [Paris?: Izdanie Tsentral'nogo Komiteta P. S.-R., 1911, 27).

23. Boris Savinkov's testimony in "Stenograficheskii otchet zasedaniia S. S. K. 9 noiabria 1910 goda," GARF, f. 1699, op. 1, d. 133, p. 20.

24. Ibid., 34.

25. Ibid., 26.

26. For Savinkov's explanation of Azef's purpose in fostering conflicts between the Central Committee and the Combat Organization members, see Boris Savinkov's testimony in "Stenograficheskii otchet zasedaniia S. S. K. 12 noiabria 1910 goda," GARF, f. 1699, op. 1, d. 133, pp. 20–21. Azef always tried and invariably succeeded in making sure that in the eyes of the party leadership the combatants appeared as a unified and cohesive group without any internal disagreements, whose members wholeheartedly trusted their representative—that is, Azef himself—to settle any disputed issue with the civilians ("Iz istorii Partii S.-R.," *Novyi zhurnal* 101 [1970]: 182).

27. Rubenstein, *Comrade Valentine*, 164.

28. Daly, *Autocracy under Siege*, 167.

29. "'Peterburgskoe' pis'mo Men'shchikova," GARF, f. 1699, op. 1, d. 4; *Zakliuchenie*, 55.

30. Rubenstein, *Comrade Valentine*, 166–67; "Pokazaniia Kubova [Argunova]," GARF, f. 1699, op. 1, d. 131, p. 18.

31. Miscellaneous notes by V. L. Burtsev, p. 1, Nic. 150-1; cited in Tiutchev, "Zametki o vospominaniiakh B. V. Savinkova," *Katorga i ssylka* 5 (12) (1924): 59. In Moscow, the SR terrorists did succeed in blowing up the Okhrana building on 9 December 1905, but according to Vladimir Zenzinov, the man in charge of this operation, Azef had nothing to do with this ad-libbed act (letter from V. M. Zenzinov to B. I. Nicolaevsky, 10 July 1931, Nic. 206-10).

32. Rubenstein, *Comrade Valentine*, 181; Daly, *Autocracy under Siege*, 167.

33. Azef had nothing to do with this act of vengeance. The SR Fedor Nazarov, commissioned by Savinkov, assassinated Tatarov in his parents'

house in Warsaw. The spy was killed in their presence, and his mother was accidentally wounded. See, for example, a letter from Senzharskii (Bleklov) to A. N. Bakh, 17 September 1910, GARF, f. 1699, op. 1, d. 81; and "Pokazaniia tt. Bobrova, Bol'shova, Kubova, Chernova, Bunakova i Moiseenko, dannye sudebno-sledstvennoi komissii," GARF, f. 1699, op. 1, d. 130, pp. 59–60; V. Denisenko, "Provokator N. Iu. Tatarov-'Kostrov'," *Katorga i ssylka* 50 (1928): 88.

34. Gerasimov, *Na lezvii*, 83.

35. Ibid., 71–72; see also a letter from B. I. Nicolaevsky to S. G. Svatikov, 30 June 1931, Nic, 416-10. Nicolaevsky suggested, albeit unconvincingly, that Rachkovskii's evasive behavior may be explained by his desire to get rid of the agent involved with criminal enterprises (letter from B. I. Nicolaevsky to V. L. Burtsev, 6 June 1931, Nic., 475-8). Most likely, Rachkovskii, a former director of the Paris and Geneva Okhrana sections, preferred to depend on his own agents, rather than to venture into a new relationship and rely on Rataev's contact among the radicals.

36. Savinkov, *Vospominaniia*, 206–8; Boris Savinkov's testimony in "Stenograficheskii otchet zasedaniia S. S. K. 12 noiabria 1910 goda," GARF, f. 1699, op. 1, d. 133, p. 2.

37. Boris Savinkov's testimony in "Stenograficheskii otchet zasedaniia S. S. K. 12 noiabria 1910 goda," GARF, f. 1699, op. 1, d. 133, p. 1.

38. Valentina Popova, "Dinamitnye masterskie 1906–1907 gg. i provokator Azef," *Katorga i ssylka* 4 (33) (1927): 64. Popova's assertion invalidates Nicolaevsky's argument that the Moscow Okhrana knew about the terrorists' plans not from Azef, but from another police agent among the local SRs, Zinaida Zhuchenko. She was not a member of the Combat Organization; nor did she stand close enough to it to know much about its internal affairs.

39. Savinkov later admitted that, incredible as it may seem, he was quite satisfied with Azef's flimsy explanation (Boris Savinkov's testimony in "Stenograficheskii otchet zasedaniia S. S. K. 12 noiabria 1910 goda," GARF, f. 1699, op. 1, d. 133, p. 1).

40. "Zaiavlenie po delu Dubasova," GARF, f. 1699, op. 1, d. 9.

41. Geifman, *Thou Shalt Kill*, 65.

42. Ibid., 65–66.

43. Feliks Lur'e, *Politseiskie i provokatory* (St. Petersburg: Chas Pik, 1992), 284–86.

44. For a discussion of the SRs' reasons for not taking responsibility for Gapon's murder, see Geifman, *Thou Shalt Kill*, 66, 282n.

45. Pokazaniia t. Bobrova (Natansona), typescript, pp. 42–43, GARF, f. 1699, op. 1, d. 123.

46. Boris Savinkov's testimony in "Stenograficheskii otchet zasedaniia S. S. K. 12 noiabria 1910 goda," GARF, f. 1699, op. 1, d. 133, p. 27.

47. Letter from B. I. Nicolaevsky to M. A. Aldanov, 17 January 1930, *Istochnik*, 2 (27) (1997): 61; Rubenstein, *Comrade Valentine*, 193.

48. Letter from Nicolaevsky to Aldanov, 17 January 1930, *Istochnik*, 61.

49. Rubenstein, *Comrade Valentine*, 197.

50. Letter from B. I. Nicolaevsky to V. M. Chernov, 24 April 1931, Nic. 476-21.

51. Rubenstein, *Comrade Valentine*, 197–200.

52. Ibid., 187.

53. Boris Savinkov's testimony in "Stenograficheskii otchet zasedaniia C. C. K. 12 noiabria 1910 goda," GARF, f. 1699, op. 1, d. 133, p. 1. Nicolaevsky, who believed that it was Azef who had been the initiator of this attempt,

describes how Rachkovskii came to assume that Azef concocted the terrorist act in Moscow: "One of the local SRs . . . [met Azef] accidentally in the street and afterwards told his comrades that he thought the attempt on Dubasoff had been organized by Azef himself. Zhuchenko hastened to report this statement to the [Moscow] Okhrana, which immediately telegraphed this news to St. Petersburg" (Nikolajewsky, *Aseff the Spy*, 160–62).

54. "Pokazaniia Iriny, Ritinoi (Rakitnikovoi), Rubanovicha, Burtseva, dannye sudebno-sledstvennoi komissii," GARF, f. 1699, op. 1, d. 129, p. 3.

55. Cited in Rubenstein, *Comrade Valentine*, 187–88. See also Tiutchev, "Zametki o vospominaniiakh B. V. Savinkova," 56.

56. "Pokazaniia Iriny, Ritinoi (Rakitnikovoi), Rubanovicha, Burtseva, dannye sudebno-sledstvennoi komissii," GARF, f. 1699, op. 1, d. 129, p. 6.

57. Savinkov, *Vospominaniia*, 208, 213.

58. "Zaiavlenie po delu Dubasova," GARF, f. 1699, op. 1, d. 9.

59. "Pokazaniia Kubova [Argunova]," GARF, f. 1699, op. 1, d. 131, p. 26.

60. Margarita Grundi, "Boris Vnorovskii (1882–1906 g.g.)," *Katorga i ssylka* 23 (1926): 236; "Zaiavlenie po delu Dubasova," GARF, f. 1699, op. 1, d. 9.

61. The revolutionary who was assigned to bring the explosive device to the would-be assassin subsequently explained that he could not fulfill his task because he was being watched by police agents and could not even leave his hotel. It is highly likely, therefore, that Azef had notified the Moscow Okhrana about the terrorist act scheduled for 23 April, and that the police took certain precautions ("Zaiavlenie po delu Dubasova," GARF, f. 1699, op. 1, d. 9).

62. Savinkov, *Vospominaniia*, 349–50.

63. "Pokazaniia V. L. Burtseva, dannye sudebno-sledstvennoi komissii po delu Azefa," GARF, f. 1699, op. 1, d. 129, p. 153.

64. Popova, "Dinamitnye masterskie," *Katorga i ssylka* 5 (34): 50. Gerasimov too believed that Azef wished to prevent this terrorist act at the last minute by his own means, but failed (Gerasimov, *Na lezvii*, 84).

65. "Zaiavlenie po delu Dubasova," GARF, f. 1699, op. 1, d. 9; Spiridovich, *Partiia sotsialistov-revoliutsionerov*, 266.

66. *Otchet o sostoiavshemsia 1/14 ianvaria 1909 g. v Parizhe sekretnom zasedanii*, Okhrana XVIc-9. See also B. Gorinson, "Na slezhke za Durnovo," *Katorga i ssylka* 7 (20) (1925): 140.

67. Tiutchev, "Zametki o vospominaniiakh B. V. Savinkova," *Katorga i ssylka* 5 (12) (1924): 57.

68. Cited in F. M. Lur'e and Z. I. Peregudova, "Tsarskaia Okhranka i provokatsiia," *Iz glubiny vremen*, 1 (1992), 57.

69. Burtsev later insisted (without substantiating his claim with any evidence) that Gerasimov persuaded Azef to continue his police service by explicit threat. "If you leave, I will expose you," he allegedly told the frustrated spy ("Pokazaniia V. L. Burtseva, dannye sudebno-sledstvennoi komissii po delu Azefa," GARF, f. 1699, op. 1, d. 129, p. 155).

70. Decoded telegram from St. Petersburg, no. 1960, 15 (28) September 1907, Okhrana XIIIc(3)-25. See also report to DPD. 20 November (3 December) 1907, Okhrana VIh-4. Moreover, after 1906 Azef was not the only informant that Gerasimov implanted in the center of the SR party; at least one other police agent, whose name was never disclosed, stood very close to the SR Central Committee, a fact that allowed a significant degree of control over Azef's activities and reports (letter from Nicolaevsky to Burtsev, 8 September 1931; miscellaneous notes by V. L. Burtsev, p. 2, Nic. 150-2; report to DPD, 3 [16] May and 31 May [13 June] 1908, Okhrana XVIb [4]-1; and police report, 10 October 1909, Okhrana XVIb [3]-1A).

71. Letter from Nicolaevsky to Agafonov, 30 October 1932, Nic. 471-9.

72. Gerasimov, *Na lezvii*, 85, 138.

73. Schleifman, *Undercover Agents*, 27.

74. In following this policy, the authorities were even forced on occasion to go against the law in order to save their agent. Thus, when the *boevik* Moiseenko was arrested and tried, the police did not reveal all the evidence provided by Azef about his participation in terrorist acts, allowing the terrorist to get away with a sentence of administrative exile instead of many years of hard labor or worse (Savinkov, *Vospominaniia*, 213; Gorbunov, "Savinkov, kak memuarist," *Katorga i ssylka* 3 [40]: 182n).

75. Gorbunov, "Savinkov, kak memuarist," 3 (40): 182.

76. Ibid.

77. Popova, "Dinamitnye masterskie," *Katorga i ssylka* 5 (34): 53.

78. Gorodnitskii, "B. V. Savinkov i udebno-ledstvennaia komissiia po delu Azefa," 213–14.

79. Zinaida Gippius in Dmitrii Zubarev, ed., "Boris Savinkov: chelovek, kotoryi khotel rasshirit' chelovecheskuiu svobodu," *Nezavisimaia gazeta* (23 May 1995), 3.

80. Letter from B. I. Nicolaevsky to V. M. Chernov, 15 October 1931, Nic. 206-6. See also Boris Savinkov's testimony in "Stenograficheskii otchet zasedaniia S. S. K. 12 noiabria 1910 goda," GARF, f. 1699, op. 1, d. 133, p. 5; and "Pokazaniia t. Bobrova (Natansona)," typescript, pp. 32, 34, GARF, f. 1699, op. 1, d. 123.

81. Savinkov, *Vospominaniia*, 283–84; Gerasimov, *Na lezvii*, 85–87. The party leaders did everything to prevent the disintegration of the Combat Organization, but the terrorists repeatedly asserted that without Savinkov and Azef they could not continue their terrorist activities. At the end of negotiations between the Central Committee and the combatants a compromise was reached: central terror would be halted for the time being, but a few former members of the Combat Organization would go to St. Petersburg with the aim of assassinating von der Launits, and several of their comrades would try their luck against General A. V. Kaul'bars in Odessa. The rest of the combatants categorically refused to comply with the Central Committee's demand that they continue with terrorist work ("Pokazaniia t. Bobrova [Natansona]," typescript, p. 36, GARF, f. 1699, op. 1, d. 123).

82. Gorodnitskii, "B. V. Savinkov i sudebno-sledstvennaia komissiia po delu Azefa," 213.

83. "Pokazaniia t. Bobrova (Natansona)," typescript, pp. 45-48, GARF, f. 1699, op. 1, d. 123; and Gorodnitskii, "B. V. Savinkov i sudebno-sledstvennaia komissiia po delu Azefa," 223.

84. Cited in Gorodnitskii, "B. V. Savinkov i sudebno-sledstvennaia komissiia po delu Azefa," 224.

85. "Pokazaniia L. G. Azef," GARF, f. 1699, op. 1, d. 126, p. 29.

86. Stenograficheskii otchet 26 zasedaniia sudebno-sledstvennoi komissii, 2 maia 1910 g., pp. 23-24, GARF, f. 1699, op. 1, d. 136.

87. "Pokazaniia t. Bobrova (Natansona)," typescript, p. 36, GARF, f. 1699, op. 1, d. 123.

88. "Pokazaniia V. L. Burtseva, dannye sudebno-sledstvennoi komissii po delu Azefa," GARF, f. 1699, op. 1, d. 129, p. 154.

89. For example, on the eve of the attack against von der Launits on 3 January 1907, he had ignored an Okhrana warning to take proper precautions (Geifman, *Thou Shalt Kill*, 64).

90. GARF, f. 102, 00 1909, d. 155, part 3, p. 2ob.

91. *Obvinitel'nyi akt ob . . . Lopukhine,* GARF, f. 102, 7 *deloproizvodstvo,* 1909, d. 891. See also "Zapiska o predpolozheniiakh i slukhakh kasatel'no sushch-estvovaniia ser'eznoi provokatsii vnutri P.S.R.," GARF, f. 1699, op. 1, d. 44; and "Pokazaniia tt. Bobrova, Bol'shova, Kubova, Chernova, Bunakova i Moi-seenko, dannye sudebno-sledstvennoi komissii," GARF, f. 1699, op. 1, d. 130, p. 38.

92. Gorodnitskii, "Tri stilia rukovodstva boevoi organizatsiei," 58.

93. *Obvinitel'nyi akt ob . . . Lopukhine,* GARF, f. 102, 7 *deloproizvodstvo,* 1909, d. 891; "Pokazaniia Iriny, Ritinoi (Rakitnikovoi), Rubanovicha, Burtseva, dan-nye sudebno-sledstvennoi komissii po delu Azefa," GARF, f. 1699, op. 1, d. 129, p. 15; Vinogradov-Iagodin and Protopopov, "Provokator-terrorist Evno Azef," GARF, f. 533, op. 1, d. 1445.

94. "Pokazaniia Iriny, Ritinoi (Rakitnikovoi), Rubanovicha, Burtseva, dan-nye sudebno-sledstvennoi komissii po delu Azefa," GARF, f. 1699, op. 1, d. 129, p. 16.

95. Nikolajewsky, *Aseff the Spy,* 259–62; and Gerasimov, *Na lezvii,* 113–14, 124–27.

96. See, for example, "Pokazaniia V. L. Burtseva, dannye sudebno-sled-stvennoi komissii po delu Azefa," GARF, f. 1699, op. 1, d. 129, pp. 307–8; and Gorodnitskii, "B. V. Savinkov i sudebno-sledstvennaia komissiia po delu Azefa," 224.

97. Nicolaevsky, *Konets Azefa,* 17n.

98. Gerasimov, *Na lezvii,* 131.

99. Nikolajewsky, *Aseff the Spy,* 266.

100. Report to DPD, 31 May [13 June] 1908, Okhrana, XVIb [4]–1; and police report, 4 September 1908, Okhrana, XVIb [3]–6.

101. Boris Savinkov's testimony in "Stenograficheskii otchet zasedaniia S. S. K." (Prilozhenie), GARF, f. 1699, op. 1, d. 133.

102. Savinkov, *Vospominaniia,* 303, 309, 358.

103. Boris Savinkov's testimony in "Stenograficheskii otchet zasedaniia S. S. K." (Prilozhenie), GARF, f. 1699, op. 1, d. 133.

104. Ibid.; and cited in Gorodnitskii, "B. V. Savinkov i sudebno-sled-stvennaia komissiia po delu Azefa," 225. Upon reviewing the evidence, Prais-man confirmed Savinkov's opinion: "Azef did not doubt that Avdeev would not shoot" (Praisman, "Fenomen Azefa," 72–73).

Chapter 5, The Exposure, 105–122

1. Cited in Praisman, "Fenomen Azefa," 65.

2. "Izveshchenie Tsentral'nogo Komiteta o provokatsii E. F. Aseva," 2, PSR, 3-168; Nicolajewsky, *Aseff the Spy,* 29; see also a letter from E. Kolosov to Valentina Kolari written in Paris, 21 October 1912, Okhrana XVIb(3)-10.

3. Letter from N. A. Rubakin to B. I. Nicolaevsky, 8 March 1935, Nic. 206-8.

4. Later the SRs received similar information from other police sources, exposing Azef along with Tatarov. See "Zapiska o predpolozheniiakh i slukhakh kasatel'no sushchestvovaniia ser'eznoi provokatsii vnutri P.S.R.," GARF, f. 1699, op. 1, d. 44.

5. L. Praisman, "Fenomen Azefa," 65. Natanson confessed that since he assumed that Plehve and the Grand Duke Sergei were killed by the Combat

Organization under Azef's direction, "any rumors of his treachery bounced off me" ("Pokazaniia M. A. Natansona," GARF, f. 1699, op. 1, d. 123, p. 74).

6. Aldanov, "Azef," *Istoki*, 409. Petr Lavrov was a celebrated Populist theorist and a great authority in the radical circles.

7. As a result of an assassination attempt that Savinkov organized in 1906, Tatarov was killed in Warsaw, in the house of his parents and in their presence. The Central Committee of the PSR was reluctant to accept responsibility for this act of brutal retribution, acknowledging it as a party deed only in 1909 ("Zaiavlenie sudebno-sledstvennoi komissii Ts.K. po delu ob ubiistve Tatarova," GARF, f. 1699, op. 1, d. 10).

8. See, for example, "Saratovskoe" pis'mo, GARF, f. 1699, op. 1, d. 5; and "Zapiska o predpolozheniiakh i slukhakh kasatel'no sushchestvovaniia ser'eznoi provokatsii vnutri P.S.R.," GARF, f. 1699, op. 1, d. 44; "Pokazaniia t. Bobrova (Natansona)," typescript, pp. 4–5, GARF, f. 1699, op. 1, d. 123. See also *Zakliuchenie*, 60–61.

9. Savinkov, *Vospominaniia*, 227, 323; M. Gorbunov, "Savinkov, kak memuarist," *Katorga i ssylka* 3 (40) (1928): 173; Tiutchev, "Zametki o vospominaniiakh B. V. Savinkova," *Katorga i ssylka* 5 (12) (1924): 57; Okhrana XIIIb [1]-1B, document no. 123, 1906; and "Zapiska o predpolozheniiakh i slukhakh kasatel'no sushchestvovaniia ser'eznoi provokatsii vnutri P.S.R.," GARF, f. 1699, op. 1, d. 44. See also unsigned manuscript (probably written by Andrei Argunov), entitled "Pervaia vstrecha s Azefom," GARF, f. 1699, op. 1, d. 78, p. 41; and "Pokazaniia Iriny, Ritinoi (Rakitnikovoi), Rubanovicha, Burtseva, dannye sudebno-sledstvennoi komissii," GARF, f. 1699, op. 1, d. 129, p. 29.

10. "Pokazaniia I. A. Rubanovicha, dannye sudebno-sledstvennoi komissii po delu Azefa," GARF, f. 1699, op. 1, d. 129, p. 69; "Zapiska o predpolozheniiakh i slukhakh kasatel'no sushchestvovaniia ser'eznoi provokatsii vnutri P.S.R.," GARF, f. 1699, op. 1, d. 44; "Pokazaniia t. Bobrova (Natansona)," typescript, p. 46, GARF, f. 1699, op. 1, d. 123.

11. Stenograficheskii otchet 26 zasedaniia sudebno-sledstvennoi komissii, 2 maia 1910 g., p. 11, GARF, f. 1699, op. 1, d. 136; "Pokazaniia Iriny, Ritinoi (Rakitnikovoi), Rubanovicha, Burtseva, dannye sudebno-sledstvennoi komissii po delu Azefa," GARF, f. 1699, op. 1, d. 129, p. 42; and "Zapiska o predpolozheniiakh i slukhakh kasatel'no sushchestvovaniia ser'eznoi provokatsii vnutri P.S.R.," GARF, f. 1699, op. 1, d. 44.

12. Aldanov, "Azef," *Istoki*, 408.

13. Untitled manuscript by Olga Chernov Andreev, p. 40, Olga Andreyev Carlisle private archive.

14. Longe and Zil'ber, *Terroristy i okhranka*, 59.

15. Untitled manuscript by Olga Chernov Andreev, pp. 40–41, Olga Andreyev Carlisle private archive.

16. *Obvinitel'nyi akt ob . . . Lopukhine*, GARF, f. 102, 7 *deloproizvodstvo*, 1909, d. 891; and "Zapiska o predpolozheniiakh i slukhakh kasatel'no sushchestvovaniia ser'eznoi provokatsii vnutri P.S.R.," GARF, f. 1699, op. 1, d. 44.

17. "Zapiska o predpolozheniiakh i slukhakh kasatel'no sushchestvovaniia ser'eznoi provokatsii vnutri P.S.R.," GARF, f. 1699, op. 1, d. 44.

18. Cited in Longe and Zil'ber, *Terroristy i okhranka*, 41.

19. Rubenstein, *Comrade Valentine*, 250. See also 18 April [1 May] 1908 report to DPD, Okhrana XIIc [1]– Sotsialistov-Revoliutsionerov" (Paris, 1 [14] January 1909), PSR 1-31.

20. Cited in Rubenstein, *Comrade Valentine*, 250. See also "Zapiska o predpolozheniiakh i slukhakh kasatel'no sushchestvovaniia ser'eznoi provokatsii

vnutri P.S.R.," GARF, f. 1699, op. 1, d. 44; and "Pokazaniia tt. Bobrova, Bol'sho-va, Kubova, Chernova, Bunakova i Moiseenko, dannye sudebno-sledstvennoi komissii," GARF, f. 1699, op. 1, d. 130, p. 52.

21. "Pokazaniia t. Bobrova (Natansona)," typescript, p. 57, GARF, f. 1699, op. 1, d. 123; unsigned manuscript (probably written by Andrei Argunov), entitled "Pervaia vstrecha s Azefom," p. 52, GARF, f. 1699, op. 1, d. 78.

22. See letter from Boris Savinkov to Victor Chernov, 8 September 1908, GARF, f. 1699, op. 1, d. 46.

23. "Kopiia protokola tovarishcheskogo treteiskogo suda (Figner, Lopatin, Kropotkin)," GARF, f. 1699, op. 1, d. 25; letter from Kropotkin to "Dear Com-rades," 7 September 1908, GARF, f. 1699, op. 1, d. 33.

24. Letter from M. A. Natanson to V. M. Chernov, 28 August 1908, GARF, f. 1699, op. 1, d. 32.

25. Unsigned manuscript (probably written by Andrei Argunov), entitled "Pervaia vstrecha s Azefom," GARF, f. 1699, op. 1, d. 78, pp. 54, 56.

26. Cited in Boris Savinkov's testimony in "Stenograficheskii otchet zasedaniia S. S. K." (Prilozhenie), GARF, f. 1699, op. 1, d. 133.

27. See an undated letter from Burtsev to V. P. Zhuk in England (enve-lope postmarked 20 January 1909), Arkhiv V. P. Zhuka, International Institute of Social History, Amsterdam; "Pokazaniia V. L. Burtseva, dannye sudebno-sledstvennoi komissii po delu Azefa," GARF, f. 1699, op. 1, d. 129, p. 144; *Otchet o zasedaniiakh levoi gruppy sotsialistov-revoliutsionerov (Iudelevskogo i Agafonova) po delu Azefa*, police report, 6 (19) January 1909, Okhrana XVIc-9; *Delo Lopukhina*, 34.

28. On his own initiative, M. E. Bakai (Mikhailovskii) applied and was accepted as an agent of the Ekaterinoslav section of the Okhrana. After sub-sequently serving in St. Petersburg and Moscow, he was transferred to War-saw, where he was implicated in corruption and extortion, leading to his forced retirement. After his dismissal in 1906, Bakai immediately switched sides and joined the revolutionaries, providing them with secret police documents. He was caught and exiled to Siberia, but with Burtsev's help managed to escape abroad (telegram from St. Petersburg signed by Orloff, dated 22 March [4 April] 1908, Okhrana XXIVb-5; and *Otchet o zasedaniiakh levoi gruppy sotsialis-tov-revoliutsionerov [Iudelevskogo i Agafonova] po delu Azefa*, police report dated 6 [19] January 1909, Okhrana XVIc-9).

29. V. Burtsev, an untitled manuscript (Paris, 29 December 1934), 5–7, Vladimir L. Burtsev Collection (cited hereafter as Burtsev with box and fold-er numbers), 2–12, Hoover Institution Archives, Stanford, California. To men-tion only one example of Bakai's penchant for storytelling, he claimed that the head of the local Okhrana in Radom was tried and sentenced to death for ille-gal operations, when in fact there was no section of the security police in that town (Stolypin, *Polnoe sobranie rechei*, 166, 168; for a similar example, see Schleifman, *Undercover Agents*, 23).

30. "Pokazaniia t. Bobrova (Natansona)," typescript, p. 60, GARF, f. 1699, op. 1, d. 123. On circumstantial evidence that Burtsev received from Bakai, see "Pokazaniia V. L. Burtseva, dannye sudebno-sledstvennoi komissii po delu Azefa," GARF, f. 1699, op. 1, d. 129, pp. 93–94. In a private letter to Burtsev, Nicolaevsky conceded that Bakai "to a great extent lived on gossip, a signifi-cant part of which was incorrect. He did not at all understand the true situa-tion in the [Police] Department and universalized *(universaliziroval)* Azef's role to the extreme" (letter from B. I. Nicolaevsky to V. L. Burtsev, 8 September 1931, Nic. 475-8).

31. *Zakliuchenie*, 71–72.

32. Letter from V. L. Burtsev to B. I. Nicolaevsky, 31 March 1931, Nic., 475-8; "Pokazaniia V. L. Burtseva, dannye sudebno-sledstvennoi komissii po delu Azefa," GARF, f. 1699, op. 1, d. 129, p. 72.

33. "Pokazaniia V. L. Burtseva, dannye sudebno-sledstvennoi komissii po delu Azefa," GARF, f. 1699, op. 1, d. 129, p. 74.

34. Ibid.

35. Ibid., 75–76, 79.

36. Ibid., 79.

37. *Obvinitel'nyi akt ob . . . Lopukhine*, GARF, f. 102, 7 *deloproizvodstvo*, 1909, d. 891. At one point, Burtsev claimed that Lopukhin, knowing that Burtsev was looking for an oportunity to talk to him, had written to him in 1908 and indicated a willingness to arrange a rendezvous. Unfortunately, Burtsev claimed, Lopukhin's letter was not delivered to him in Paris because of an incorrect address ("Pokazaniia V. L. Burtseva, dannye sudebno-sledstvennoi komissii po delu Azefa," GARF, f. 1699, op. 1, d. 129, p. 102). The story cannot be confirmed and appears to be highly implausible, especially since Lopukhin never confirmed it.

38. Nikolajewsky, *Aseff the Spy*, 21.

39. Rubenstein, *Comrade Valentine*, 249, 251, 255.

40. Aldanov, "Azef," *Istoki*, 409–10.

41. Undated letter from Burtsev to Zhuk, Arkhiv V. P. Zhuka; *Zakliuchenie*, 85.

42. "Obvinitel'nyi akt ob . . . Lopukhine," *Byloe* 9–10 (1909): 227; and Zenzinov, "Razoblachenie provokatsii Azeva," 6, Nic. 205-18.

43. Rubenstein, *Comrade Valentine*, 260–61.

44. *Delo Lopukhina*, 14. The SRs, however, hesitated to acknowledge this publicly until late January 1909 (Nic. 112-11).

45. Rubenstein, *Comrade Valentine*, 261.

46. Both Chernov and Savinkov denied that they had disclosed this information to Azef, as did Argunov, who later claimed that Azef's wife knew the purpose of Argunov's mission prior to his departure for St. Petersburg (Rubenstein, *Comrade Valentine*, 262; Boris Savinkov's testimony in "Stenograficheskii otchet zasedaniia S. S. K. 9 noiabria 1910 goda," GARF, f. 1699, op. 1, d. 133, p. 33; and unsigned manuscript [probably written by Andrei Argunov], entitled "Pervaia vstrecha s Azefom," GARF, f. 1699, op. 1, d. 78, p. 56; see also a letter from Senzharskii [Bleklov] to Bakh, 11 October 1910, GARF, f. 1699, op. 1, d. 56; and "Pokazaniia V. L. Burtseva, dannye sudebno-sledstvennoi komissii po delu Azefa," GARF, f. 1699, op. 1, d. 129, p. 120).

47. Pavlov and Peregudova, *Pis'ma Azefa*, 167.

48. F. M. Lur'e, *Khraniteli proshlogo* (Leningrad: Lenizdat, 1990), 91; *Obvinitel'nyi akt ob . . . Lopukhine*, GARF, f. 102, 7 *deloproizvodstvo*, 1909, d. 891.

49. *Obvinitel'nyi akt ob . . . Lopukhine*, GARF, f. 102, 7 *deloproizvodstvo*, 1909, d. 891. For the same document see *Byloe* 9–10 (1909) and *Novoe vremia* 11899 (29 April [12 May] 1909).

50. At his trial Lopukhin claimed that during their rendezvous Gerasimov was so insolent that Lopukhin felt an urge to slap his face. Gerasimov resorted to threats, Lopukhin said, and he was forced to ask his uninvited guest to leave his house (police report, 28 April 1909, GARF, f. 102, 7 *deloproizvodstvo*, 1909, d. 891). For his part, during this interview Gerasimov became convinced that Lopukhin might indeed turn out to be a traitor and decided not to transmit the spy's letter to him, so as to prevent the revolutionaries from acquiring

this irrefutable piece of written evidence of Azef's involvement with the police (*Obvinitel'nyi akt ob . . . Lopukhine,* GARF, f. 102, 7 *deloproizvodstvo,* 1909, d. 891).

51. *Otchet o sostoiavshemsia 1/14 ianvaria 1909 g. v Parizhe sekretnom zasedanii,* Okhrana XVIc-9; unsigned manuscript (probably written by Andrei Argunov), entitled "Pervaia vstrecha s Azefom," GARF, f. 1699, op. 1, d. 78, pp. 58–59; Gerasimov, *Na lezvii,* 133; Savinkov, *Vospominaniia,* 341. Azef later wrote to Gerasimov: "It was a fateful mistake for you and me to visit L. When God wishes to punish someone, He deprives him of reason" (cited in Aldanov, "Azef," *Istoki,* 420–22).

52. Savinkov, *Vospominaniia,* 344.

53. For a summary of Azef's deposition before the SRs, see GARF, f. 1699, op. 1, d. 7. In his letter of 25 December 1909 he wrote to Gerasimov: "Everything might have ended not so badly, and perhaps even well, had it been possible to establish an alibi. But this did not work out" because SR V. O. Fabrikant, who had gone to Berlin on a mission to verify the spy's testimony, reported to the party leaders that Azef's alibi was flawed. "Of course, I could not describe the room in which I stayed or to give its number," Azef complained, because "in spite of my request, you did not provide me with this information" (cited in Aldanov, "Azef," *Istoki,* 420, and in Ruud and Stepanov, *Fontanka,* 16, 193).

54. Cited in Aldanov, "Azef," *Istoki,* 409.

55. K. V. Gusev, *Partiia eserov: Ot melkoburzhuaznogo revoliutsionarizma k kontrrevoliutsii* (Moscow, 1975), 71.

56. 16 (29) March 1909 report to DPD, Okhrana XIIIb (1)-1A, Outgoing Dispatches, doc. 164; coded telegram from St. Petersburg, 23 January (5 February) 1909, Okhrana XIIIc (3)-28.

57. Nicolaevsky assumed incorrectly that "Nikolai" was an alias of revolutionary Ian Berdo (Nikolaevskii, *Konets Azefa,* 7n). K. N. Morozov, ed., "B. V. Savinkov i Boevaia Organizatsiia PSR v 1909–1911," *Minuvshee* 18 (Moscow-St. Petersburg: Atheneum-Feniks, 1995), 246–47). Asef always recommended "Nikolai" as the person closest to him and his future replacement in the Combat Organization. According to Natansov, the three men were selected to negotiate with Azef because he would have refused to have any dealing with anyone else in the party at that point ("Pokazaniia M. A. Natansona," GARF, f. 1699, op. 1, d. 123, pp. 67–68).

58. Nikolaevskii, *Konets Azefa,* 8.

59. "Pokazaniia L. G. Azef," GARF, f. 1699, op. 1, d. 126, p. 41; Savinkov, *Vospominaniia terrorista,* 348–53.

60. *Zakliuchenie,* 69; unsigned manuscript (probably written by Andrei Argunov), entitled "Pervaia vstrecha s Azefom," GARF, f. 1699, op. 1, d. 78, p. 65. According to Mark Aldanov, a contemporary and student of the Azef affair, the spy "was not killed because everybody was totally confused" (M. Aldanov, "Azef," *Poslednie novosti* [1924], Nic. 205-19). For his part, Mark Natanson argued that to kill Azef then would have unleashed "a total internal strife within the party" ("Pokazaniia M. A. Natansona," GARF, f. 1699, op. 1, d. 123, p. 62). At the same time, it appears that Burtsev was unfair in suggesting that the SR leaders deliberately allowed Azef to flee because they did not want to kill him in Paris—an act that would undoubtedly have resulted in the arrest and deportation of many Russian political émigrés by the French authorities (Report to DPD, 30 December 1908 [12 January 1909], Okhrana XIIc [1]-2a). For his part, Burtsev seemed to be interested not so much in killing Azef, but in interrogating and extracting police secrets from him ("Pokazaniia tt. Bobrova, Bol'shova, Kubova, Chernova, Bunakova i Moiseenko, dannye sudebno-sledstvennoi komissii," GARF, f. 1699, op. 1, d. 130, p. 17). Similarly,

Natanson notes that it was so important for the SRs to obtain Azef's confession that they were prepared to resort to "interrogation with application of physical pressure (*[dopros s pristrastiem]*," "Pokazaniia M. A. Natansona," GARF, f. 1699, op. 1, d. 123, pp. 62, 64).

The SRs suspended the surveillance of Azef's house, which made it possible for him to escape, but there is evidence that at the time of his disappearance the party leaders had already initiated preparations for a plan to induce Azef to come to Italy with them, supposedly for the purpose of his taking part in the trial, but, in fact, so that they would be able to do away with him in a prearranged secluded place without stirring a police and public scandal in France ("Pokazaniia Kubova [Argunova]," GARF, f. 1699, op. 1, d. 131, p. 66; "Pokazaniia M. A. Natansona," GARF, f. 1699, op. 1, d. 123, pp. 64–65). In any case, years later Chernov told a family member that he and Savinkov had not had the heart to kill Azef in his home in the presence of his wife and children on the evening of his escape (S. Sosinskii-Semikhat, "Pis'ma iz derevni v epokhu perestroiki zastoia" [unpublished manuscript, 1992], 3). Chernov had previously confessed, however, that in accordance with a prior agreement, all three comrades went to Azef's house unarmed for fear of the French police. Upon leaving the house, all three decided that tomorrow Azef would surely escape. Yet, at the same time, they still hoped that perhaps he would not ("Pokazaniia tt. Bobrova, Bol'shova, Kubova, Chernova, Bunakova i Moiseenko, dannye sudebno-sledstvennoi komissii," GARF, f. 1699, op. 1, d. 130, pp. 91, 93; *Zakliuchenie*, 88). For his part, soon after the spy's exposure Savinkov confessed that for several years his "feeling toward Azef resembled brotherly sentiments." Even when he became "intellectually" convinced that Azef was a police agent, Savinkov "did not apprehend this emotionally." Savinkov admitted to have "voted . . . to kill him . . . in a purely logical way," knowing that at the moment he had no emotional stamina to kill Azef (Boris Savinkov's testimony in "Stenograficheskii otchet zasedaniia S. S. K. 9 noiabria 1910 goda," GARF, f. 1699, op. 1, d. 133, p. 34).

61. See, for example, V. Burtsev, "Pravda o Lopukhine" (newspaper clipping), PSR 3-279; Vladimir Burtsev, untitled manuscript (Paris, 29 December 1934), p. 8, Burtsev 2–12. On at least one occasion Burtsev even claimed that Lopukhin had purposely informed him about his travel plans in a telegram, giving the spy hunter an opportunity to arrange the meeting on the train ("Pokazaniia V. L. Burtseva, dannye sudebno-sledstvennoi komissii po delu Azefa," GARF, f. 1699, op. 1, d. 129, p. 102).

62. Nikolajewsky, *Aseff the Spy*, 4.

63. Letter from B. I. Nicolaevsky to L. P. Men'shchikov, 19 August 1931, Nic. 179-24. General-Adjutant Count Sviatopolk-Mirskii, who knew Lopukhin well and served as a witness at his trial, claimed that even after Lopukhin's retirement from state service, his attitude toward the revolutionaries was "unconditionally negative" (police report, 28 April 1909, GARF, f. 102, 7 *deloproizvodstvo*, 1909, d. 891). Prior to Azef's 11 November conversation with the retired police chief, Gerasimov "did not allow for the possibility of any association between Lopukhin and the revolutionaries" (*Obvnitel'nyi akt ob . . . Lopukhine*, GARF, f. 102, 7 *deloproizvodstvo*, 1909, d. 891).

64. Letter from B. I. Nicolaevskii to S. G. Svatikov, 30 June 1931, Nic., 416-10. Even after his retirement, Lopukhin judged it proper to maintain contact with Gapon, his double-dealing notwithstanding (letter from B. I. Nicolaevsky to V. K. Agafonov, 30 October 1932, Nic. 471-9).

65. Letter from B. I. Nicolaevskii to V. L. Burtsev, 6 June 1931, Nic. 475-8. According to the latest research, Lopukhin "almost certainly supported" Azef's

advancement in the terrorist organization at the time (Daly, *Autocracy under Siege*, 136).

66. Daly, *Autocracy under Siege*, 152.

67. Letter from B. I. Nicolaevsky to V. K. Agafonov dated 30 October 1932, Nic. 471-9.

68. *Delo Lopukhina*, 97; see also A. B. Gerasimov, "E. Azef i A. A. Lopukhin" (undated manuscript), p. 10, Nic. 206–14. In his Duma speech, Stolypin argued that it would have been certainly a more appropriate course for Lopukhin to appeal to the government than to join with the revolutionaries allegedly to fight provocation (Stolypin, *Polnoe sobranie rechei*, 170). This was also a key argument of the prosecution at Lopukhin's trial (police report, 29 April 1909, GARF, f. 102, 7 *deloproizvodstvo*, 1909, d. 891). For his part, Lopukhin subsequently claimed, but presented no evidence, that in 1906, having found out that Azef had returned to police serivce, the retired official warned Stolypin about Azef's criminal activities and even threatened that he would "take measures toward . . . [Azef's] exposure"; only after this proved to no avail did he agree to unmask Azef before the revolutionaries. Lopukhin then insisted, equally unconvincingly, that during his trial he had tried to explain this, but was silenced ("Pokazaniia, dannye Chrezvychainoi sledstvennoi kommissii . . . A. A. Lopukhin," 2–3; see also miscellaneous noted by V. L. Burtsev, p. 3, Nic., 150-2; and *Delo Lopukhina*, 116). Notably, Nicolaevsky refers to a marked contradiction between Lopukhin's claim and his other assertion; namely, that he kept silent about Azef's exploits assuming that the radicals had killed his agent together with Tatarov (letter from B. I. Nicolaevsky to V. L. Burtsev, 6 June 1931, Nic. 475-8).

69. Gerasimov, *Na lezvii*, 8, 132; 28 January (10 February) 1909 report to DPD, Okhrana XXVIId-3; see also Schleifman, *Undercover Agents*, 93.

70. "Pokazaniia V. L. Burtseva 1 aprelia 1917 g.," *Padenie tsarskogo rezhima*, vol. 1 (Leningrad, 1925): 309.

71. "Pokazaniia V. L. Burtseva, dannye sudebno-sledstvennoi komissii po delu Azefa," GARF, f. 1699, op. 1, d. 129, p. 103.

72. Cited in "Kratkie svedeniia ob upominaemykh litsakh (Lopukhin)," in Gerasimov, *Na lezvii*, 197. A. S. Lopukhin's manuscript is said to be held among materials in the Rodzianko family private archive.

73. 14 (27) October 1907 decoded telegram signed by M. I. Trusevich, Okhrana XIIIc(3)-26.

74. Telegram signed by the director of the Police Department, Trusevich, in St. Petersburg to "Chef de Police Sir Henry" in London, no. 2174 (copy no. 2175), 14 (27) October 1907, "Deloproizvodstvo o docheri Deistvitel'nogo Statskogo Sovetnika Varvare Alekseevne Lopukhinoi," GARF, f. 102, 00, 1907, d. 611.

75. See, for example, a later reference to the 1907 events in "Arrest of M. Lopukhin," *Daily Chronicle* (1 February 1909), PSR 3-189.

76. "Protsess Lopukhina," *Novoe vremia* 11900 (30 April [13 May] 1909), PSR 3-167.

77. For a long time Burtsev believed that the primary goal of any revolutionary organization was to kill the tsar, and even criticized the SRs for choosing governors and ministers as their targets instead of striking at the very heart of the autocracy (V. A. Posse, *Moi zhiznennyi put'* [Moscow-Leningrad, 1929], 311; and V. Burtsev, "Sotsialisty-revoliutsionery i narodovol'tsy," *Narodovolets* 4 [1903]: 20, PSR 1-19). On Burtsev's arrest, trial, and eighteen-month imprisonment in London in 1898 for preaching regicide, see V. Burtsev, *Doloi tsaria!* (London, n.d.), 44–56, PSR 1-19; and 4 December 1903 police report,

Okhrana XIIIc (2)-2c. Later, Burtsev liked to say about himself: "Now I am no longer a socialist or even a terrorist, but simply a *bombist*" (untitled, unsigned, and undated manuscript, p. 7, Nicolaevsky, 384–85). On Burtsev's personal involvement in terrorist plots, see, for example, a 9 (22) March 1904 report to DPD, Okhrana XVIId—1A; and a 8 (21) May 1907 report to DPD, Okhrana XVIb (1)–1; as well as Okhrana XVIId-1A, and XXVIIb-1.

78. 22 September [5 October] 1907 report to DPD, Okhrana XVIa-2; see also Walter Laqueur, *Terrorism* (Boston-Toronto, 1977), 106.

79. Spiridovich, *Partiia sotsialistov-revoliutsionerov,* 423–24.

80. Burtsev refused to follow this option alledgedly because he was afraid that such an action might cause a vicious feud and genuine carnage *(ponozhov-shchina)* in the SR circles ("Pokazaniia V. L. Burtseva, dannye sudebno-sledstvennoi komissii po delu Azefa," GARF, f. 1699, op. 1, d. 129, pp. 141, 143).

81. Downplaying all indirect and inconclusive clues about Azef's police connections, the SRs considered Lopukhin's testimony to be "the main and sole evidence for Azef's exposure" (*Obvinitel'nyi akt ob . . . Lopukhine,* GARF, f. 102, 7 *deloproizvodstvo,* 1909, d. 891).

82. "Obvinitel'nyi akt ob . . . Lopukhine," *Byloe* 9–10 (1909): 229; *Delo Lopukhina,* 21–22.

83. *Obvinitel'nyi akt ob . . . Lopukhine,* GARF, f. 102, 7 *deloproizvodstvo,* 1909, d. 891.

84. *Delo Lopukhina,* 13; A. I. Spiridovich, *Partiia sotsialistov-revoliutsionerov i ee predshestvenniki (1886–1916)* (Petrograd, 1918), 423–24; *Zakliuchenie,* 70.

85. *Zakliuchenie,* 68.

86. See, for example, Savinkov, *Vospominaniia,* 343; and unsigned manuscript (probably written by Andrei Argunov), entitled "Pervaia vstrecha s Azefom," GARF, f. 1699, op. 1, d. 78, pp. 59–60. All subsequent attempts to portray Lopukhin as a good samaritan in the Azef affair are in sharp contrast to the SRs' earlier views on this tsarist official. The SR leaders felt that they had every reason not to trust this man of obscure political and ethical credo, since, for instance, while contributing to Gapon's recruitment as a police agent, the retired bureaucrat simultaneously sought to enter the Kadet party ("Pokazaniia t. Bobrova [Natansona]," typescript, p. 61, GARF, f. 1699, op. 1, d. 123).

87. *Obvinitel'nyi akt ob . . . Lopukhine,* GARF, f. 102, 7 *deloproizvodstvo,* 1909, d. 891. Police sources show profound concern about the possibility that Lopukhin would provide the revolutionaries with classified information on subjects other than Azef. For conflicting opinions on this matter, see, for example, 14 (27) January and 28 January (10 February) 1909 reports to DPD, Okhrana XXVIId-3; and a decoded telegram, 30 December 1908 (12 January 1909), Okhrana XIIc (1)-1B.

88. *Delo Lopukhina,* 96.

89. Gerasimov, *Na lezvii,* 134; *Obvinitel'nyi akt ob . . . Lopukhine,* GARF, f. 102, 7 *deloproizvodstvo,* 1909, d. 891.

90. In fact, the revolutionaries did not even try to conceal their main source of information and revealed the details of their cooperation with Lopukhin to newspaper reporters ("Obvinitel'nyi akt ob . . . Lopukhine," *Byloe* 9–10 [1909]: 225).

91. The SR leaders clearly realized that many ordinary party members, and especially the terrorists, were bound to condemn the Central Committee for persecuting Azef unless it could justify its actions with indisputable evidence, such as a confession from Azef's former employer. For discussions among the SRs about the possible ramifications of the Azef affair, see Savinkov, *Vospominaniia,* 347.

92. Spiridovich, *Partiia sotsialistov-revoliutsionerov*, 425.

93. Pokazaniia t. Bobrova (Natansona), typescript, p. 61, GARF, f. 1699, op. 1, d. 123.

94. *Obvinitel'nyi akt ob . . . Lopukhine*, GARF, f. 102, 7 *deloproizvodstvo*, 1909, d. 891.

95. Unsigned manuscript (probably written by Andrei Argunov), entitled "Pervaia vstrecha s Azefom," GARF, f. 1699, op. 1, d. 78, p. 63.

96. 14 (27) January 1909 report to DPD, Okhrana XXVIId-3.

97. "Protsess Lopukhina," *Novoe vremia* 11899 (29 April [12 May] 1909).

98. See copies of Lopukhin's letter to Stolypin, 21 November 1908 in RGIA, f. 1278, op. 2, d. 2528, pp. 19–19ob. and in GARF, f. 1699, op. 1, d. 2; see also *Obvinitel'nyi akt ob . . . Lopukhine*, GARF, f. 102, 7 *deloproizvodstvo*, 1909, d. 891.

99. Unsigned article, translated from the German and entitled "Kozel otpushcheniia Lopukhin. Neosnovatel'nost' obvineniia," typescript, GARF, f. 102, 7 *deloproizvodstvo*, 1909, d. 891.

100. "Obvinitel'nyi akt ob . . . Lopukhine," 224, 227; Savinkov, *Vospominaniia*, 341; unsigned manuscript (probably written by Andrei Argunov), entitled "Pervaia vstrecha s Azefom," GARF, f. 1699, op. 1, d. 78, p. 61; Lur'e, *Khraniteli proshlogo*, 93. See also *Delo Lopukhina*, 16.

101. *Lur'e, Khraniteli proshlogo*, 93; *Obvinitel'nyi akt ob . . . Lopukhine*, GARF, f. 102, 7 *deloproizvodstvo*, 1909, d. 891; and *Otchet o sostoiavshemsia 1/14 ianvaria 1909 g. v Parizhe sekretnom zasedanii iskliuchitel'no chlenov "pravoi" gruppy partii sotsialistov-revoliutsionerov po delu Azeva*, Okhrana XVIc-9. Gerasimov, who knew Lopukhin well, also believed that he would have written the letter only "under the influence of someone else's will." Gerasimov, "E. Azef i A. A. Lopukhin," 7.

102. "Arkhiv obshchestvennoi zhizni," *Poznanie Rossii* 2 (February 1909): 251; Aldanov, "Azef," *Istoki*, 415.

103. Unsigned manuscript (probably written by Andrei Argunov), entitled "Pervaia vstrecha s Azefom," GARF, f. 1699, op. 1, d. 78, p. 61.

104. Cited in *Delo Lopukhina*, 38; and in "K delu Azefa-Lopukhina," *Russkie vedomosti* 31 (January 1909), PSR 2-157.

105. Savinkov, *Vospominaniia*, p. 336. In a contradictory statement, Argunov later asserted that Lopukhin explicitly indicated his wish to have no further dealings with Burtsev (unsigned manuscript [probably written by Andrei Argunov], entitled "Pervaia vstrecha s Azefom," GARF, f. 1699, op. 1, d. 78, p. 63).

106. According to Argunov, in London Lopukhin agreed to meet with the SRs again, should this become necessary. Argunov explained Lopukhin's "bravery" away by stating bluntly, if unconvincingly, that the former police chief "trusted us, the party's representatives" (unsigned manuscript [probably written by Andrei Argunov], entitled "Pervaia vstrecha s Azefom," GARF, f. 1699, op. 1, d. 78, pp. 61, 63).

107. See, for example, a citation from the London *Times* in "Arkhiv obshchestvennoi zhizni," p. 251, Nic. 205-20.

Chapter 6, The Public Scandal, 123–141

1. Cited in S. Kh. Karin, *V mire mudrykh myslei* (Moscow: Znanie, 1962), 89 (author's translation).

2. GARF, f. 102, 00 1909, d. 155, part 3, p. 1.

3. Untitled article from *Russkoe znamia* (25 February 1909), GARF, f. 102, op. 147, 7 *deloproizvodstvo*, 1909, d. 891.

4. Letter from Ivan Shcheglovitov to P. A. Stolypin, 25 February 1909, GARF, f. 102, op. 147, 7 *deloproizvodstvo*, 1909, d. 891; and "Vsepoddaneishii doklad Ministra Iustitsii," RGIA, f. 1405, op. 521, d. 464, pp. 78–79.

5. Excerpt from *Birzhevye vedomosti* (28 March 1909); excerpt from *Vecher* (4 April 1909); and excerpt from *Rech'* (26 February 1909), GARF, f. 102, op. 147, 7 *deloproizvodstvo*, 1909, d. 891.

6. Reference to *Kievskie vesti* (4 April 1909), GARF, f. 102, op. 147, 7 *deloproizvodstvo*, 1909, d. 891.

7. Excerpts from *Vecher* (6 March and 4 April, 1909), GARF, f. 102, op. 147, 7 *deloproizvodstvo*, 1909, d. 891.

8. See, for example, handwritten excerpt from the Polish newspaper *Nowa Reforma*, p. 2, GARF, f. 219, op. 1, d. 60.

9. N. Irten'ev, "Sotrudnichestvo," excerpt from the newspaper *Priamur'e* (11 April 1909), GARF, f. 102, op. 147, 7 *deloproizvodstvo*, 1909, d. 891.

10. Police report, 29 April 1909, GARF, f. 102, op. 147, 7 *deloproizvodstvo*, 1909, d. 891.

11. Police report, 29 April 1909, GARF, f. 102, op. 147, 7 *deloproizvodstvo*, 1909, d. 891. Passover presented similar arguments in his 13 May 1909 appeal letter (RGIA, f. 1354, op. 6, d. 1239, pp. 4–5). In a private conversation, the defense lawyer characterized the charges against Lopukhin as "vulgar grotesque" (Ruud and Stepanov, *Fontanka*, 16, 216).

12. Police report, 29 April 1909, GARF, f. 102, op. 147, 7 *deloproizvodstvo*, 1909, d. 891.

13. Police report, 30 April 1909, GARF, f. 102, op. 147, 7 *deloproizvodstvo*, 1909, d. 891; see also RGIA, f. 1354, op. 6, d. 1239, p. 2. For a copy of Lopukhin's verdict, see RGIA, f. 1405, op. 530, d. 1121, pp. 319–20.

14. "Vsepoddaneishii doklad Ministra Iustitsii o lishenii prav sostoianiia A. A. Lopukhina," RGIA, f. 1405, op. 521, d. 465, p. 20a. See also *Delo Lopukhina*, 4, 6.

15. *Delo Lopukhina*, 71–72.

16. Police report addressed to M. I. Trusevich, 24 October 1907, "Deloproizvodstvo o docheri Deistvitel'nogo Statskogo Sovetnika Varvare Alekseevne Lopukhinoi," GARF, f. 102, 00, 1907, d. 611.

17. Police report on Lopukhin's trial, 28 April 1909, GARF, f. 102, op. 147, 7 *deloproizvodstvo*, 1909, d. 891; Ruud and Stepanov, *Fontanka*, 16, 216.

18. "V parlamente," *Vecher* (2 May 1909), GARF, f. 102, op. 147, 7 *deloproizvodstvo*, 1909, d. 891.

19. Undated report from Minister of Justice I. G. Shcheglovitov to Nicholas II, RGIA, f. 1405, op. 521, d. 472, pp. 143–44.

20. RGIA, f. 1405, op. 521, d. 472, p. 141; Gerasimov, *Na lezvii*, 135.

21. "Protsess Lopukhina," *Novoe vremia* 11899 and 11900; *Obvinitel'nyi akt ob . . . Lopukhine*, GARF, f. 102, 7 *deloproizvodstvo*, 1909, d. 891.

22. Letter from B. I. Nicolaevsky to V. K. Agafonov, 30 October 1932, Nic. 471-9.

23. A. V. Bel'gard, "Bor'ba pravitel'stva s revoliutsionnym dvizheniem i direktor departamenta A. A. Lopukhin" (typescript), Nic. 774-12. There is a pencil rough draft of a letter allegedly written by Ekaterina Lopukhina to Burtsev (dated 23 March with the year omitted), in which she underscores that her husband's motifs for exposing Azef were entirely altruistic. The letter contains no reference to the kidnapping incident; its style and tone render its authenticity highly questionable (Nic. 150-2).

24. World-famous writer Maksim Gor'kii, for instance, wrote to Burtsev: "I bow to the ground, expressing my exultation before you with all my soul" (cited in Nic. 615-11).

25. "Police Spy Scandal," *Reynolds's* (22 August 1909), PSR 1-78.

26. Report to DPD, 30 July (12 August) 1909, Okhrana XVIId-1A.

27. *Otchet o sostoiavshemsia 1/14 ianvaria 1909 g. v Parizhe sekretnom zasedanii,* Okhrana XVIc-9. See also a letter from "Maksim" in France to F. Ia. Zimovskii in St. Petersburg, 22 March 1909, Okhrana XIIIc (1)-1B, Incoming Dispatches, document no. 346, 1909.

28. Longe and Zil'ber, *Terroristy i okhranka,* 26.

29. Many well-known SRs criticized the party leadership for this initial reaction. See, for example, a copy of a letter from E. E. Lazarev to M. A. Natanson in Paris, 4 (17) January 1909, Okhrana XIIc (1)-1B.

30. "Izveshchenie Tsentral'nogo Komiteta," 1, PSR 3-168.

31. V. Kosovskii, "Azefshchina," *Otkliki Bunda* 1 (March, 1909): 13, Nic. 205-21.

32. See copy of Burtsev's undated appeal to the Central Committee, GARF, f. 1699, op. 1, d. 72. Some prominent SRs argued from the outset of the party scandal that they must enter an agreement, "a certain entente," with Burtsev (letter from Lazarev to Natanson, 4 [17] January 1909, Okhrana XIIc [1]-1B).

33. "Izveshchenie Tsentral'nogo Komiteta," 1, PSR 3-168.

34. "Protsess Lopukhina," *Novoe vremia,* 11899 (29 April [12 May] 1909), PSR 3-167.

35. Gerasimov, *Na lezvii,* 136; *Otchet o sostoiavshemsia 1/14 ianvaria 1909 g. v Parizhe sekretnom zasedanii,* Okhrana XVIc-9. For more on the anecdote about romantic rivalry between Plehve and Bogdanovich see V. D. Novitskii, *Iz vospominanii zhandarma* (Moscow: Izdatel'stvo Moskovskogo Universiteta, 1991), 179–80, and Spiridovich, *Zapiski zhandarma,* 132).

36. These allegations appeared incredible even to some of the leading SRs. Egor Lazarev, one of the party's veterans, warned his comrades against political opportunism, imploring them to adhere to the facts and not to be "seduced by the temptation to accuse the Okhrana" of sponsoring political assassinations (copy of a letter from E. E. Lazarev to M. A. Natanson in Paris, 20 January 1909, Okhrana XIIIb (1)-1A, Outgoing Dispatches, document no. 28). These warnings notwithstanding, the public, and especially the left-wing public, accepted this interpretation without question, readily adopting the SR argument that "all sensational terrorist acts . . . were organized and carried out . . . according to plans developed by Azef together with the de facto head of the Russian political police, Rachkovskii" (Kosovskii, "Azefshchina," 12).

37. See, for example, copies of Burtsev's appeals to Count Sergei Witte: letter, 9 December 1910, RGIA, f. 1622, op. 1, d. 305, pp. 1–2; and letter, 9 March 1911, RGIA, f. 1622, op. 1, d. 304, p. 1. See also "K vozobnovleniiu dela Azefa (V. L. Burtsev's appeal submitted to the Minister of Justice and the Procurator of the St. Petersburg Sudebnaia Palata)," GARF, f. 1699, op. 1, d. 144; and untitled and unsigned manuscript, p. 9, Nic. 384-5. Burtsev also made appeals to several Duma deputies, urging them to revitalize the Azef controversy. GARF, f. 102, 00 1909, d. 155, part 3; and B. Koz'min, ed., "K istorii razoblacheniia Azefa," *Katorga i ssylka* 3 (32) (1927), 104–6).

38. Letter from V. L. Burtsev to B. V. Savinkov, 22 December 1910, GARF, f. 5831, op. 1, d. 37.

39. Longe and Zil'ber, *Terroristy i okhranka,* 169. For materials concerning the interpolation, see RGIA, f. 1278, op. 2, d. 2528. Having accepted the Kadet

inquiry in principle, the Duma's special committee "left the inquirers responsible for the evidence, noting that it would be naive simply to believe the SR Central Committee, and hoping that the authors of the interpolation would provide some probable proof of the existence of provocation." And yet, the Kadet party Deputy, O. Ia. Pergament, while defending the legitimacy of the interpolation on 11 February, merely reaffirmed the accusations against the government for its alleged use of provocation, providing no information essentially different from the official statements of the SRs. (*Tret'ia Gosudarstvennaia Duma. Materialy dlia otsenki ee deiatel'nosti* [St. Petersburg: Izdatel'stvo parlamentskoi fraktsii Partii Narodnoi Svobody, 1912], 121–22).

40. Stolypin, *Polnoe sobranie rechei*, 158. See also *Gosudarstvennaia Duma. III sozyv. Stenograficheskie otchety*, 1419.

41. Cited in Rubenstein, *Comrade Valentine*, 269–70.

42. *Tret'ia Gosudarstvennaia Duma*, 119; for an example of official regulations to heads of the Okhrana sections, see "Vremennoe polozhenie ob Okhrannykh Otdeleniiakh," PSR 1-26.

43. Vladimir Nabokov, "Ugolovnaia otvetstvennost' agenta-provokatora," Manuscript published in the journal *Pravo* in 1909, Nic. 205-20.

44. Stolypin, *Polnoe sobranie rechei*, 158. See also *Gosudarstvennaia Duma. III sozyv. Stenograficheskie otchety*, 1420. For the similar view of the director of the Police Department Mikhail Trusevich, see "Dopros M. I. Trusevicha 4 maia 1917 goda," *Padenie tsarskogo rezhima*, 3 (Leningrad, 1925): 212.

45. "Dopros A. I. Spiridovicha 28 aprelia 1917 goda," *Padenie tsarskogo rezhima*, vol 3 (Leningrad, 1925): 32.

46. *Tret'ia Gosudarstvennaia Duma*, 122–23.

47. Ruud and Stepanov, *Fontanka*, 16, 194.

48. "Pokazaniia V. L. Burtseva ... po delu Azefa," GARF, f. 1699, op. 1, d. 129, p. 154.

49. Nabokov, "Ugolovnaia otvetstvennost' agenta-provokatora," Nic. 205-20.

50. See, for example, Burtsev, "Azef i ego uchastie v terroristicheskikh aktakh," Nic. 205-21.

51. "Sprawa Aziewa," newspaper clipping from *Nowa reforma* (5 February 1909), GARF, f. 219, op. 1, d. 59.

52. "Police Spy Scandal," *Reynolds's* (22 August 1909), PSR 1-78.

53. Octobrist leader Aleksandr Guchkov implied in a later conversation with Burtsev that his exposure of the master spy indirectly served to benefit the government's cause by "demoralizing the revolutionary circles" (cited in Aldanov, "Azef," *Istoki*, 417n).

54. Praisman, "Fenomen Azefa," 65.

55. Aldanov, "Azef," Nic. 205-19; *Otchet o sostoiavshemsia 1/14 ianvaria 1909 g. v Parizhe sekretnom zasedanii iskliuchitel'no chlenov "pravoi" gruppy partii sotsialistov-revoliutsionerov po delu Azefa*, in a 6 (19) January 1909 report to DPD, Okhrana XVIc-9; V. Zenzinov, "Razoblachenie provokatsii Azeva" (New York, 1924), 9, Nic. 205-18. Karpovich later denied having ever made such threats (letter from P. V. Karpovich to B. V. Savinkov, 1 June 1911, GARF, f. 5831, op. 1, d. 84).

56. "Pokazaniia M. A. Natansona," GARF, f. 1699, op. 1, d. 123, p. 62.

57. Ibid., 65.

58. Ibid., 64.

59. While considering the police depiction an overstatement, Aldanov acknowledges that "the shock within the socialist-revolutionary circles was terrible of course" (cited in Aldanov, "Azef," *Istoki*, 419n).

60. "Pokazaniia Kubova [Argunova]," GARF, f. 1699, op. 1, d. 131, p. 67.

61. *Zakliuchenie*, 1.

62. Anna Geifman, "Aspects of Early Twentieth-Century Russian Terrorism: The Socialist-Revolutionary Combat Organization," *Terrorism and Political Violence* 4, no. 2 (Summer 1992), 23–46.

63. Letter from Senzharskii (Bleklov) to A. N. Bakh, 3 October 1911, GARF, f. 1699, op. 1, d. 65.

64. A. Argunov, "Azef v partii S.-R.," 181, Nic. 633-2.

65. Boris Savinkov's testimony in "Stenograficheskii otchet zasedaniia S. S. K. 9 noiabria 1910 goda," GARF, f. 1699, op. 1, d. 133, pp. 37–38; see also report to DPD, 22 October [4 November] 1912, Okhrana XVIc-2. According to Chernov, Azef received only 125 rubles per month from the Central Committee, but this figure is clearly an understatement. For very sketchy records of the Central Committee and Combat Organization funds dispensed to Azef between 1904 and 1907, see GARF, f. 1699, op. 1, d. 1. Natanson claimed that if the Combat Organization consisted of approximately twenty people, and the monthly maintenance of each person was estimated roughly as 250 rubles, the cost of the terrorist unit was around 5000 rubles per month. This amount did not include sums provided by the Central Committee for the "extraordinary expenses" of the combatants ("Pokazaniia t. Bobrova [Natansona]," typescript, p. 20, GARF, f. 1699, op. 1, d. 123).

66. Vladimir Khludov and Andrei Iashlavskii, "Evangelie ot Azefa," *Moskovskii komsomolets* (22 September 1996), 4. According to Natanson, Azef and Gershuni were the only people involved with the plan to build a "flying apparatus"—a project that they initiated in the summer of 1907. Natanson suggests that Azef appropriated approximately two thousand rubles from the total sum of twenty thousand ("Pokazaniia M. A. Natansona," GARF, f. 1699, op. 1, d. 123, pp. 69–70). Aldanov correctly characterizes Azef's administration of this project as but "sheer derision at the terrorists" (Aldanov, "Azef," *Istoki*, 422n).

67. "Pokazaniia Kubova [Argunova]," GARF, f. 1699, op. 1, d. 131, p. 68; "Pokazaniia M. A. Natansona," GARF, f. 1699, op. 1, d. 123, pp. 72–73.

68. Unsigned manuscript (probably written by Andrei Argunov), entitled "Pervaia vstrecha s Azefom," GARF, f. 1699, op. 1, d. 78, p. 23.

69. "Pis'mo M. A. Natansona v sudebno-sledstvennuiu komissiiiu," 1 April 1911, GARF, f. 1699, op. 1, d. 114.

70. Letter from P. V. Karpovich to B. V. Savinkov, 1 June 1911, GARF, f. 5831, op. 1, d. 84.

71. Cited in Gorodnitskii, "B. V. Savinkov i sudebno-sledstvennaia komissiia po delu Azefa," 234.

72. Cited in ibid., 233.

73. Letter from Senzharskii (Bleklov) to A. N. Bakh, 1 May 1911, GARF, f. 1699, op. 1, d. 63.

74. Letter from A. Agafonov to Senzharskii, 4 May 1910, GARF, f. 1699, op. 1, d. 91.

75. Letter from P. V. Karpovich to B. V. Savinkov, 14 July 1911, GARF, f. 5831, op. 1, d. 84. Gorodnitskii discusses some obvious biases of the Committee in "B. V. Savinkov i sudebno-sledstvennaia komissiia po delu Azefa," 201–3.

76. Boris Savinkov's testimony in "Stenograficheskii otchet zasedaniia S. S. K. 9 noiabria 1910 goda," GARF, f. 1699, op. 1, d. 133, p. 33.

77. Chernov admitted that while there were many courageous characters and talented propagandists among the Russian revolutionaries, gifted practical organizers were extremely rare (A. B. [V. Tuchkin], *Za kulisami okhrannogo otdeleniia*, 130).

78. Trotskii, "Evno Azef," 233.
79. "Pokazaniia Kubova [Argunova]," GARF, f. 1699, op. 1, d. 131, p. 67; Rubenstein, *Comrade Valentine*, 273.
80. Schleifman, *Undercover Agents*, 89–90.
81. Ibid., 94.
82. Cited in Rubenstein, *Comrade Valentine*, 273.
83. "Pokazaniia Kubova [Argunova]," GARF, f. 1699, op. 1, d. 131, p. 67.
84. See, for example, a letter from P. V. Karpovich to B. V. Savinkov, 6 (19) May 1909, GARF, f. 5831, op. 1, d. 84; and a report to DPD, 22 October [4 November] 1912, Okhrana XVIc-2. Even the veteran terrorist "Nikolai," one of the three SRs who had interrogated Azef on the fateful night of his escape, fell under suspicion in the summer of 1909 (Morozov, "B. V. Savinkov i Boevaia Organizatsiia," 246–47).
85. Cited in Praisman, "Fenomen Azefa," 73.
86. See, for example, a report to DPD, 23 January (5 February) 1909, Okhrana XIIc(1)-1b.
87. "Pokazaniia Kubova [Argunova]," GARF, f. 1699, op. 1, d. 131, p. 67.
88. Untitled manuscript by Olga Chernov Andreev, p. 45, Olga Andreyev Carlisle private archive; Morozov, "B. V. Savinkov i Boevaia Organizatsiia," 257. When interrogated by the Investigatory-Judiciary Committee, Lapina fell under suspicion of having known about Azef's police connections, and this misconception might have induced her to take her own life (V. L. Burtsev, "Kak ia razoblachil Azefa" in *Shchegolev, Provokator*, 285; see also V. L. Burtsev, *V pogone za provokatorami* [Moscow: Sovremennik, 1989]: 155–56).
89. Report to DPD, 22 October [4 November] 1912, Okhrana XVIc-2; Aldanov, "Azef," *Istoki*, 419n.
90. Cited in Schleifman, *Undercover Agents*, 86; see also "Pokazaniia tt. Bobrova, Bol'shova, Kubova, Chernova, Bunakova i Moiseenko, dannye sudebno-sledstvennoi komissii," GARF, f. 1699, op. 1, d. 130, pp. 28–29.
91. Undated letter from P. V. Karpovich to B. V. Savinkov, GARF, f. 5831, op. 1, d. 84.
92. Il'ia Erenburg cited in Dmitrii Zubarev, ed., "Boris Savinkov: chelovek, kotoryi khotel rasshirit' chelovecheskuiu svobodu," *Nezavisimaia gazeta* (23 May 1995), 3; and Mogil'ner, "Boris Savinkov," 89.
93. Cited in "Pis'mo S. V. Zubatova A. I. Spiridovichu," 282.
94. Cited in Schleifman, *Undercover Agents*, 95. See also Spence, *Boris Savinkov*, 75.
95. Gorodnitskii, "Tri stilia rukovodstva boevoi organizatsiei," 59; Morozov, "B. V. Savinkov i Boevaia Organizatsiia," 244–45.
96. Morozov, "B. V. Savinkov i Boevaia Organizatsiia," 244.
97. Ibid., 253.
98. Gorodnitskii, "Tri stilia rukovodstva boevoi organizatsiei," 62; Gorodnitskii, "B. V. Savinkov i sudebno-sledstvennaia komissiia po delu Azefa," 229. Evidence suggests that the two men were in fact guiltless of secret dealings with the police. Having found out the reason for his discharge from the Combat Organization, one of them, Ian Berdo, committed suicide in November 1910; his partner in misfortune, Vatslav Komorskii, also took his life in 1911, having asked in his farewell letter to be buried next to Berdo (Morozov, "B. V. Savinkov i Boevaia Organizatsiia," 255–56).
99. Cited in Gorodnitskii, "Tri stilia rukovodstva boevoi organizatsiei," 62.
100. Gorodnitskii, "B. V. Savinkov i sudebno-sledstvennaia komissiia po delu Azefa," 229.
101. Of about a dozen members of the Combat Organization recruited since the fall of 1909, eight either left voluntarily or were dismissed by

Savinkov in the course of the next year and a half (Morozov, "B. V. Savinkov i Boevaia Organizatsiia," 256).

102. Gorodnitskii, "Tri stilia rukovodstva boevoi organizatsiei," 63; and Gorodnitskii, "B. V. Savinkov i sudebno-sledstvennaia komissiia po delu Azefa," 229–30. In the years between 1911 and 1914, Savinkov led a life of tedious "non-existence" in a small French village and then in Nice, until the outbreak of the Great War, which delivered him from his melancholy by flinging him back into the whirlpool of European politics (Mogil'ner, "Boris Savinkov," 90).

103. Schleifman, *Undercover Agents,* 193.

104. Cited in B. V. Levanov, *Iz istorii bor'by bol'shevistskoi partii protiv eserov v gody pervoi russkoi revoliutsii* (Leningrad: Izdatel;stvo Leningradkogo Universiteta, 1974), 144.

105. A. V. Amfiteatrov cited in Gorodnitskii, "Tri stilia rukovodstva boevoi organizatsiei," 62.

106. Aldanov, "Azef," Nic. 205-19.

107. Report to DPD, 22 October [4 November] 1912, Okhrana XVIc-2.

108. In 1912 and in the spring of 1914 the SRs did make attempts to revive the Combat Organization, but their efforts were to no avail (Morozov, "B. V. Savinkov i Boevaia Organizatsiia," 261).

Chapter 7, Fugitive Incognito, 143–166

1. Cited in Karin, *V mire mudrykh myslei,* 127 (author's translation).

2. "Pokazaniia L. G. Azef," GARF, f. 1699, op. 1, d. 126, pp. 13, 17–19.

3. See, for example, ibid., 25.

4. Savinkov, *Vospominaniia revoliutsionera,* 343.

5. Aldanov, "Azef," *Istoki,* 405.

6. "Pokazaniia L. G. Azef," GARF, f. 1699, op. 1, d. 126, p. 26.

7. Aldanov, "Azef," *Istoki,* 405.

8. "Stenograficheskii otchet 26-ogo zasedaniia sudebno-sledstvennoi komissii. 2 Maia 1910 g.," GARF, f. 1699, op. 1, d. 136, p. 4.

9. Letter from L. G. Azef to B. V. Savinkov, 15 March 1907, GARF, f. 5831, op. 1, d. 19. A police report mentions that Azef's wife was named a representative of the Central Committee in Paris, and prior to May 1906, even had access to party funds, which she allegedly "used without any control." Report to DPD, 3 (16) May 1906, p. 2, Okhrana XIc [5]-1. This information is not confirmed by any other source and therefore should be disregarded as inaccurate.

10. "Pokazaniia L. G. Azef," GARF, f. 1699, op. 1, d. 126, p. 17.

11. Ibid., 27, 31–32.

12. Menkina also remembered that when members of the Combat Organization visited Azef hoping to reassure and comfort him, he pretended that it was emotionally unbearable for him to face his comrades. In fact, his wife claimed, he was simply afraid that the *boeviki* had already established his guilt and had come to kill him (ibid., 32–33).

13. Ibid., 36.

14. Menkina's testimony contradicts any stereotyped sentimental description of Azef, the loving father, kissing his children before his hasted departure. See, for example, Rubenstein, *Comrade Valentine,* 268. Azef did tell his wife that

he would not want the children to become revolutionaries ("Pokazaniia L. G. Azef," GARF, f. 1699, op. 1, d. 126, p. 42).

15. Rubenstein, *Comrade Valentine*, 267–68; "Pokazaniia M. A. Natansona," GARF, f. 1699, op. 1, d. 123, p. 66.

16. "Pokazaniia L. G. Azef," GARF, f. 1699, op. 1, d. 126, pp. 42–43.

17. Rubenstein, *Comrade Valentine*, 268.

18. Shchegolev, "Istoricheskii Azef," 8; cited in Nikolaevskii, *Konets Azefa*, 13. Nicolaevsky claims that Hedwig Klöpfer was one of the "entertainers" escorting Grand Duke Kirill Vladimirovich in his train returning from the Far East in 1905 (ibid., 12).

19. See, for example, Gor'kii, "O predateliakh," 193.

20. Cited in ibid., 192; and Aldanov, "Azef," *Istoki*, 420, 437.

21. "Pokazaniia V. L. Burtseva, dannye sudebno-sledstvennoi komissii po delu Azefa," GARF, f. 1699, op. 1, d. 129, p. 146.

22. Frau Hedwig Klöpfer asserted that at one point Azef had made a secret trip to Paris, and unexpectedly showed up at his wife's apartment, but was forced to leave immediately because Liubov' grabbed a revolver the moment she saw him. Menkina did not mention a word about this incident to her SR comrades; hence, the story is probably fictitious (Lur'e, *Politseiskie i provokatory*, 369; and Nikolaevskii, *Konets Azefa*, 28n).

23. Copy of Azef's letter, 7 January 1909, GARF, f. 1699, op. 1, d. 3. See also Pavlov and Peregudova, *Pis'ma Azefa*, 166.

24. Copy of a letter from P. A. Kropotkin to M. A. Bobrov (Natanson), 30 March 1909, GARF, f. 1699, op. 1, d. 110.

25. "Vyderzhka iz pokazanii Lapina (Iudelevskogo)," GARF, f. 1699, op. 1, d. 134, p. 5; see also "Zaiavlenie L. G. Azef v sudebno-sledstvennuiu komissiiu," 25 May 1909, GARF, f. 1699, op. 1, d. 29.

26. "Pokazaniia L. G. Azef," GARF, f. 1699, op. 1, d. 126, p. 40.

27. "Zaiavlenie L. G. Azef v sudebno-sledstvennuiu komissiiu," 10 May 1909, GARF, f. 1699, op. 1, d. 30; and "Zaiavlenie L. G. Azef v sudebno-sledstvennuiu komissiiu," 17 April 1911, GARF, f. 1699, op. 1, d. 27.

28. "Pokazaniia V. L. Burtseva, dannye sudebno-sledstvennoi komissii po delu Azefa," GARF, f. 1699, op. 1, d. 129, p. 146. The SRs did not find out about Azef's escape until two days later because Menkina denied knowing where he was ("Pokazaniia M. A. Natansona," GARF, f. 1699, op. 1, d. 123, p. 68).

29. See, for example, "Vyderzhka iz pokazanii Lapina (Iudelevskogo)," GARF, f. 1699, op. 1, d. 134; and "Zaiavlenie L. G. Azef v sudebno-sledstvennuiu komissiiu," dated 25 May 1909, GARF, f. 1699, op. 1, d. 29.

30. Olga Chernov lost contact with Leonid and Valentin in 1911. Their mother, having obtained a divorce from Azef, later married one of his former party colleagues, Aleksandr Gurevich, whom Menkina and her children accompanied to America shortly before the outbreak of World War I. Liubov' and her family settled in New York, where she lived until her death in 1958. Olga Chernov eventually found out that Azef's older son had committed suicide, while the younger one became a scientist, devoting his life to the fight against cancer. Chernov's stepdaughter and Azef's son saw each other again only once—in 1952 in New York, at the funeral of Viktor Chernov, to whom Valentin wished to pay his last respects (untitled manuscript by Olga Chernov Andreev, p. 41, Olga Andreyev Carlisle private archive; Rubenstein, *Comrade Valentine*, 292; and a letter from B. I. Nicolaevsky to M. A. Aldanov, 25 January 1930, *Istochnik*, 2 (27) [1997]: 65–66n).

31. Azef's letter to L. G. Menkina, 13 April 1909, GARF, f. 1699, op. 1, d. 20.

32. Azef's letter to L. G. Menkina, postmarked 28 November 1910, GARF, f. 1699, op. 1, d. 23; and Azef's letter to L. G. Menkina, 13 April 1909, GARF, f. 1699, op. 1, d. 20.

33. Stenograficheskii otchet 26-ogo zasedaniia sudebno-sledstvennoi komissii, 2 maia 1910 g., p. 25, GARF, f. 1699, op. 1, d. 136.

34. Boris Savinkov's testimony in "Stenograficheskii otchet zasedaniia S. S. K. 9 noiabria 1910 goda," GARF, f. 1699, op. 1, d. 133, p. 21.

35. "Pokazaniia Iriny, Ritinoi (Rakitnikovoi), Rubanovicha, Burtseva, dan-nye sudebno-sledstvennoi komissii po delu Azefa," GARF, f. 1699, op. 1, d. 129, p. 30.

36. "Pokazaniia L. G. Azef," GARF, f. 1699, op. 1, d. 126, p. 20.

37. Ibid., 19.

38. "Pokazaniia V. L. Burtseva, dannye sudebno-sledstvennoi komissii po delu Azefa," GARF, f. 1699, op. 1, d. 129, p. 160.

39. Ibid., 161–62.

40. Ibid., 162; see also Longe and Zil'ber, *Terroristy i okhranka*, 52; and "Pokazaniia tt. Bobrova, Bol'shova, Kubova, Chernova, Bunakova i Moi-seenko, dannye sudebno-sledstvennoi komissii," GARF, f. 1699, op. 1, d. 130, p. 185.

41. Ibid.

42. A. B. (V. Tuchkin), *Za kulisami okhrannogo otdeleniia*, 34.

43. Azef's letter to L. G. Menkina, 13 April 1909, GARF, f. 1699, op. 1, d. 20; and Azef's letter to L. G. Menkina, postmarked 14 May 1909, GARF, f. 1699, op. 1, d. 21. See also "Priznanie Azefa," *Budushchee* (5 November 1911), PSR, 3–279.

44. Azef's letter to L. G. Menkina, 13 April 1909, GARF, f. 1699, op. 1, d. 20; and copy of an undated letter from Azef to L. G. Azef, GARF, f. 1699, op. 1, d. 86, pp. 7–8.

45. Azef's letter to L. G. Menkina, 13 April 1909, GARF, f. 1699, op. 1, d. 20.

46. Azef's letter to L. G. Menkina, postmarked 14 May 1909, GARF, f. 1699, op. 1, d. 21.

47. Ibid.

48. Aldanov, "Azef," *Istoki*, 425.

49. Cited in Karin, *V mire mudrykh myslei*, 129.

50. Azef's letter to L. G. Menkina, postmarked 14 May 1909, GARF, f. 1699, op. 1, d. 21; and Azef's letter to L. G. Menkina, 13 April 1909, GARF, f. 1699, op. 1, d. 20.

51. Azef's letter to L. G. Menkina, 13 April 1909, GARF, f. 1699, op. 1, d. 20; and Azef's letter to L. G. Menkina, postmarked 14 May 1909, GARF, f. 1699, op. 1, d. 21.

52. Cited in Gor'kii, "O predateliakh," 192.

53. Azef's letter to L. G. Menkina, postmarked 28 November 1910, GARF, f. 1699, op. 1, d. 23.

54. Undated testimony by Iur'ev (Zenzinov), GARF, f. 1699, op. 1, d. 71.

55. Reference to the newspapers *Zemshchina* and *Rannee utro* in a Police Department dispatch, 6 January 1913, Okhrana, VIIIa-1; report to DPD, 19 January (1 February) 1913, Okhrana, XIIc(1)-1C.

56. A. B. (V. Tuchkin), *Za kulisami okhrannogo otdeleniia*, 11.

57. Rubenstein, *Comrade Valentine*, 2.

58. Untitled manuscript by Olga Chernov Andreev, p. 39, Olga Carlisle private archive; see also Boris Savinkov's testimony in "Stenograficheskii otchet zasedaniia S. S. K. 12 noiabria 1910 goda," GARF, f. 1699, op. 1, d. 133, p. 7.

59. Chernov reverberated Gots almost verbatim (Aldanov, "Azef," *Istoki*, 406). Savinkov also admired Azef's "beautiful eyes" ("Iz istorii Partii S.-R.," *Novyi zhurnal*, 101 [1970]: 189).

60. Longe and Zil'ber, *Terroristy i okhranka*, 46.

61. "Pokazaniia Iriny, Ritinoi (Rakitnikovoi), Rubanovicha, Burtseva, dannye sudebno-sledstvennoi komissii," GARF, f. 1699, op. 1, d. 129, p. 4.

62. Untitled manuscript by Olga Chernov Andreev, p. 39, Olga Carlisle private archive; see also Longe and Zil'ber, *Terroristy i okhranka*, 46–47.

63. Ivanovskaia, "Delo Pleve," 190-91; Aldanov, "Azef," *Istoki*, 406; Budnitskii, *Zhenshchiny-terroristki v Rossii*, 69. According to an alternative description, Azef's face was "dull and expressionless" (Ia. Akimov, "*Ne mogu molchat'!*" [New York, 1912], 17).

64. Tolstoi, "Azef, kak teatral'naia maska," 15.

65. Cited in Shchegolev, "Istoricheskii Azef," 7–8.

66. Lur'e, *Khraniteli proshlogo*, 87–88; Vladimir Khludov and Andrei Iashpavskii, "Evangelie ot Azefa," *Moskovskii komsomolets* (22 September 1996), 4.

67. See, for example, "Pokazaniia V. L. Burtseva, dannye sudebno-sledstvennoi komissii po delu Azefa," GARF, f. 1699, op. 1, d. 129, p. 72; and Vladimir Khludov and Andrei Iashlavskii, "Evangelie ot Azefa," *Moskovskii komsomolets* (22 September 1996), 4. This assertion, found only in Burtsev's testimonies, is probably just another invention of his, as is his highly improbable declaration that as early as 1893, Burtsev's radical acquaintances from Darmstadt had considered Azef to be a police spy. (It may be helpful to remember that Azef moved to Darmstadt only in 1896.) Both claims, however, were essential for Burtsev's version of his role in the Azef affair: they served as convenient explanations for the murky business of how the spy hunter originally came to suspect Azef of police connections.

68. Longe and Zil'ber, *Terroristy i okhranka*, 47.

69. "Pokazaniia M. A. Natansona," GARF, f. 1699, op. 1, d. 123, p. 76; "Pokazaniia Iriny, Ritinoi (Rakitnikovoi), Rubanovicha, Burtseva, dannye sudebno-sledstvennoi komissii po delu Azefa," GARF, f. 1699, op. 1, d. 129, pp. 8–9; Longe and Zil'ber, *Terroristy i okhranka*, 45.

70. Stenograficheskii otchet 26-ogo zasedaniia sudebno-sledstvennoi komissii, 2 maia 1910 g., p. 27, GARF, f. 1699, op. 1, d. 136.

71. Unsigned manuscript (probably written by Andrei Argunov), entitled "Pervaia vstrecha s Azefom," GARF, f. 1699, op. 1, d. 78, p. 16.

72. Unsigned letter (possibly from Mendel' Levin), 23 January 1909, GARF, f. 1699, op. 1, d. 42; see also "Stenograficheskii otchet 26-ogo zasedaniia sudebno-sledstvennoi komissii. 2 Maia 1910 g.," GARF, f. 1699, op. 1, d. 136, p. 3.

73. "Stenograficheskii otchet 26-ogo zasedaniia sudebno-sledstvennoi komissii. 2 Maia 1910 g.," GARF, f. 1699, op. 1, d. 136, p. 3.

74. "Pervaia vstrecha s Azefom," GARF, f. 1699, op. 1, d. 78, p. 18.

75. Boris Savinkov's testimony in "Stenograficheskii otchet zasedaniia S. S. K. 9 noiabria 1910 goda," pp. 23, 35 and in "Stenograficheskii otchet zasedaniia S. S. K. 12 noiabria 1910 goda," GARF, f. 1699, op. 1, d. 133, p. 7.

76. "Iz istorii Partii S.-R.," *Novyi zhurnal*, 101 (1970): 189.

77. See "Protokol pokazanii v spetsial'nuiu komissiiu, naznachennuiu TsK dlia rassledovaniia slukhov o provokatsii Azefa," GARF, f. 1699, op. 1, d.

95; A. B. (V. Tuchkin), *Za kulisami okhrannogo otdeleniia*, 18; and Akimov, *"Ne mogu molchat'!,"* 18, 20.

78. "Otkrytoe pis'mo Azefa," published in a Polish journal of Leo Bel'mont, GARF, f. 1699, op. 1, d. 145.

79. Azef's letter to L. G. Menkina, postmarked 14 May 1909, GARF, f. 1699, op. 1, d. 21; and Azef's letter to L. G. Menkina, postmarked 28 November 1910, GARF, f. 1699, op. 1, d. 23.

80. "Beseda s Azefom," GARF, f. 219, op. 1, d. 59.

81. Newspaper clipping from *Varshavskoe ekho*, no. 36, 5 (16; sic.) February, 1909, GARF, f. 219, op. 1, d. 59. See also Vladimir Burtsev, untitled manuscript (Paris, 29 December 1934), p. 2, Burtsev 2-12.

82. Rubenstein, *Comrade Valentine*, ix.

83. Clipping from newspaper *Nowa reforma* (11 February 1909), GARF, f. 219, op. 1, d. 59.

84. "Sprawa Aziefa," newspaper clipping from *Nowa reforma* (25 February 1909), GARF, f. 219, op. 1, d. 59.

85. See, for example, clippings from *Peterburgskaia gazeta, Russkoe slovo*, and *Rech'* (22 September 1910); coded telegram to DPD, 25 September 1910, GARF, f. 102, 00 1909, d. 155, part 3; and clipping from *Russkoe slovo* (10 February 1909), PSR 2-132.

86. "Pokazaniia V. L. Burtseva ... po delu Azefa," GARF, f. 1699, op. 1, d. 129, pp. 148–49; clipping from newspaper *Nowa reforma* (8 February 1909), GARF, f. 219, op. 1, d. 59; "Vesti ob Azefe," clipping from newspaper *Novyi den'* (12 October 1909), GARF, f. 102, 1909, d. 155, part 3; and Rubenstein, *Comrade Valentine*, x.

87. "Pokazaniia Kubova [Argunova]," GARF, f. 1699, op. 1, d. 131, p. 68; Aldanov, "Azef," *Istoki*, 419.

88. D. A. Lutokhin, "V. M. Chernov: Portret bez retushi," *Revoliutsionnaia Rossiia* 7 (20) (1992): 5.

89. Letter from "Evgenii" to V. I. Zasulich, 30 October 1909, Okhrana XIb-1.

90. See, for example, Galchenok, "Dnevnik Veburtseva," *Byvshie liudi* 1 (1910):, 2.

91. Bakai, *O razoblachiteliakh i razoblachitel'stve*, 60.

92. O. V. Budnitskii, "Vladimir Burtsev i ego korrespondenty," *Otechestvennaia istoriia* 6 (1992): 110.

93. Mikhail Reisner, Professor of International Law at Tomsk University, whom Burtsev incorrectly labeled an employee of the secret police, was subjected to public ostracism, which nearly drove him to suicide (Vadim Andreev, *Detstvo* [Moscow: Sovetskii pisatel', 1966], 67; see also miscellaneous notes by V. L. Burtsev, p. 2, Nic. 150-2). For similar examples, see Bakai, *O razoblachiteliakh i razoblachitel'stve*, 59–60; and a letter from "Evgenii" to V. I. Zasulich, 30 October 1909, Okhrana XIb-1. When confronted with evidence demonstrating the baselessness of his allegations against fellow revolutionaries, Burtsev did everything to elude public acknowledgment of his mistakes (see, for example, Akimov, *"Ne mogu molchat'!"* 30, 35–41, 46–47).

94. Cited from an untitled and unsigned manuscript, p. 10, Nic. 384-5.

95. One of them was Lerois *(Lerua)*, formerly an Okhrana surveillance agent stationed abroad. See, for example, a report to DPD, 29 April [12 May] 1914, Okhrana XXIVa-5k, and a report to DPD, 23 June [6 July] 1910, Okhrana XVIIp-1i.

96. See, for example, a report to DPD, 8 (21) August 1909, Okhrana, XXIVc-2S.

97. M. Bakai, *O razoblachiteliakh i razoblachitel'stve (Pis'mo k V. Burtsevu)* (New York: n. p., 1912), 46; and Vladimir Burtsev, untitled manuscript (Paris, 29 December 1934), p. 5, Burtsev 2-12.

98. Police report, 24 January 1910, Okhrana, XVId-1.

99. Some of Burtsev's informants who had defected from the government camp, most notably Bakai, shared this opinion and blamed him for inflating the value of his accomplishments. Bakai, *O razoblachiteliakh i razoblachitel'stve*, 50, 52.

100. See, for example, a letter from Georgii Nosar' in Paris to V. L. Burtsev in Petrograd, 11 February 1915, Okhrana, XVIId-1B; see also Bakai, *O razoblachiteliakh i razoblachitel'stve*, 43.

101. Schleifman, *Undercover Agents*, 190, 192.

102. Cited in ibid., 190.

103. Burtsev's descriptions of his encounter with Azef in 1912 is rather nebulous. See, for example, "Russian Spy Admits Guilt," *The Sun* (15 September 1912), PSR 1-19. It is not entirely clear why Azef, circumspect as he always was, dared to agree to a meeting that could have easily been a setup contrived by Burtsev and the SRs. Burtsev's explanation was obviously less than adequate: having accidently found out Azef's address, "I wrote to him, proposing a meeting. I promised him not to set up a trap for him. He believed my promise and agreed to see me" on 15 August (Vladimir Burtsev, untitled manuscript [Paris, 29 December 1934], p. 2, Burtsev 2-12). Needless to say, Azef had serious misgivings about his prospective rendezvous with Burtsev; on 14 August he wrote a will, consigning all his property to Hedy. Lur'e, *Khraniteli proshlogo*, 94. A serious incentive for Azef to yield to Burtsev's request must have been the following sentence in Burtsev's letter to the exposed spy: "In case you fail to respond . . . I will transfer all information [about your address—A.G.] to the press, while simultaneously giving it to the SR party" (Pavlov and Peregudova, *Pis'ma Azefa*, 184).

104. Report to DPD, 22 October [4 November] 1912, Okhrana XVIc-2; Lur'e, *Politseiskie i provokatory*, 371; Pavlov and Peregudova, *Pis'ma Azefa*, 182.

105. Letter from B. V. Savinkov to V. M. Chernov, 26 August 1912, Okhrana, XVIId-1B.

106. Cited in Schleifman, *Undercover Agents*, 191.

107. In September 1912 Azef wrote to Burtsev, outlining his conditions for a revolutionary trial. He promised to recognize any verdict of his former comrades; in case of a death sentence, Azef demanded the right to execute it upon himself within twenty-four hours after its issuance. There is little doubt that the exposed spy had no intention of appearing as a defendant before the revolutionary court; he was merely testing the SRs, seeking to clarify their intentions and giving them three months to respond to his proposal—which they never acknowledged (letter from Azef to Burtsev dated 2 September 1912, Nic. 112-16; see also Pavlov and Peregudova, *Pis'ma Azefa*, 187–88).

108. Believing that "it was possible to kill Azef a long time ago," some SRs blamed their party leaders for disregarding the urgency of this measure and procrastinating, as well as for allowing Burtsev to meet with the exposed spy and to let him get away unharmed (report to DPD, 22 October [4 November] 1912, Okhrana XVIc-2). According to police sources, in 1913 the SRs tried again to establish Azef's whereabouts in order to execute the party's death sentence, but these halfhearted attempts produced no results (report to DPD, 23 March [5 April] 1913, Okhrana XIIc(1)-1C).

109. Schleifman, *Undercover Agents*, 191–92.

110. Cited in ibid., 192–93. All criticism notwithstanding, Burtsev continued his antigovernment crusade in the years preceding the outbreak of the First World War. In 1914, however, he adjourned his revolutionary activity for the duration of the war and returned to Russia, where he was arrested, tried, and exiled to Siberia. Owing to the public campaign on his behalf, in November 1915, Burtsev was freed and allowed to settle in St. Petersburg (Vladimir Burtsev, untitled manuscript [Paris, 29 December 1934], p. 13, Burtsev 2-12). After the collapse of the tsarist regime in March 1917, Burtsev proved himself a bitter enemy of Lenin and his followers, whom he accused of being paid agents of the German government. After the Bolshevik takeover Burtsev was arrested and, after several months in the Peter and Paul fortress, in the spring of 1918 he emigrated abroad. For the rest of his life he lived in Paris, where he died of starvation during the Nazi occupation (Burtsev's biographical materials in Nic. 615-5).

111. Aldanov, "Azef," *Istoki*, 422; Gor'kii, "O predateliakh," 192; Shchegolev, "Istoricheskii Azef," 9.

112. "Pokazaniia L. G. Azef," GARF, f. 1699, op. 1, d. 126, pp. 14–15. See also Aldanov, "Azef," *Istoki*, 408, 412.

113. Nikolaevskii, *Konets Azefa*, 19–20; see also Pavlov and Peregudova, *Pis'ma Azefa*, 167.

114. Coded telegram to acting DPD, 6 September 1910, GARF, f. 102, 00 1909, d. 155, part 3.

115. Azef's passport with the name of Neumayer is held in GARF, f. 1699, op. 2, d. 142.

116. Aldanov, "Azef," *Istoki*, 423; and Nikolaevskii, *Konets Azefa*, 21–22.

117. Aldanov, "Azef," *Istoki*, 423–24.

118. Overstreet, *Understanding Fear*, 6.

119. Aldanov, "Azef," *Istoki*, 429.

120. Ibid.

121. Rubenstein, *Comrade Valentine*, 282; and Nikolaevskii, *Konets Azefa*, 36.

122. Gor'kii, "O predateliakh," 192–93.

123. Aldanov, "Azef," *Istoki*, 431; Shchegolev, "Istoricheskii Azef," 12. Lieutenant Alfred Dreyfus was the innocent victim of a scandalous anti-Semitic conspiracy in France in the 1890s.

124. Rubenstein, *Comrade Valentine*, 283.

125. Cited in Nikolaevskii, *Konets Azefa*, 37. See also Shchegolev, "Istoricheskii Azef," 11.

126. His newly acquired interest in religion notwithstanding, Azef did not neglect strictly earthly matters, such as persistent appeals to the Red Cross and various other philanthropic societies for material aid. Thus, on 17 January 1917, Azef petitioned the "High Committee of Her Imperial Highness the Grand Duchess Tat'iana Nikolaevna," a humanitarian agency in Stockholm, to consider the seriousness of his health problems and to send consumable products to him in prison (GARF, f. 1699, op. 2, d. 142; see also Pavlov and Peregudova, *Pis'ma Azefa*, 223–25).

127. Postcards from Mariia to Azef, 28 January and 11 April 1918, GARF, f. 1699, op. 2, d. 143.

128. Postcard from Mariia to Azef, 13 April 1918, GARF, f. 1699, op. 2, d. 143.

129. Postcard from Mariia to Azef, 28 January 1918; and letter from Mariia to Azef, 1 March 1918, GARF, f. 1699, op. 2, d. 143.

130. Undated letter from Mariia to Azef; and letter, 29 March 1918, GARF, f. 1699, op. 2, d. 143.
131. Letters from Mariia to Azef postmarked 19 April 1918, 24 April 1918, and 28 June 1918, GARF, f. 1699, op. 2, d. 143.
132. Unsigned letter from Mariia to Azef, 28 June 1918, and undated and unsigned letter to Azef from Mariia, GARF, f. 1699, op. 2, d. 143.
133. Ibid; postcards from Mariia to Azef, 28 January and 2 (15) February 1918; and letter from Mariia to Azef, 19 April 1918, GARF, f. 1699, op. 2, d. 143.
134. Undated letters from Mariia to Azef; letters, 29 March and 8 April 1918; and postcard from Mariia to Azef, 11 April 1918, GARF, f. 1699, op. 2, d. 143.
135. Mariia mentioned once that she had published two of Azef's letters to her in a newspaper. Letters from Mariia to Azef, 4 April and 8 April 1918, GARF, f. 1699, op. 2, d. 143.
136. Reference in Rubenstein, *Comrade Valentine,* 285; Nikolaevskii, *Konets Azefa,* 43.
137. Nikolaevskii, *Konets Azefa,* 38; Rubenstein, *Comrade Valentine,* 284–85.
138. Rubenstein, *Comrade Valentine,* 15, 284–85.
139. Ibid., 285.
140. Aldanov, "Azef," *Istoki,* 432; Rubenstein, *Comrade Valentine,* 286.
141. Shchegolev, "Istoricheskii Azef," 12; and Rubenstein, *Comrade Valentine,* 286.
142. Unsigned letter from Mariia to Azef postmarked 28 June 1918, GARF, f. 1699, op. 2, d. 143. In one of her last dispatches, Mariia declared that she was entirely unconcerned about the political situation in Russia, the establishment of the Bolshevik regime, or any "other nonsense": "All this is transient. And the eternal is my love for You" (postcard from Mariia to Azef postmarked 12 August 1918, GARF, f. 1699, op. 2, d. 143).
143. Rubenstein, *Comrade Valentine,* x.

Epilogue, 167–181

1. M. A. Bulgakov, *Master i Margarita* (Ann Arbor: Ardis, 1979), 301, 315 (author's translation).
2. Those responsible for the protection of the tsarist regime operated under the notion that in order to be able to prevent crimes, they had to commit them (L. P. Men'shchikov, "Secrets of the Russian Safety," p. 32, Nic. 179-25).
3. Rubenstein, *Comrade Valentine,* 270.
4. Letter from Nicolaevsky to Burtsev, 8 September 1931, Nic. 475-8; "Pokazaniia V. L. Burtseva, dannye sudebno-sledstvennoi komissii po delu Azefa," GARF, f. 1699, op. 1, d. 129, p. 116; and *akliuchenie,* 1. For a similar usage of the word "provocateur" see, for example, K., "Ivan Timenkov," *Byloe* 14 (1921): 45; and "Prilozhenie k #21-22 'Znameni Truda'," PSR, 8-650.
5. For the corroboration of the figure of ten thousand secret agents, see Z. I. Peregudova, "Deiatel'nost' komissii Vremennogo pravitel'stva i sovetskikh arkhivov po raskrytiiu sekretnoi agentury tsarskoi okhranki," *Otechestvennye arkhivy* 5 (1998): 10–22. For detailed figures, see also Lur'e and Peregudova, "Tsarskaia Okhranka i provokatsiia," 61; Praisman, "Fenomen Azefa," 65; and Daly, *Autocracy under Seige,* 91. For the distribution of secret agents according

to party membership and varying wages between 1902 and 1914, see Schleifman, *Undercover Agents,* 54, 61.

6. For information about the depraved and illicit machinations of one such agent see "K arestu aferista Rabinovicha," *Novoe vremia,* no. 12842 (24 November 1911), Okhrana VIL-2.

7. See, for example, E. K. Klimovich, a one-time director of the Police Department, and Gerasimov cited in Zinaida Peregudova, "Metody bor'by Departamenta politsii s revoliutsionnym dvizheniem," *Fakel 1990: Istoriko-revoliutsionnyi al'manakh* (Moscow: Politizdat, 1990), 202.

8. Z. I. Peregudova, ed., *Tainy politicheskogo syska: instruktsiia o rabote s sekretnymi sotrudnikami* (St. Petersburg: Izdanie Sankt-Peterburgskogo universiteta, 1992), 2. See also *Instruktsiia po organizatsii i vedeniiu vnutrennego (agenturnogo) nabliudeniia* in Lur'e and Peregudova, "Tsarskaia Okhranka i provokatsiia," 71; and Peregudova, "Metody bor'by Departamenta politsii s revoliutsionnym dvizheniem," 201.

9. "Dopros Gerasimova 26 aprelia 1917 goda," *Padenie tsarskogo rezhima,* 3 (Leningrad, 1925), 3.

10. Cited in Lur'e and Peregudova, "Tsarskaia Okhranka i provokatsiia," 57.

11. "Dopros M. I. Trusevicha," 218.

12. *Instruktsiia po organizatsii i vedeniiu vnutrennego (agenturnogo) nabliudeniia* in Lur'e and Peregudova, "Tsarskaia Okhranka i provokatsiia," 72–73.

13. Ibid., 74. The idea that the police authorities frequently knew that their agents initiated and participated in terrorist acts, but declined to take legal action against them, must be dismissed as an unjustified accusation. For information on agents suspended and convicted for malfeasance (including provocation), see, for example, *Obvinitel'nyi akt o meshchanakh Movshe-Arone Davidove Zakgeime i Tsirle Khaimovoi Shkol'nik,* PSR, 9-778; and police circular #110455, 26 November 1911, Okhrana VIL-3.

14. "Otvety," Argunov's handwritten manuscript, 26 April (no year), GARF, f. 1699, op. 1, d. 101.

15. *Zakliuchenie,* 11–12.

16. Ibid., 23. See also Ruud and Stepanov, *Fontanka,* 16, 181.

17. Following the assassination of Plehve, Sazonov wrote to his parents: "I was not insane when I decided and carried out my act . . . I am not a child . . . and therefore could realize what I was doing, and was not a toy in the hands of some evil people, hiding behind my back" ("Iz pisem E. Sazonova," letter, May 1906, 3–4; see also Gerasimov, *Na lezvii,* 139).

18. *Zakliuchenie,* 24; Amy Knight, "Female Terrorists in the Russian Socialist Revolutionary Party," *The Russian Review* 38, no. 2 (April 1979): 149; see also Stenograficheskii otchet 26-ogo zasedaniia sudebno-sledstvennoi komissii, 2 maia 1910 g., p. 11, GARF, f. 1699, op. 1, d. 136.

19. Cited in Schleifman, *Undercover Agents,* 94.

20. Boris Savinkov's testimony in "Stenograficheskii otchet zasedaniia C. C. K. 6 noiabria 1910 goda," GARF, f. 1699, op. 1, d. 133, p. 6.

21. Gerasimov, *Na lezvii,* 139.

22. Boris Savinkov's testimony in "Stenograficheskii otchet zasedaniia C. C. K. 9 noiabria 1910 goda," GARF, f. 1699, op. 1, d. 133, p. 14; see also A. B. (V. Tuchkin), *Za kulisami okhrannogo otdeleniia,* 36.

23. Gerasimov, *Na lezvii,* 85.

24. Letter from V. M. Chernov to B. I. Nicolaevsky, 7 October 1931, Nic. 206-6. Gerasimov explained this tactic by classifying Azef as "a dogged opponent

of revolution who recognized reforms alone—and only those which were implemented with great consistency. He almost extolled Stolypin's agrarian reforms and often said that the main vice in Russia was in the absence of private property" in the countryside (cited in Praisman, "Fenomen Azefa," 69).

25. Even the revolutionaries never advanced this claim, which Nicolaevsky defended until the early 1960s. Nor did Nicolaevsky find incredible a story told by Lopukhin's widow about Witte, who during secret negotiations in 1903 allegedly attempted to persuade Lopukhin to permit the revolutionaries to assassinate Nicholas II (letter from B. I. Nicolaevsky to L. P. Men'shchikov, 19 August 1931, Nic. 179-24; letter from B. I. Nicolaevsky to Bertram Wolfe, 8 May 1958, Nic. 508-41; and Nikolajewsky, *Aseff the Spy*, 17).

26. See, for example, Lur'e, *Politseiskie i provokatory*, 308–10.

27. Even Nicolaevsky found this contention impossible. Letter from B. I. Nicolaevsky to V. K. Agafonov, 25 April 1931, Nic. 471-9; letter from B. I. Nicolaevsky to L. P. Men'shchikov, 19 August 1931, Nic. 179-24; letter from B. I. Nicolaevsky to N. E. Andreev, 17 October 1961, Nic. 471-30; letter from B. I. Nicolaevsky to V. L. Burtsev, 6 June 1931, Nic. 475-8; and letter from B. I. Nicolaevsky to S. G. Svatikov, 30 June 1931, Nic. 416-10.

28. Rataev, "Evno Azef," 192; see also *Delo Lopukhina*, 59. See also "Razoblachennyi Azef," *Byloe* 2 (24) (August 1917): 212; and letter from Nicolaevsky to Svatikov, 30 June 1931, Nic. 416-10. Nicolaevsky's evidence confirms that Azef had no dealings with Rachkovskii prior to August 1905; therefore, Lopukhin's assertion that in 1902 Rachkovskii gave Azef five hundred rubles for Gershuni's dynamite laboratory was based on a misunderstanding ("Pokazaniia dannye Chresvychainoi sledstvennoi komissii dlia rassledovaniia protivozakonnykh po dolzhnosti deistvii byvshikh ministrov i proch. A. A. Lopukhin," 6 November 1917, Nic. 12-12; N. [L. P. Men'shchikov], "Novoe ob Azefe," manuscript, 23 March 1925, Nic. 179-26; "Obvinitel'nyi akt ob Lopukhine," GARF, f. 102, 7 *deloproizvodstvo*, 1909, d. 891; letter from B. I. Nicolaevsky to S. G. Svatikov, 30 June 1931, Nic. 416-10; letter from B. I. Nicolaevsky to V. L. Burtsev, 6 June 1931, Nic. 475-8; and letter from B. I. Nicolaevsky to V. K. Agafonov, 30 October 1932, Nic. 471-9).

29. "Pis'mo S. V. Zubatova A. I. Spiridovichu," 282.

30. *Zakliuchenie*, 25n.

31. Burtsev admitted that some of his newspaper interviews had indeed insinuated Azef's collaboration with the Police Department in his murderous intrigues against high-posted statesmen—an unfortunate misunderstanding for which Burtsev blamed his interviewers, who had allegedly misinterpreted his words ("Pokazaniia V. L. Burtseva 1 aprelia 1917 g.," *Padenie tsarskogo rezhima*, vol. 1 [Leningrad, 1925], 302, 304; Burtsev, an unsigned manuscript, p. 9). See also "Pokazaniia V. L. Burtseva, dannye sudebno-sledstvennoi komissii po delu Azefa," GARF, f. 1699, op. 1, d. 129, p. 155; and Istorik, "Azef v izobrazhenii P. E. Shchegoleva," 248.

32. "Pokazaniia V. L. Burtseva 1 aprelia 1917 g.," 305.

33. In his analysis of the spy's activity, Aldanov is correct in emphasizing this point. Aldanov, "Azef," *Istoki*, 434.

34. While believing Azef to be a "person of rare selfishness" who would not shun any means to achieve his egotistic objective, the leading gendarme officer Aleksandr Spiridovich considered him to be a veritable revolutionary and terrorist. Cited in Gorodnitskii, "Tri stilia rukovodstva boevoi organizatsiei," 58–59.

35. "Pokazaniia V. L. Burtseva, dannye sudebno-sledstvennoi komissii po delu Azefa," GARF, f. 1699, op. 1, d. 129, p. 156.

36. Police officials were well aware that Azef appropriated large amounts of money from the treasury of the SR Combat Organization for his private needs, although they probably did not know how gainful he in fact was. Unaware that Azef's efficiency in this regard hardly required encouragement, Gerasimov even incited him to steal from the SRs, justifying the theft by the fact that the agent thus inflicted additional damage on the terrorists (*Otchet o sostoiavshemsia 1/14 ianvaria 1909 g. v Parizhe sekretnom zasedanii*, Okhrana, XVIc-9; Gerasimov, *Na lezvii*, 86). On Azef's appropriation of party funds, see also a report to DPD, 22 October (4 November) 1912, Okhrana, XVIc-2.

37. P. Struve, *Patriotica* (St. Petersburg, 1911): 256.

38. Rataev, "Evno Azef," 194.

39. Nikolajewsky, *Aseff the Spy*, 65; and Judge, *Plehve*, 224–25. The SR Investigatory Committee report mentions nothing of Azef's involvement in the act against Bogdanovich ("Izveshchenie Tsentral'nogo Komiteta," 2).

40. For various terrorist undertakings that the police were able to prevent largely owing to Azef, see *Delo Lopukhina*, 10–13, 56–57; and Stolypin, *Polnoe sobranie rechei*, 162.

41. Rubenstein, *Comrade Valentine*, 65; "Pokazaniia V. L. Burtseva, dannye sudebno-sledstvennoi komissii po delu Azefa," GARF, f. 1699, op. 1, d. 129, p. 157.

42. See, for example, L. P. Men'shchikov, "Secrets of Russian Safety" (unpublished manuscript in English), pp. 24–25, Nic., 179-25.

43. Nikolajewsky, *Aseff the Spy*, 16.

44. "Pis'mo S. V. Zubatova A. I. Spiridovichu," 282. Interestingly, Savinkov seemed to share Zubatov's opinion of Azef, considering "cowardice and avarice" to be the driving forces of his personality (cited in Gorodnitskii, "Tri stilia rukovodstva boevoi organizatsiei," 59).

45. Rataev, "Evno Azef," 200, 203.

46. Norman Naimark, "Terror and the Fall of Imperial Russia," published lecture (Boston University, 14 April 1986), 19.

47. Rataev, "Evno Azef," 200.

48. *Otchet o zasedaniiakh levoi gruppy sotsialistov-revoliutsionerov (Iudelevsko-go i Agafonova) po delu Azefa*, police report, 6 (19) January 1909, Okhrana XVIc-9.

49. Gerasimov, *Na lezvii*, 73. According to official sources, information reported by Azef at the time "becomes so regular and so complete that not one plot of the Central Committee is carried out, and all attempts of the Combat Organization to stage terrorist acts are prevented by the police" (*Obvinitel'nyi akt ob . . . Lopukhine*, GARF, f. 102, 7 deloproizvodstvo, 1909, d. 891). "If it were necessary," Gerasimov asserted subsequently, "Azef would have been paid not one thousand [rubles] a month, but five thousand" (cited in Aldanov, "Azef," *Istoki*, 423).

50. Popova, "Dinamitnye masterskie," *Katorga i ssylka* 5 (34): 59.

51. See, for example, [Burtsev], "Gerasimov i Azef," in which the author incorrectly holds Azef responsible for the assassination of General Dumbadze. Burtsev based his accusations on the totally unsubstantiated testimony of a revolutionary named Nina Vengerova (report to DPD, 14 [27] October 1913, Okhrana XXIVa-1B; see also Burtsev, "Azef i ego uchastie v terroristicheskikh aktakh," and his article in *Budushchee* [31 March 1912], both in Nic., 205-21). Azef was even accused of participating in the terrorist activities of various groups other than the SRs, and of having connections with right-wing terrorist organizations. See, for example, "Azef i Lbov," *Russkoe slovo* 27 (4 February 1909), PSR 2-157; and "Arkhiv obshchestvennoi zhizni," *Poznanie Rossii* 2 (Feb-

ruary 1909): 262–63, Nic., 205-20. Finally, Rataev came to believe that "Azef not only worked for the Russian revolution, but also trained foreign revolutionaries" (Rataev, "Evno Azef," 189).

52. Gerasimov, *Na lezvii*, 141. This condition became quite satisfactory for the police after the Second Congress of the PSR, held on 12–15 February 1907 in Tammerfors, Finland, passed a resolution allowing "terrorist acts of primary importance to be carried out only under the direction and control of the Central Committee" (Okhrana XVIb [3]-1A).

53. Letter to the Editor, 20 December 1911, *Budushchee* (24 December 1911), Nic. 205-21.

54. Gerasimov, *Na lezvii*, 141.

55. "Pokazaniia Iriny, Ritinoi (Rakitnikovoi), Rubanovicha, Burtseva, dannye sudebno-sledstvennoi komissii," GARF, f. 1699, op. 1, d. 129, p. 7.

56. Gerasimov, *Na lezvii*, 99–101. For other information that the police received from Azef on terrorists outside the Combat Organization, see "Pokazaniia, danye Chrezvychainoi sledstevennoi kommissii dlia rassledovaniia protivozakonnykh po dolzhnosti deistvii byvshikh ministrov i proch. A. A. Lopukhin," 6 November 1917, p. 4, Nic. 12-12.

57. Gerasimov, *Na lezvii*, 141.

58. Rataev, "Evno Azef," 191.

59. Ibid., 189, 192. See also Gorbunov, "Savinkov, kak memuarist," *Katorga i ssylka* 3 (40): 173–74.

60. "Pokazaniia, dannye Chrezvychainoi slestvennoi kommissii dlia rassledovaniia protivozakonnykh po dolzhnosti deistvii byvshikh ministrov i proch. A. A. Lopukhin (6 November 1917)," 1-2, Nic. 12-12.

61. Cited in Rubenstein, *Comrade Valentine*, 55.

62. Burtsev, untitled manuscript, 8. Even according to Burtsev's version of the story, it was he who did all the talking during their encounter on the train, and it was he who succeeded in convincing Lopukhin that Azef was a criminal (police report, 28 April 1909, GARF, f. 102, 7 *deloproizvodstvo*, 1909, d. 891; and "Pokazaniia V. L. Burtseva, dannye sudebno-sledstvennoi komissii po delu Azefa," GARF, f. 1699, op. 1, d. 129, p. 104).

63. "Opravdatel'naia zapiska Azefa," 62.

64. Spiridovich, *Partiia sotsialistov-revoliutsionerov i ee predshestvenniki*, 429; Nikolajewsky, *Aseff the Spy*, 291; N. (L. P. Men'shchikov), "Novoe ob Azefe," Nic. 179-26. Some historians even went as far as to insinuate baselessly that the Russian police authorities wanted to assassinate Azef and "did not kill the provocateur because they hoped the SRs would do so for them" (Lur'e, *Politseiskie i provokatory*, 368).

65. Danilo Kis, *A Tomb for Boris Davidovich* (New York: Penguin Books, 1980), 81.

66. Nicolaevsky, *Konets Azefa*, 11.

67. Gerasimov, *Na lezvii*, 137.

68. Nicolaevsky, *Konets Azefa*, 11.

69. Gor'kii, "O predateliakh," 191, 195.

70. Trotskii, "Evno Azef," 228. Aldanov seems to concur on this point, wondering if "perhaps Azef did not have an actual inner world at all" (Aldanov, "Azef," *Istoki*, 437).

71. Trotskii, "Evno Azef," 229.

72. "Pokazaniia tt. Bobrova, Bol'shova, Kubova, Chernova, Bunakova i Moiseenko, dannye sudebno-sledstvennoi komissii," GARF, f. 1699, op. 1, d. 130, p. 87; and Pavlov and Peregudova, *Pis'ma Azefa*, 132.

73. "Pokazaniia tt. Bobrova, Bol'shova, Kubova, Chernova, Bunakova i Moiseenko, dannye sudebno-sledstvennoi komissii," GARF, f. 1699, op. 1, d. 130, p. 85.

74. "Pokazaniia Iriny, Ritinoi (Rakitnikovoi), Rubanovicha, Burtseva, dannye sudebno-sledstvennoi komissii po delu Azefa," GARF, f. 1699, op. 1, d. 129, p. 20.

75. In much the same way, Azef never attempted to harmonize his less-than-revolutionary views with the official position of the PSR leadership—something any other secret agent would probably have done. Instead, he succeeded in winning the SRs' respect and trust by manifesting his courage and integrity while defending his unorthodox position against the rest of the party (Praisman, "Fenomen Azefa," 70).

76. Ibid.

77. Ibid., 68.

78. "Pokazaniia M. A. Natansona," GARF, f. 1699, op. 1, d. 123, p. 76.

79. "Iz istorii Partii S.-R.," *Novyi zhurnal* 101 (1970): 195; see also A. B. (V. Tuchkin), *Za kulisami okhrannogo otdeleniia*, 21.

80. Nikolajewsky, *Aseff the Spy*, vi. This explanation of Azef's motives coincided entirely with the opinion of Zubatov, who argued that avidity for money was always the driving force behind Azef's behavior.

81. Among these motives Chernov considered the thrill of exhibiting "power and the danger of walking on the edge of the abyss," the memory of a difficult childhood in a poor Jewish family, personal scores, and the role that he played in the party (untitled manuscript by Olga Chernov Andreev, p. 39, Olga Andreyev Carlisle private archive).

82. V. Zenzinov, "Provokator Azef," unpublished manuscript (New York, 30 March 1934), 13, Nic. 205-18.

83. Tolstoi, "Azef, kak teatral'naia maska," 15.

84. Cited in Gorodnitskii, "Tri stilia rukovodstva boevoi organizatsiei," 58–59.

85. Zubatov's assessment in "Protsess Lopukhina," *Novoe vremia* 11900 (30 April [13 May], 1909). See also Gerasimov, *Na lezvii*, 71–72, 138.

86. Aleksei Tolstoi seems to be over-stressing his point in declaring: "Azef loved power. His one word, usually uttered reluctantly, gloomily, over his shoulder. . . was enough for a person to go to his death without any vacillation. The tsar could not dictate as much as Azef did" (Tolstoi, "Azef, kak teatral'naia maska," 15).

87. P. S. Ivanovskaia cited in Budnitskii, ed., *Zhenshchiny-terroristki v Rossii*, 113.

88. Sophocles, *Acrisius*, quoted in *The Merriam-Webster Dictionary of Quotations*, 142.

89. Tolstoi, "Azef, kak teatral'naia maska," 16.

90. Cited in Rubenstein, *Comrade Valentine*, 2.

91. P. S. Ivanovskaia cited in Budnitskii, ed., *Zhenshchiny-terroristki v Rossii*, 113.

Selected Bibliography

This selected bibliography contains only works cited in the notes, and excludes separate references for archival documents and for memoirs published as articles in frequently cited journals.

Archives

Arkhiv-Biblioteka Rossiiskogo Fonda Kul'tury, Moscow, Russia.
Olga Andreyev Carlisle private archive, San Francisco, California
Gosudarstvennyi Arkhiv Rossiiskoi Federatsii (GARF), Moscow, Russia
Hoover Institution Archives, Stanford University, Stanford, California:
    Arkhiv Zagranichnoi Agentury Departamenta Politsii (Okhrana Collection)
    Vladimir L. Burtsev Collection
    Boris I. Nicolaevsky Collection
International Institute of Social History, Amsterdam:
    Arkhiv L. P. Men'shchikova
    Arkhiv Partii Sotsialistov-Revoliutsionerov
    Arkhiv V. P. Zhuka
Rossiiskii Gosudarstvennyi Istoricheskii Arkhiv (RGIA), St. Petersburg, Russia

Published Documents and Periodicals

"Arkhiv obshchestvennoi zhizni." *Poznanie Rossii* 2 (February 1909).
Bakai, M. *O razoblachiteliakh i razoblachitel'stve (Pis'mo k V. Burtsevu).* New York, 1912.
Byloe [The Past].
Delo A. A. Lopukhina v osobom prisutstvii pravitel'stvuiushchego Senata. Stenograficheskii otchet. St. Petersburg, 1910.
"Dopros A. I. Spiridovicha 28 aprelia 1917 goda." In *Padenie tsarskogo rezhima*, vol. 3. Leningrad, 1925.
"Dopros A. V. Gerasimova 26 aprelia 1917 goda." In *Padenie tsarskogo rezhima*, vol. 3. Leningrad, 1925.
"Dopros M. I. Trusevicha 4 maia 1917 goda." In *Padenie tsarskogo rezhima*, vol. 3. Leningrad, 1925.

Gosudarstvennaia Duma. III sozyv. Stenograficheskie otchety. St. Petersburg, 1909.

Istochnik 2 (27) (1997).

Katorga i ssylka.

Krasnyi arkhiv.

Minuvshee 18. Moscow-St. Petersburg: Atheneum-Feniks, 1995.

Morison, Elting E., ed. *The Letters of Theodore Roosevelt.* Cambridge, MA: Harvard University Press, 1951.

Novoe vremia.

Novyi zhurnal.

Pavlov, D. B., and Z. I. Peregudova, eds. *Pis'ma Azefa (1893–1917).* Moscow: Terra, 1994.

Pistsovaia kniga grodnetskoiekonomii s pribavleniiami, izdannaia vilenskoiu komissieiu dlia razbora drevnikh aktov, pt. 1. Vil'na, 1881.

"Pokazaniia V. L. Burtseva 1 aprelia 1917 g." In *Padenie tsarskogo rezhima,* vol. 1. Leningrad, 1925.

Stolypin, P. A. *Nam nuzhna velikaia Rossiia.* Moscow: Molodaia gvardiia, 1991.

———. *Polnoe sobranie rechei predsedatelia Soveta ministrov P. A. Stolypina v Gosudarstvennoi dume I Gosudarstvennom sovete (1907–1911 gg.).* New York: Teleks, 1990.

Tret'ia Gosudarstvennaia Duma. Materialy dlia otsenki ee deiatel'nosti. St. Petersburg: Izdatel'stvo parlamentskoi fraktsii Partii Narodnoi Svobody, 1912.

Zakliuchenie sudebno-sledstvennoi komissii po delu Azefa. [Paris?], Izdanie Tsentral'nogo Komiteta P. S.-R., 1911.

Memoirs

Budnitskii, O. V., ed. *Zhenshchiny-terroristki v Rossii.* Rostov-on-Don: Feniks, 1996.

Burtsev, V. L. *V pogone za provokatorami.* Moscow: Sovremennik, 1989.

Chernov, V. M. *Pered burei.* New York: Izdatel'stvo imeni Chekhova, 1953.

Gerasimov, A. V. *Na lezvii s terroristami.* Paris: YMCA-Press, 1985.

Gershuni, Grigorii. *Iz nedavnego proshlogo.* Paris: Tribune Russe, 1908.

Savinkov, B. V. *Vospominaniia terrorista.* Kharkov: Proletarii, 1926.

Spiridovich, A. I. *Zapiski zhandarma.* Moscow: Proletarii, 1991.

Secondary Works

A. B. [V. Tuchkin]. *Za kulisami okhrannogo otdeleniia.* Berlin, Heinrich Gaspari Verlagsbuchhandlung, 1910.

Aizenberg, L. "Na slovakh i na dele (Po povodu memuarov S. Iu. Vitte i A. A. Lopukhina." *Evreiskaia letopis'* 3. Leningrad-Moscow, 1924.

Akimov, Ia. *"Ne mogu molchat'!"* New York, 1912.

Aldanov, Mark. "Azef." In *Istoki*. Moscow: Izvestiia, 1991.

Andreev, Vadim. *Detstvo*. Moscow: Sovetskii pisatel', 1966.

An-skii, S. A. "Evreiskoe narodnoe tvorchestvo." In *Evrei v Rossiiskoi imperii 18–19 vekov: sbornik trudov evreiskikh istorikov,* edited by A. Lokshin. Moscow and Jerusalem: Gesharim, 1995.

Bernstein, L. *L'Affaire Azeff: Histoire et documents.* Paris: Société des amis du peuple russe, 1909.

Bezrodnyi, Mikhail. *Konets tsitaty.* St. Petersburg: Izdatel'stvo Ivana Limbakha, 1996.

Blok, Aleksandr. *"The Intelligentsia and the Revolution."* In *Russian Intellectual History: an Anthology,* edited by Mark Raeff. New Jersey: Humanities Press, 1978.

Budnitskii, Oleg V. "The Jews in Rostov-on-Don in 1918–1919." In *Jews and Jewish Topics in the Soviet Union and Eastern Europe.* Jerusalem: The Hebrew University of Jerusalem, Winter 1993.

———. "Political Leaders among Jews in Rostov-on-Don, 1900–1920." In *Proceedings of the Eleventh World Congress of Jewish Studies,* Division B (The History of the Jewish People). Vol. 3. Jerusalem, 1994.

———. "Vladimir Burtsev i ego korrespondenty." *Otechestvennaia istoriia* 6 (1992).

Daly, Jonathan W. *Autocracy under Seige: Security Police and Opposition in Russia, 1866–1905.* DeKalb, IL: Northern Illinois University Press, 1998.

Davydov, Iuri. *Tainaia liga.* Moscow: Izdatel'stvo Pravda, 1990.

Galchenok. "Dnevnik Veburtseva." *Byvshie liudi* 1 (1910).

Gary, Romain. *White Dog.* New York: World Publishing Company, 1970.

Geifman, Anna. "Aspects of Early Twentieth-Century Russian Terrorism: The Socialist-Revolutionary Combat Organization." *Terrorism and Political Violence* 4, no. 2 (Summer 1992).

———. *Thou Shalt Kill. Revolutionary Terrorism in Russia, 1894–1917.* Princeton: Princeton University Press, 1993.

———. "Zinaida F. Zhuchenko." In *Modern Encyclopedia of Russian and Soviet History.* Vol. 55. Gulf Breeze, FL: Academic International Press, 1993, 230–31.

Gor'kii, Maksim. "O predateliakh." *Sobranie sochinenii.* Vol. 25. Moscow: Gosudarstvennoe izdatel'stvo khudozhestvennoi literatury, 1953.

Gorodnitskii, R. A. "Tri stilia rukovodstva boevoi organizatsiei partii sotsialistov-revoliutsionerov: Gershuni, Azef, Savinkov." *Individual'nyi politicheskii terror v Rossii XIX–nachalo XX v.* Moscow: Memorial, 1996.

Gray, Jeffrey A. *The Neuropsychology of Anxiety: An Enquiry into the Functions of the Septo-Hippocampal System.* New York: Oxford University Press, 1982.

Gul', Roman. *Azef.* New York: Most, 1974.

Gusev, K. V. *Partiia eserov: ot melkoburzhuaznogo revoliutsionarizma k kontrrevoliutsii.* Moscow, 1975.

Hailparn, Diane F. *Fear No More.* New York: St. Martin's Press, 1988.

Hampden-Turner, Charles. *Radical Man.* New York: Anchor Books, 1971.

Izrecheniia kitaiskogo mudretsa Lao-Tze. Moscow: Izdatel'stvo MGIK, 1992.

Judge, Edward H. *Plehve: Repression and Reform in Imperial Russia 1902–1904.* Syracuse, NY: Syracuse University Press, 1983.

Karin. S. Kh. *V mire mudrykh myslei.* Moscow: Znanie, 1962

Khludov, Vladimir, and Andrei Iashlavskii. "Evangelie ot Azefa." *Moskovskii komsomolets,* 22 September 1996.

Kis, Danilo. *A Tomb for Boris Davidovich.* New York: Penguin Books, 1980.

Knight, Amy. "Female Terrorists in the Russian Socialist Revolutionary Party." *Russian Review* 38, no. 2 (April 1979).

Kopp, Sheldon. *Raise Your Right Hand against Fear.* Minneapolis, MN: CompCare Publishers, 1988.

Kundera, Milan. *Immortality.* London and Boston: Faber and Faber, 1991.

Laqueur, Walter. *Terrorism.* Boston, 1977.

Levanov, B. V. *Iz istorii bor'by bol'shevistskoi partii protiv eserov v gody pervoi russkoi revoliutsii.* Leningrad: Izdatel'stvo Leningradskogo Universiteta, 1974.

Longe, Zh., and G. Zil'ber. *Terroristy i okhranka.* Moscow, 1991.

Lunacharskii, A., K. Radek, and L. Trotskii. *Siluety: Politicheskie portrety.* Moscow: Izdatel'stvo politicheskoi literatury, 1991.

Lur'e, F. M. *Khraniteli proshlogo.* Leningrad: Lenizdat, 1990.

———. *Politseiskie i provokatory.* St. Petersburg: Chas pik, 1992.

Lur'e, F. M., and Z. I. Peregudova. "Tsarskaia Okhranka i provokatsiia." *Iz glubiny vremen.* Vol. 1. St. Petersburg: Elektrotekhnicheskii institut sviazi imeni M. A. Bonch-Bruevicha, 1992.

Lutokhin, D. A. "V. M. Chernov: portret bez retushi." *Revoliutsionnaia Rossiia* 7 (20) (1992).

The Merriam-Webster Dictionary of Quotations. Springfield, MA: Merriam-Webster, 1992.

Miller, Alice. *Prisoners of Childhood.* New York: Basic Books, 1981.

Mogil'ner, Marina. "Boris Savinkov: 'podpol'naia' I 'legal'naia' Rossiia v peripetiiakh odnoi sud'by." *Obshchestvennye nauki i sovremennost' (ONS).* New York, 1995.

Mommsen, Wolfgang J. and Gerhard Hirschfeld, eds. *Social Protest, Violence and Terror in Nineteenth- and Twentieth-Century Europe.* New York: St. Martin's Press, 1982.

Naimark, Norman M. "Terror and the Fall of Imperial Russia." Published lecture. Boston University, 14 April 1986.

———. *Terrorists and Social Democrats: The Russian Revolutionary Movement under Alexander III.* Cambridge, MA: Harvard University Press, 1983.

Nikolaevskii, Boris I. *Konets Azefa*. Leningrad: Gosudarstvennoe izdatel'stvo, 1926.

Nikolajewsky, Boris I. *Aseff the Spy: Russian Terrorist and Police Stool*.

Novitskii, V. D. *Iz vospominanii zhandarma*. Moscow: Izdatel'stvo Moskovskogo Universiteta, 1991.

Overstreet, Bonaro W. *Understanding Fear*. New York: Harper, 1951.

Pavlov, D. B. *Esery-maksimalisty v pervoi Rossiiskoi revoliutsii*. Moscow, 1989.

———. Preface to "Pis'ma Azefa." *Voprosy istorii* 4 (1993).

Peregudova, Z. I. "Deiatel'nost' komissii Vremennogo pravitel'stva i sovetskikh arkhivov po raskrytiiu sekretnoi agentury tsarskoi okhranki." *Otechestvennye arkhivy* 5 (1998).

———. "Metody bor'by Departamenta politsii s revoliutsionnym dvizheniem." *Fakel 1990: Istoriko-revoliutsionnyi al'manakh*. Moscow: Politizdat, 1990.

Peregudova, Z. I., ed. *Tainy politicheskogo syska: instruktsiia o rabote s sekretnymi sotrudnikami*. St. Petersburg: Izdanie St. Peterburgskogo universiteta, 1992.

Posse, A. *Moi zhiznennyi put'*. Moscow and Leningrad, 1929.

Praisman, Leonid. *"Fenomen Azefa": Individual'nyi politicheskii terror v Rossii XIX-nachalo XX v.* Moscow: Memorial, 1996.

Reich, Walter, ed. *Origins of Terrorism*. Cambridge, U.K.: Cambridge University Press, 1990.

Riha, Thomas. *A Russian European: Paul Miliukov in Russian Politics*. Notre Dame: University of Notre Dame Press, 1969.

Rostov-na-Donu: Ocherki o gorode. Rostov: Rostovskoe knizhnoe izdatel'stvo, 1973.

Rubenstein, Richard E. *Comrade Valentine*. New York: Harcourt Brace and Company, 1994.

Ruud, Charles, and Sergei Stepanov. *Fontanka, 16: Politicheskii sysk pri tsariakh*. Moscow: Mysl', 1993.

Schleifman, Nurit. *Undercover Agents in the Russian Revolutionary Movement: The SR Party, 1902–1914*. New York: St. Martin's Press, 1988.

Shchegolev, P. E., ed. *Provokator*. Leningrad: Priboi, 1929.

Shvetsov, S. *V starom Rostove*. Rostov: Rostovskoe knizhnoe izdatel'stvo, 1971.

Spence, Richard B. *Boris Savinkov: Renegade on the Left*. Boulder, CO: East European Monographs, 1991.

Spiridovich, A. I. *Partiia Sotsialistov-revoliutsionerov i ee predshestvenniki (1886–1916)*. Petrograd, 1918.

Struve, P. *Patriotica*. St. Petersburg, 1911.

Tolstoi, A., and P. Shchegolev, eds. *Azef*. Leningrad: Academia, 1926.

Vishniak, Mark. *Dan' proshlomu*. New York: Izdatel'stvo imeni Chekhova, 1954.

Zborowski, Mark, and Elizaberh Herzog. *Life Is with People: The Culture of the Shtetl*. New York: Schocken Books, 1952.

Zubarev, Dmitrii, ed. "Boris Savinkov: chelovek, kotoryi khotel rasshirit' chelovecheskuiu svobodu." *Nezavisimaia gazeta*, 23 May 1995.

Index